D1632051

Opting for Elsewhere

Opting
for Elsewhere

Lifestyle Migration
in the American Middle Class

BRIAN A. HOEY

Vanderbilt University Press • *Nashville*

© 2014 by Vanderbilt University Press
Nashville, Tennessee 37235
First printing 2014

This book is printed on acid-free paper.
Manufactured in the United States of America

Frontispiece: © Jdgrant | Dreamstime

Library of Congress Cataloging-in-Publication Data on file
LC control number   2014008051
LC classification number   HQ2044.U6H64 2014
Dewey class number   305.5'50973—dc23

ISBN 978-0-8265-2005-0 (cloth)
ISBN 978-0-8265-2007-4 (ebook)

Contents

PART V

Conclusions

Preface

Due to the historical development of anthropology as a discipline—emerging as it did within the context of colonialism—anthropologists have tended to conduct their research among people deemed exotic or simply those who could be considered "the other." This proclivity has led to a preponderance of fieldwork in geographically remote places or, if not in foreign places, then among the relatively "alien" at home. With a Fulbright grant in hand and in keeping with disciplinary traditions, my own interests in family, work, and community led me first to rural Indonesia in 1998.[1] My research focused on community building in migrant villages fashioned wholesale from the ground up in an isolated river valley on the island of Sulawesi following relocation of hundreds of families from the island of Bali who had been displaced by a cataclysmic volcanic eruption a generation earlier. Though this relocation was exceptional given the circumstances, under both colonial and postcolonial governments the *transmigration* program was intended to lessen population pressures in heavily populated areas of the country while encouraging development in far-flung destination areas. For the transmigrants who participated voluntarily, there were parallels to homestead programs during frontier settlement in the United States.

My work among these transmigrants revealed how they dealt, individually and collectively, with profound disorientation of resettlement and their attempts to establish socially, economically, and ecologically sustainable communities in places much different from those that they left. I was interested not simply in migration, but rather with what we might call the coping strategies of migrants. How did they collectively struggle to create viable communities? In my research on migration in the United States, I continue to concentrate less on migration as a demographic process—how it affects population structure and dynamics—than on what relocation *means* for both the people and the places involved. This is at least in part a distinction between my qualitatively oriented approach to research as opposed to the generally quantitative approaches taken by demographers and others interested in migration trends.

Upon my return from a year in Indonesia, I accepted an offer to start a different project in the United States through a newly formed Alfred P. Sloan Foundation Center for the Study of Working Families at the Institute for Social Research in Ann Arbor, Michigan. Thus, I was thinking about how I would overcome my own disorientation of starting over as I began fieldwork in the midwestern United

States. Following the Sloan Foundation's mandate, my research needed to address changing conditions of work and family in the American middle class—an atypical research agenda for an anthropologist. Indeed, that was one of Sloan's goals: to encourage more qualitative research on the subject and, specifically, up close studies of everyday lives that characterize the methods of cultural anthropologists. Such ethnographic work, as the methodology is called, promised to both humanize and contextualize predominantly statistical data.

I knew from my fieldwork in Indonesia that challenges and opportunities presented by resettlement are rich with meaning for individuals, families, and places. Using statistical data, I began exploring broad migration trends in the United States. Having examined deliberate community building among transmigrants, I considered the "back-to-the-land" movement and so-called intentional communities born out of communitarian desires to create places to live and work according to utopian ideals. Eventually I came upon literature on what demographers have called *noneconomic* migration and applied to behavior where people relocate not to maximize individual earning potential but rather to pursue things less easily quantified by social scientists.

Following this lead, I arrived at *quality of life* as a kind of touchstone. It seemed that towns around the country now spoke explicitly about wanting to preserve or create it. Place-rating publications such as the popular *Places Rated Almanac* claimed to measure it. In the emerging high-tech economy of the 1990s, it had become shorthand for a set of practices aimed at creating a happier, more productive workplace. Could personal concern for quality of life, as opposed to individual economic maximization, be something that motivated would-be migrants not only to relocate but, more importantly, to undergo potentially transformative redefinitions of work and family in the process?

The ascendant status of quality of life as a category of public interest at this time was later confirmed when it gained unprecedented national status during the 2000 presidential campaign. As candidates for the Democratic nomination, both Al Gore and Bill Bradley issued detailed policy statements on quality of life and "livability" to address questions about urban and regional planning. How was it that something like suburban sprawl could now surface as a matter of substance for a political platform?

The geographer Robert Rogerson provides a possible explanation in his observation that at a time of profound globalization "[financial] capital is fragmenting into many parts with considerable volatility in the desires and demands of capital—both in terms of production needs and consumption—quality of life within its relative ubiquity provides an important anchor attached to which those involved in shaping the visions and trajectories of [places] can build."[2] Had concern for quality of life become a means for dealing with conditions of uncertainty inherent in a thoroughly globalized economy? For communities, this focus could offer them relative stability in an apparent desire for quality of life among current or prospective residents faced with fathoming vagaries of corporate decision making in a highly delocalized economy. Already, increasing numbers of companies severed attachments to particular places while opting for the inexpensive labor and material costs found elsewhere. For families, a focus on quality of life might allow a small measure of inner guidance in a tumultuous world.

In 2000, I attended the Michigan Legislative and Business Leaders Public Policy Forum titled "Building Tomorrow's Economy." Focusing on quality-of-life initiatives in urban and regional planning, forum organizers suggested that "If you build it, they will come." One promotional brochure stated emphatically, "There's growing recognition in Michigan that improving quality of life for our citizens is an important factor in ensuring continued economic growth and prosperity. As the ability to attract workers becomes an increasingly important competitive advantage, how to provide workers with urban vitality, a clean environment, quality education, affordable housing, and efficient transportation becomes a central question for business and political leaders alike."[3]

Looking to find a site in the Midwest where I could explore the social and cultural significance of quality of life for work and family, I recalled my experiences vacationing in the Grand Traverse region of northwestern Lower Michigan.[4] People told me how they had moved away from heavily populated urban areas, often leaving behind corporate jobs, in order to live there. A good number seemed to treat the area as part-time refuge before "pulling up stakes," as some would tell me in animated conversation, in order to relocate their lives. Their motivation sounded as if based in concern for quality of life. What did this decision to relocate mean to them and, ultimately, for the destination community? I began to see how quality of life pointed at individual needs and desires that I could interpret as having to do with lifestyle choices. Marking them *lifestyle migrants*, as I chose to do, emphasized choice and suggests consumptive practices. Lifestyle migration offered me an opportunity to look at how people struggle with competing obligations between work and family at a time when cultural models and moral frameworks that inform critical decisions appeared to be changing. We may define lifestyle migration broadly as the movement of individuals at all stages of the life course who relocate either full- or part-time to geographic places made personally meaningful by belief in the potential of their own act of relocation and the places themselves to improve quality of life. This book contributes to our understanding of this contemporary phenomenon—as observed in the United States—as well as its cultural and historical roots.

Once in the field in early 2000, I limited my study area to Grand Traverse, Leelanau, Antrim, and Benzie Counties. This restricted the project to a manageable scope with no more than a forty-five-minute drive from my home base in the central social and economic hub of Traverse City. This allowed me to get a sense of daily life in the region without spreading myself too thin. Physically speaking, all these counties are similar in that they have extensive coastlines either on Lake Michigan itself or on Grand Traverse Bay.

The responses that I got from people during the early days, when local news agencies learned of my study, were telling. Many told me, "Sounds like you want to talk to me!" Others assumed that my work was somehow allied with local boosters like the chamber of commerce. Given that for most of this century the region's elected and unelected representatives have toiled to attract both vacationers and

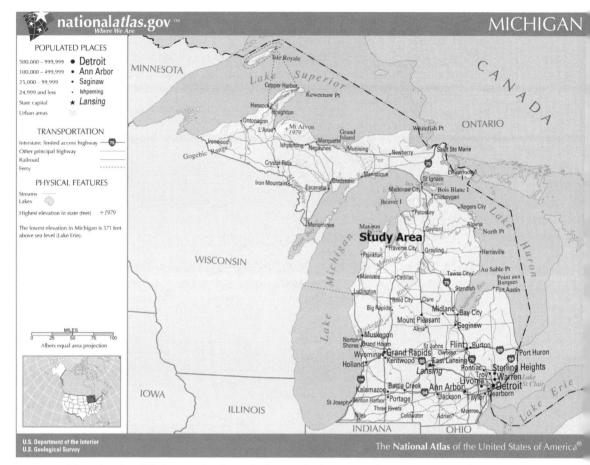

Map showing Michigan, the Great Lakes, and adjacent midwestern states—the
study area is marked in the northwestern portion of the state's Lower Peninsula.
National Atlas of the United States, March 5, 2003, *nationalatlas.gov*

residents, this is not surprising. Many found it easiest to understand the project as
a study of "why people are moving to Traverse City." Their assumption was that I
wanted to know what people find so attractive about the place. Following this assumption, they tended not to see it properly as a study of *why* people move or what
moving might mean for them. This misconception caused some to roll their eyes
in apparent frustration that someone would study a question with so obvious an
answer. I received an e-mail following a local TV news report that illustrates this
sentiment.

> I saw your project in the news and felt compelled to send you a brief mes-
> sage. Although I don't live in Traverse City, I do have a lot of dealings there
> as I live within forty-five minutes' drive. I don't mean this to be insulting in
> any way, but as a blue-collar worker from the Flint area [an industrial town
> roughly three hours' drive south of Traverse City], I feel it should be obvi-

ous to the most casual observer the reasons for leaving the heavily populated industrialized areas of the state, as it was to my wife and I when we decided to leave. [We] have discussed this many times as we have watched the population of even our small local area grow.

The more cynical tended to question the merit of a project in which they assumed I would spend my days cavorting with people of privilege. This attitude is not unique to non-academics. For example, in a thorough study of gentrification in a variety of small-town and urban neighborhoods of the United States, sociologist Japonica Brown-Saracino attempts to explain why the academic literature has tended to greatly oversimplify the phenomenon—making generalizations that were dramatically inconsistent with her own findings. Gentrification typically describes a process whereby comparatively affluent people move to a distinct urban or even a rural area—a phenomenon that may lead to increasing property values and rent as well as changes in the character and culture of this place. Used negatively, the term has come to suggest displacement of poor residents by wealthy outsiders. Despite this common use, its effects are complex and may be contradictory. Among Brown-Saracino's explanations for the oversimplification are that previous researchers have overlooked important elements simply because they found the motivations and beliefs of a category of persons—the gentry—unworthy of attention given what she describes as an inclination in the social sciences to use scholarship to advocate for marginal populations in a given society. Further, she refers to a predisposition of scholars to focus on the relative structural *position* of white middle- and upper-class Americans and, in the case of gentrification, the potential impact of their behavior on the disenfranchised, rather than on cultural variation—meaningful differences in motivations, beliefs, or practices—*within* these social classes.[5]

Let's be clear that the ability to relocate as seen in lifestyle migration is reasonably understood to be at least partly contingent on financial well-being and attendant social status. The majority of people with whom I worked had not only the economic wherewithal but also a personal background capable of facilitating their decision to move. This background may entail personal histories that made them more optimistic about taking risks associated with relocation—including, in many cases, a significant career change. Their economic resources may constitute sufficient personal finances to assure them at least some cushion during disruptive transition that comes with relocation from one place to another regardless of distance. When compared with others of different personal backgrounds, with troubled financial history or credit standing, lifestyle migrants may be more likely to have success securing loans for starting businesses and/or buying homes. This is a matter all the more significant in light of recent economic turmoil. As it was put to me by one of my project participants, no doubt referencing the perennially popular self-help book for those thinking about shifting career paths titled *What Color Is Your Parachute*, "You need to first *have* a parachute before you can worry about what color it might be."

Thus, upon hearing that I am looking at people relocating for reasons of lifestyle it isn't surprising that some came to equate this as a concern for what sociologist Thorstein Veblen called the "leisure class" a century earlier.[6] While some move to this region with expansive wealth compared to neighbors of decidedly middling conditions, I do not concern myself with these particular newcomers. Although I would not be opposed to applying the term *lifestyle migration* to a wide cross-section of the US population who choose to relocate in order to emphasize quality of life, whether this be rural- or urban-bound, I do not work with or represent all cases of such migration or socioeconomic tiers of American society.

When compared to people with average income, the affluent need be concerned far less with financial considerations of relocation. In such a privileged position, local work is seldom at issue as lives in any given place may subsidized from outside what a local economy can provide. This is also true for senior citizens who may retire on pensions and, in some areas of the country, contribute to formation of "mailbox economies" where retirement payments—now more likely to be direct deposited—have, for at least the last fifty years, helped shape local economic conditions in a variety of places in the United States. In these cases, migration may be about lifestyle, but they generally do not present the researcher with the same opportunities to examine changing cultures of work and family as among a working middle class.

While lifestyle is generally understood as an expression of individual choice and attributed to the realm of leisure, it does not follow that lifestyle migration is an exclusive privilege of members of Veblen's leisure class. Local author Sandra Bradshaw once said that in order to live year-round in the study area, you need to be one of what she calls the "3 Rs." Her simple 3-R characterization involves being rich, retired, or resourceful.[7] While the region attracts both the rich and retired—particularly during warmer months when numerous second homes are seasonally occupied—year-round migrants with whom I work tend to be a highly *resourceful* lot.

As I narrow the focus to working individuals and families of middling conditions, how then should we define the middle class for practical purposes of sampling and inclusion, among other things? I turn to the sociologist Alan Wolfe for whom middle-class status in America is as much state of mind as level of wealth or income. In an extensive survey of Americans, he found that income levels considered middle class among those interviewed ranged from $50,000 to roughly $200,000. While economically based definitions may change, he learned that it was the moral and cultural meanings of middle class as a social category that persist and define it for people in their everyday lives.[8]

Opting for Elsewhere explores the decisions of everyday Americans who choose relocation as a way of charting courses for themselves and their families and, in so doing, suggest possible futures for the meaning of work, family, and community in America. While not all forms of lifestyle migration fit this format, research presented here was concerned with migration to rural and small-town areas. Typically the concern of rural sociologists, geographers, and economists interested in development in such areas, I instead approach this migration from the perspective of a cultural anthropologist using the principal method of this discipline. An ethnographic methodology allows people to tell me about their relocation in detail so that I could see the process by which they construct a sense of self as *narrators*. What do they feel is their story? While I worked from a guide for our initial meeting, thereafter participants decided what to discuss and how to treat the topic. They gave their own continuity and context to an unfolding narrative told in many cases over the course of months or—in some cases—years of contact.[9] Working from such a microlevel, this approach encourages me to then link individual lives at a midlevel of the communities that simultaneously work to attract residents and capital through initiatives sensitive to consumer demands as well as deal with potential problems of in-migration-induced growth. I further locate lifestyle migration within the macrolevel setting for these individual lives and communities—a larger context that cultural, social, and economic changes in the United States continue to reshape. This book is a glimpse into the lived experience of those changes from the perspective of lifestyle migrants.

Acknowledgments

Without doubt, I am genuinely indebted to the participants in my fieldwork who have given willing access into their stories and lives. It must be understood that without such willingness ethnographic research would not be possible. While I cannot name them all, I want each and every one of them to know (again) how very moved I have been by their experiences. I have learned from them in a multitude of ways—lessons for which I am very grateful.

Accounting for all the many instances in which someone has made a contribution to my work in the conduct of this research and the writing of this book is not an easy task. There are countless times that I have been given some new bit of insight and thus benefited from the feedback of such people as participants in, and audience members at, the sessions that I have organized on subjects related to this research at a variety of academic conferences, as well as anonymous reviewers of this book and earlier publications in a variety of journals and books. I would like to single out Janet Finn, Melissa Fischer, and Denise Lawrence-Zuniga, with whom I worked closely in preparation for a session that I organized at the American Anthropological Association's annual meetings and subsequently as I guest edited a special edition of the journal *City and Society*. They are first-rate scholars who gave me a great deal of helpful feedback on my work. I appreciate the labor of many fine editors with whom I have worked over the years as their efforts helped hone the presentation of my scholarship in a variety of venues. Here, I will direct specific praise to Eli Bortz of Vanderbilt University Press, who recognized the potential for this book in a much earlier manuscript. I will also give thanks to Kathleen Kageff for her adept copyediting skills.

Financial support from the Alfred P. Sloan Foundation provided through the Center for the Ethnography of Everyday Life at the University of Michigan enabled my early fieldwork. I benefited tremendously from my experiences with the center and particularly through my close association with supportive colleagues there—including Lara Descartes, Janet Dunn, Sallie Han, Pete Richardson, Elizabeth Rudd, and Rebecca Upton. Further support from the Research Committee at Marshall University permitted me to conduct follow-up research and to complete the writing of this book.

I have had the good fortune of working with several excellent mentors during my undergraduate and graduate studies—from many of whom I continue to seek advice. Surely much of my earliest appreciation for and understanding of "place," so essential to my conceptualization of lifestyle migration, comes from my work with Peter Owens, a landscape architect and planner, and Richard Borden, an environmental psychologist, at the College of the Atlantic, where I earned my undergraduate degree in human ecology. In graduate school at the University of Michigan, I worked with many fine scholars, who each made their contribution. Among those most responsible for my training are Conrad Kottak, Roy "Skip" Rappaport, and Tom Fricke. In particular, Tom has left the indelible mark of his deeply moral understanding of culture and the conduct of ethnographic field-work—the sense that these are both essentially built on linkages of obligation and commitments to "the good." I have been inspired by his sensitive insight. Finally, I acknowledge the incalculable contributions to my sense of the world provided by my parents, Nancy and James Hoey, as well as my wife, Bonnie Marquis.

Chapter 9 utilizes—with permission—material that previously appeared in Brian A. Hoey, "Place for Personhood: Individual and Local Character in Lifestyle Migration," *City and Society* 22, no. 2 (2010): 237–61.

PART I

Introductions

CHAPTER 1

Reinvent or Die

Released in 1968, the poignant, nostalgic song "America" captured the character of an especially restive time in American history. Written while singer-songwriter Paul Simon visited Saginaw, Michigan, for a concert at the local YMCA, it was released just as he and partner, Art Garfunkel, were becoming a national sensation. Simon's experience inspired him to pen a song of two lovers who strike out from the city—one reflecting during their journey that "Michigan seems like a dream to me now. / It took me four days to hitchhike from Saginaw. / I've come to look for America."[1] Though Simon and Garfunkel were heading to fame and fortune, it was not by way of Saginaw—its fortunes were headed elsewhere. At this juncture, the city was poised unwittingly to leave behind glory as a star in the constellation of midwestern industrial might. Today the city has been hollowed out by cost-cutting closings of General Motors factories—with its ripple effect into local businesses—and an ensuing hemorrhage of population.

In the 2010 census, some fifty-one thousand people called Saginaw home. That's just shy of half the high-water mark set in 1960. In the past decade alone, ten thousand residents called it quits to find their fortune elsewhere. To the extent that Saginaw continues to show life—at least from afar—one might say it is largely through persistent longing. In late 2010, a reporter for the *Saginaw News* documented appearance of what he came to understand was a coordinated effort by a mural painter who had returned to Saginaw after leaving many years earlier. He began spray-painting lyrics from Simon and Garfunkel's "America" on abandoned structures around town, over two dozen altogether.[2] Notably, those who left Saginaw in increasing numbers over the past few decades left not so much to "look for America" as to look for improved economic prospects somewhere else within it. They opted for elsewhere.

This book is about an *option of elsewhere* seen in the behavior of migrants who decide on relocation as a means of starting over—here according to a personal *lifestyle commitment* within an overarching concern for quality of life.[3] I aim to contextualize lifestyle migration within a discussion of significant processes of cultural, social, and economic change and debates about the meaning of such basic categories as work, family, and community. I have structured the book into five sections. Part I foregrounds essential elements of the story of lifestyle migration through introducing processes for individual and collective construction of "the good"—something basic to the relocation decisions of lifestyle migrants—together with a perspective on how this entails taking a moral orientation that is inherently *spatial.* I also offer a descriptive discussion of the physical setting for this research. Part II draws on the accounts of migrants as well as a historical discussion of relevant migration trends in the United States to establish an appreciation of what is at stake in lifestyle migration for people and the places that are affected by their relocation decisions. Part III furthers an examination of essential elements by exploring the changing meaning of work in the lives of lifestyle migrants as well as the importance of a cultivated sense of place in an emerging identity facilitated by the act of relocation. Part IV explores the complex dimensions and tensions entailed in the paths that lifestyle migrants take as they navigate between actual and—what we may think of as—*potential* selves. Part V concludes my analysis by examining dynamics between migrants and longtime residents in destination communities and tying up threads from the book as a whole in order to succinctly situate lifestyle migration in what appear as contemporary cultural trends. Finally, the Epilogue extends our consideration of what lifestyle migration might be able to tell us about what's next in American society while rounding out the stories of three central characters. I have included a discussion of methods as well as a copy of my initial interview guide in the Appendixes.

Given that the area that I chose for examining this migration phenomenon—and what it might imply about both shifting meanings and structural conditions—is in a state where stories of in-migration run very much counter to a prevailing contemporary story of exodus, I have chosen to focus the introductory chapter on the current state of Michigan in light of the aforementioned cultural, social, and economic changes. In this way, I introduce my approach to lifestyle migration, which is to explore the accounts of these migrants for what we can learn about changing cultural understandings in the United States.

Michigration

In an apparent slip of the tongue, a TV reporter out of Grand Rapids, Michigan, coined a term for contemporary out-migration from the state when she inadvertently combined two words during her commentary to form the catchy "Michigration" while reporting on a study conducted by United Van Lines and released in early 2008. The study was well timed for the gaffe, coming just as a deep recession took hold of the nation. One of the country's largest moving companies, United reported that in 2007 Michigan was number one among all states for *outbound* moves handled by the company at 67.8 percent of all contracts (both inbound and outbound for the state). Nearly 110,000 more people left the state from 2007 to 2008 than moved in.[4]

While many have already left Michigan, there is evidence that during the past several years many more would have moved out of state. Even in instances where skilled workers have job offers out of state, they remain saddled with homes that have lost so much value that many are now "underwater" on mortgages—a term that appropriately captures a sense of drowning. Mortgages that are underwater have home owners who own more on their loan than the value of the house and land. In real estate parlance, these homes are "distressed properties." Clearly, it isn't only the properties that are troubled. In this state, worried home owners have been unwilling or unable to leave. Many became, in effect, economic detainees of a deflated housing market. They are an opposing category to the "equity migrants" who, in better economic times, used value in houses sold in one location to fund relocations to other places. Before the economic crisis, many lifestyle migrants spoke to me of how they were able to take advantage of home equity—the value of ownership that they had built up in a home representing current market value less any mortgage balance. The relative prosperity of the 1990s and early 2000s enabled them to subsidize potentially risky career moves before the housing market collapsed. Far fewer are capable of putting to use such a strategy today.

Taking on the question of how the 2008 stock market and housing market crash may reshape the social and economic landscape of America, urban studies theorist Richard Florida fundamentally challenges home ownership as a long-privileged center to the US economy and central tenet of a normative American dream. Referring to what he terms "distortive incentives," ranging from government tax breaks to artificially low interest rate for mortgages coming into the crisis, Florida concludes that despite compelling reasons for home ownership—including higher levels of engagement in civic life—our fixation has proven too costly to the economy.[5] An unprecedented level of home ownership—on the order of 70 percent nationally before the bust—created a workforce too often trapped in a location with few prospects at the very time that flexibility and mobility become imperatives of an emerging economy fundamentally different from the one that once established Michigan as an industrial powerhouse a century ago. The ability, if not desire, to relocate is an obligation for life in a highly globalized world.

With home ownership dropping from a historic high, the challenges of an emerging economic order on families preoccupy those who make it their job to sell houses. A recent National Association of Realtors (NAR) report gives special attention to strategizing how to convince an entire generation known by most as Millennials—now in their twenties and thirties—that owning is preferable to renting.[6] Also called Generation Y, this birth cohort significantly outnumbers my own Generation X that preceded them. In fact, these so-called Echo Boomers—born between the early 1980s and 2000 and named by some to denote them as a demographic reverberation of the Baby Boom—number some eighty million strong. This figure puts them ahead of that earlier, swollen cohort born from the end of World War II to the early 1960s. Thus, the answer to how and where Generation Y will decide to reside is one many would like to know given that it will have substantial impact not only on the economic welfare of real estate agents but also on the economy as a whole as well as for patterns of internal migration in the United States for years to come.

Echo Boomers—many of whom were just poised to launch their adult lives and careers—have witnessed the nation's current economic and political turmoil born, in large part, by a burst housing bubble. Thus, the NAR report suggests the belief among some Realtors that this generation may no longer hold that home ownership represents the American Dream. So outward is the Millennials' apparent aversion to buying a home—now perceived as risky behavior—that economist Todd Buchholz has declared them a "Go-Nowhere Generation" to emphasize how the number of young adults living with their parents had nearly doubled by 2008 compared to 1980 (when members of that cohort were first born). Importantly, his data was collected even before the so-called Great Recession had taken hold. Similarly, while 80 percent of eighteen-year-olds in 1980 had obtained a driver's license, by 2008 that number had dropped by 15 percent.[7] According to Nicolas Meilhan, an automotive analyst with Frost and Sullivan in Paris, "Owning a car is thought to be very stupid by Generation Y . . . [who] are moving from car ownership to renting. The business model of the future is to rent."[8] Have we gone all the way from the driveway-mechanic-fashioned muscle car to the on-demand rental car popularized by emerging companies like Zipcar in little more than a generation? Does any of this suggest a generation who, unlike their parents and grandparents, is disinclined to hit the road—whether they are hitchhiking or behind the wheel—in order "to look for America?"

Of further concern to the National Association of Realtors is the fact that their own data suggests that there may be significant shifts in consumer attitudes and behaviors. For example, just before the turmoil that began in 2007, home owners expected to stay in their properties for eight years, according to the annual "Profile of Home Buyers and Sellers" report by the NAR released in 2006. In the report issued in 2011, the expectation had nearly doubled to fifteen years.

Like many around the country that have played a waiting game, would-be migrants in Michigan have waited hoping that the housing and job markets would improve. While they waited, the broader economy deteriorated further until jobs that might have been found outside the state had disappeared as well. In Metro Detroit, the median sale price for a home dropped by two-thirds between January 2005 and January 2009.[9] Ironically, in places like Detroit and nearby Youngstown, Ohio—communities tied to the auto industry—by 2012 a worker might expect no more from the sale of his or her home for than the retail price of the midsized cars that workers themselves were building on the job. Thus, for those who wanted to leave, it appeared that they had lost their chance—unless willing to sell at fire-sale prices in an act of desperation that would only further drive down prices on remaining homes and increase the challenges facing others who might want to leave.

Despite worries about the generation as a whole, many of those leaving the state are recent college graduates, twenty-somethings—most of whom did not own homes and are thus relatively untethered when compared to most working families. While nearly 40 percent of those leaving had at least a four-year college degree, only one-quarter of those who remain are degree holders. Although, through a legislative effort to boost Michigan's fortunes, the numbers of graduates at all levels of postsecondary education are up, as much as 53 percent of native-born University of Michigan graduates left the state in 2008 when the recession began. The loss of revenue is staggering—billions in lost paychecks and taxes. The income leaving the state cost Michigan over $100 million in 2007 alone, at a time that it could ill afford such losses.[10] Departing twenty-somethings are leaving behind an aging population burdened with expensive infrastructure built for many more than those remaining—a problem felt most acutely by Detroit, which has lost some two-thirds of its population over the past half century. According to the United States Census Bureau, Detroit's population peaked in 1950 at 1.8 million residents. As of the 2010 census, the city had just over 714,000 people—a whopping 25 percent drop since the census just ten years earlier. Saginaw too saw heavy losses during the last census period, having lost 17 percent of its already greatly diminished midcentury population.

Clearly, such out-migration of the state's young is not what was intended for its investment in higher education. Who then benefits from the considerable value that this training represents? In the nearby Chicago area, expatriate communities of graduates from Michigan's largest universities are greater than concentrations of their graduates within the state. Three times as many Michigan State University graduates call Chicago home than Detroit. In the state of Washington—some two thousand miles away—the influx of college-educated workers from Michigan to work at companies such as Boeing and Microsoft over the past few years has been of sufficient volume to earn public recognition by state legislators there. Washington state representative Glenn Anderson, ranking Republican on the state's Higher Education Committee, acknowledged, "We are importing intellectual capital at a very low cost to ourselves."[11] Apparently, this cheap capital import has made it difficult for the politician to increase funding for students in his home state. Why pay at home for what you can get for free from elsewhere?

During recent economic downturns in the state, Michigan's more educated workers were recruited by or sought work with the country's top companies. Many wage laborers flocked to boomtowns in the southwest such as Las Vegas. Construction and other jobs associated with the city's growth attracted well over ten thousand Michigan residents from 2001 to 2007 according to IRS figures. In 2008, however, Vegas lost thousands of construction jobs as a bubble of speculative growth burst with a housing market collapse.[12] This gambling boomtown appeared to have gone bust. As recently as mid-2012, the state of Nevada as a whole ranked number one for home foreclosures.

Labor migration from Michigan is not new. The state has experienced many periods of economic hardship. The state's industrial economy has been wholly reinvented at least once. At the end of the nineteenth century, the state's industry began shifting from timber and other natural resource extraction to complex manufacturing with the automobile and, specifically, Henry Ford's vision not only for production but also for a consumption-driven economy that would come to define the aspirations of a burgeoning American middle class. Ford understood that the mass production that he implemented in assembly-line factories would require mass consumption in order to be profitable and sustainable. This meant paying higher wages that created opportunity for many to achieve a growing dream of both home and automobile ownership.

During much of the twentieth century, Michigan experienced booms and busts as an increasingly global economy shaped consumption of goods like cars. When times got bad, cyclical migration patterns developed in which many out-of-work residents relocated to other parts of the country not hit by a drop in demand for cars and trucks that would lead to layoffs in the auto industry. Working out of state for a period of months or even years, these *economic migrants* supported family back home in Michigan in order to keep hard-earned "blue-collar" middle-class homes and land paid for by hard work on the shop floors of Fordist industry.

When jobs returned to Michigan during a return to profit for the automakers, so did these laborers.

This time seems different, however. When I recently spoke to people from cities like Detroit, Flint, and Saginaw, they seemed to wonder if their state would ever fully recover. Can industry in the state reinvent itself again? Without such a wholesale rebirth, the fate of the state as a whole might be like that of these cities, each of which seems caught in a protracted, downward spiral—motor cities now out of gas. Chatting with a resident of Saginaw during a roadside stop just outside the city on my way north to the study area in summer 2012, I was presented with his surreal assessment that watching the deterioration and depopulation of his hometown was as if witnessing the same wrath that Hurricane Katrina unleashed on New Orleans but only in slow motion and without the benefit of government-subsidized rebuilding in its aftermath. What could I say? I murmured "Good luck." I meant it, but in truth I am sure that luck has nothing to do with what's been going on there.

Option of Elsewhere

Coining a term in the 1960s to describe an American frontier ethic rendered for the economic sphere, the economist Kenneth Boulding cautioned against the destructive potential of what he called a "cowboy economy" that uses up one place in order to seek opportunity beyond a real or imagined horizon.[13] Robert Beckley, dean of the University of Michigan's Taubman College of Architecture and Urban Planning, addressed the term's contemporary relevance for describing the experience of Saginaw's sister city of Flint, which he too suggests has experienced Katrina-like devastation—albeit from a wholly unnatural disaster.[14] In his address, Beckley spoke to how Flint gained notoriety by way of the activist-filmmaker Michael Moore's now iconic early film *Roger and Me*, which Moore intended as documentation of the real costs of the cowboy economy for places and people left behind. Specifically, in the film Moore chronicles the social effects of General Motors plant closings in his hometown with his now familiar style of ornery reportage.

Moore relocated his production company to northwestern Lower Michigan, where he has renovated a stately old theatre and begun the now internationally renowned Traverse City Film Festival. When I returned to Traverse City in the summer of 2010 for follow-up research, word on the street was that Californians ("film industry types") were buying up stylish new downtown condos. Indeed, the parking garage had many fine cars with California plates and long-term permit stickers. While *Roger and Me* resonates more than ever and Moore's investments in my study area have made a significant contribution to an increasingly diverse and relatively stable economy in northern Lower Michigan, like that of many other former industrial centers, Flint's fortunes appear set for continuing decline. During the recent recession, General Motors cut its workforce in the city from a high of eighty thousand to around fifteen thousand.

Ironically, even while Robert Beckley uses Boulding's thesis of the cowboy economy to attack the guiding ethic of industrial capitalists that have devastated local economies in Michigan and elsewhere, he speaks wistfully of a tradition of

Front Street in Traverse City during the Traverse City Film Festival of 2012. Photo by Brian Hoey

reinvention in Flint's economy. I would argue that any such "tradition" is part and parcel of a fundamentally American belief in the capacity to remake oneself through sheer force of will—a faith central to the relocation decision making of lifestyle migrants that I document in this book. Such faith is vital to a robust capitalism that holds that "creative destruction" and renewal are essential elements to economic growth. Writing in 1942 about this notion in the book that popularized it, the economist Joseph Schumpeter asserted: "The opening up of new markets, foreign or domestic, and the organizational development from the craft shop and factory to such concerns as U.S. Steel illustrate the same process of industrial mutation—if I may use that biological term—that incessantly revolutionizes the economic structure from within, incessantly destroying the old one, incessantly creating a new one. This process of creative destruction is the essential fact about capitalism. It is what capitalism consists in and what every capitalist concern has got to live in."[15] Belief in the prospect of rebirth through such creative destruction, or at least the *option of elsewhere*, drives both companies and people from one place to another. While it is hard to find virtue in this behavior given costs to those left behind in particular communities, in this drive forward we find an optimistic faith in the possibility of redemption or revitalization through confident change. Oddly, even while wholly uprooted in this manifestation, it is the same dream that Paul Simon's anonymous hitchhiker invokes in his desire to go and look for America by leaving places like Saginaw behind. It is faith in rebirth, reinvention. If Saginaw or Flint can pull through, it will take genuine commitment to fulfilling a vision for starting over—though one that must be *rooted* in that place.

In this odd confluence of dispositions, we can appreciate how the United States has a history of conflicting but largely balanced tendencies with respect to individual and community life. On the one hand, Americans have long embraced an individualistic, *centrifugal* pattern that inspires outward mobility where meaning and identity are found "on the road." On the other hand, we have had a complementary, communally focused *centripetal* pattern that has centered on domestication, settling down, and place-based identity formation. At least since the 1970s, however, this national balancing may have been put into jeopardy as the centrifugal tendency became increasingly pervasive throughout all domains of life. Recent history suggests that the scales might have been tipped by the sheer weight of a consumer capitalism that goes beyond consumption of goods as a virtue to instill values that encourage people to constantly seek to begin again, overturn the past, and neglect existing attachments. The lifestyle migration documented in this book occurs at the cusp between these competing tendencies and suggests ways in which at least some Americans are attempting to find balance again.

CHAPTER 2

Constructing the Good

While this book is not based on a community study, per se, such studies typically engage with the same on-the-ground, bread-and-butter issues as those addressed here—questions, for example, about how individuals struggle to negotiate variously contending economic imperatives, moral obligations, and personal expectations. As suggested in my assessment of Michigan's exceptional challenges in the previous chapter, the problems facing many communities are varied and potentially overwhelming. Homelessness, ineffectual schools, crumbling infrastructure, and distressed families are just a few of many difficulties that exact high societal costs (both in dollars and lost potential) as people struggle first to achieve financial stability and further to lead personally fulfilling and culturally meaningful lives.

Community, both real and imagined, plays an essential role in the public debate over the impacts of profound cultural, social, and economic changes on people and places just as it does in the lives of ordinary people who search for their own solutions to everyday problems. In searching for a compelling reason to explain why some people stay or even return to depressed, rural communities that he terms "rural ghetto" in his investigation into economic and population decline in agriculturally dominated places of the United States over the second half of the twentieth century, the writer Osha Gray Davidson describes a shared longing to feel that we belong to a group that is "larger than family but more embraceable than a nation."[1] This longing is at the base of the centripetal pattern—to which I referred earlier—at work in shaping certain critical elements of the American physical and social landscape since its beginning as a nation. For lifestyle migrants, such a sense of belonging is sought through community believed rooted in a location or even "based on geography"—as one migrant so tellingly put it. Still, as evident from the many layers of emotional meaning attached to the word or idea of community, the concept has meaning that goes beyond mere geographic place or local activity. It implies expectation for a special quality of human relationship.[2]

In her article "Fieldwork in the Postcommunity," the anthropologist Sherry Ortner considers the meaning of community for ethnographic studies when most Americans "live in a condition in which the totality of their relations is precisely not played out within a single geographic location and a single universe of known others, both at a given point in time and across time."[3] Ortner explores its usefulness as a concept in anthropology considering—among other postcommunal characteristics—the many aspects of hypermobility that characterize contemporary society. She concludes that community remains useful as a concept so long as we do not identify it with harmony and cohesion or describe it as something bounded, discrete, and particular to a single people in a specific place, that is, as localized, on-the-ground entities—something that has been done for much of the history of ethnographic studies. My own use of the term should be considered apart from a theoretical and methodological debate over its usefulness as an analytical construct. I am talking about community as perception, as imagining, and as something experienced or sought in the lives of migrants—as what we might call a *structure of feeling*.[4]

Citing a study by Joseph Gusfield, the sociologist David Hummon notes in his own study of community as idea and lived experience that the "enduring power of the concept of community must be found, not in its scientific utility, but in its 'poetic' meanings: its power as an expressive metaphor and myth to *evaluate* human relations."[5] Community as evoked both in public discourse and individual thought is thus properly seen as always involving a *moral* perspective through which people may take a stand and weigh the extent to which present relations among individuals in a given time and place fulfill an idealized vision. Basically, though academics may wrangle over the meaning or worth of community as an analytical concept, the fact remains that it matters as an idea in people's everyday lives and is an important category to examine in order to understand a given culture. Hummon's study investigates popular American beliefs and sentiments about the city, suburb, and small town in terms of what he calls distinct "community ideologies" as a way of providing a broader interpretation of American culture in the late twentieth century.

In a manner akin to notions of culture expounded by the anthropologist Clifford Geertz, Hummon defines such ideologies as involving "system[s] of belief that use conceptions of community to describe, evaluate, and explain social reality, and that [do] so in such a manner so as to motivate commitment to community."[6] Geertz notably asserted that "culture is public, because meaning is" and that thought is largely the same throughout humanity even while symbols that people in different cultures use to communicate their ideas may be quite dissimilar.[7] In this understanding, symbols shared among members of a given culture are not studied to gain access to private mental processes, that is, to get inside people's heads, but rather as a basis for interpreting observable social phenomena in a specific cultural context. That is how I approach my own ethnographic work. Similarly, in Hummon's usage, *community ideologies*—as symbolic forms that legitimate individual and collective commitments to particular forms of community—are therefore essential to understanding the "symbolic resources" available to people for creating and sustaining these commitments and, in particular, how they put them to use in their everyday lives. Given this, fieldwork in communities should entail determining not only similarities and differences between what may be distinct ideological forms among local groups but also the means by which people come to hold particular moral orientations constructed from these resources.

It is useful further to note that Geertz stressed that culture may be productively thought of as consisting of particular models for understanding the world. Specifically, he saw culture as fundamentally "models of" and "models for" reality. As models *of* reality, cultural patterns such as Hummon's community ideologies constitute the perceived worlds of human actors. They speak to how the world is actually believed to be. Thus, they represent a certain conception of reality *as it is*. On the other hand, as models *for* reality, such cultural patterns offer the ethnographer ways of seeing into moral worlds and allow analysis of the sense of obligation to others and to particular ideals that people may feel based on shared categories of meaning within a particular group. Here cultural patterns speak to how those that hold these categories of meaning believe the world *should be*. Hence, they represent certain moral sensibilities and, indeed, are basic to any understanding of what constitutes *the good*—as in what goes into making "the good life." We can easily see why such a view is useful to understanding social phenomenon, including such things as lifestyle migration. Together, these models (of and for reality) allow people, individually and collectively, to make sense of the world and their place in it—they give form and meaning to life while legitimating commitments to particular ways of believing and acting in the world.[8]

In her community study of Viroqua, Wisconsin, sociologist Lyn MacGregor examines how three distinct "cultures of community," representing what amounts to distinct *community ideologies* as they were conceptualized in Hummon's study, go about living and working together in this small town—a town that like Traverse City in my own study area has many outward markers and symbols that continue to characterize an idealized American community of an imagined past.[9] Members of these groups, identified by the social scientist as "Alternatives," "Main Streeters," and "Regulars," each assert that they value community and a personal sense of community; however, they have quite different understandings of what constitutes community and how people should go about making it. These differences contribute to important distinctions among individuals and groups and to organization of the town's social life. Speaking in terms that reflect Geertz's notion of culture, MacGregor states, specifically, that residents of Viroqua "had differing ideas about how community *worked* and—more important—how it *ought* to work."[10]

Much as I would say is true of lifestyle migrants in my study, in her study of newcomers engaging in what is generally referred to as "gentrification" in a variety of places, Brown-Saracino found they "vary in terms of impetus for their relocation, their ideological orientation to the place of residence, longtimers [longtime local residents], gentrification, and their practices."[11] Like these other community-oriented studies, Brown-Saracino also attempts to place persons in her study into analytically meaningful categories defined by their ideological distinctions vis-à-vis community. In each of these cases, it boils down to what I would characterize as models *of* and models *for* community—complete with distinct moral orientations and particular sets of possibilities and limitations for individual belief and behavior.

Like Hummon and Brown-Saracino, MacGregor is interested not in seeing if people in her study measure up to an arbitrary definition of community in their attempts to create it; rather she wants to see how assumptions inherent in their distinct orientations to—or "styles" of—community making variously enable or constrain them as individuals and groups in that particular place and time. The question is essentially then "What did it *mean* for them in terms of their everyday lives?" rather than "How successful were these groups at enacting their particular form of community?" Thus, we may say that she was interested in the "poetic" meanings to which Hummon refers. Community becomes a symbolic expression of varied cultural understandings and values to which we have access as social scientists. In speaking about what this cultural approach revealed to her as a sociologist conducting fieldwork in this small Wisconsin town, MacGregor avows that her "biggest surprise was . . . [finding] ideas about obligation and agency, and specifically about the degree to which it is necessary or good to try to bring one's life into precise conformance with a set of larger goals, turned out to have replaced more traditional markers of social belonging, such as occupation or ethnicity."[12]

Much more significant than her contribution of another typology, MacGregor establishes that distinct "ethics of agency" and "logics of commitment" informed the ways that residents in her study created community—indeed, how it structured belief and behavior in many facets of their lives. As for an ethic of agency, MacGregor defines this as "the view one takes of the moral value of individual deliberation and choice" where, in Viroqua, some residents "operated on the assumption that deliberation and individual choice was the basis of any moral action . . . [and] others thought it more valuable to accept one's situation as part of some 'natural' order of things."[13] The first of these is akin to the commitment seen in "weighing" behavior to which I will refer in the accounts of lifestyle migrants. One can see this similarity in MacGregor's definition of logic of commitment as "a set of ideas about how one is connected to and obligated to the communities in one's life . . . [that] provides a basis for ordering priorities and evaluating options."[14] Again, we are returned to moral orientation as entailed in these ideas of obligation as well as to how people may now, if not by more "traditional" means, come to hold their particular understandings of *the good* and how a person must, through individual agency, negotiate a process of forging identity and establishing their own social belonging.

The Great Northern Dream

As in other parts of the United States, in the Grand Traverse region of Michigan there are chambers of commerce, boards of real estate, and others who serve as professional boosters by promoting economic development through relocation to their geographic areas of concern.[15] The job isn't easy in difficult economic times. In places like Saginaw and Flint, it must seem downright impossible nowadays. As they have for nearly a century, in Northern Michigan such promoters spin elaborate, even captivatingly literary, visions of lifestyle dreams fulfilled by moving "Up North," a term of local vernacular importance to which I will return. In what amounts to a kind of guided visualization, we can see how these boosters translate a normative American dream regarding home ownership into a locally germane version that they call the "Great Northern Dream."

> Go ahead; indulge yourself in the Great Northern Dream—owning a condo on the lake, hunting cabin in a hardwood forest, or an upscale natural log home. Then make your dream reality. You can fill your fondest housing

fantasy in Northwest Michigan, whether it is residential, vacation or rental property. Real estate here is geared to complement every lifestyle from active to reclusive. Our diverse geography provides home settings along scenic coastlines, in thick piney woods and within charming historic towns. We have a variety of developments: world-class lakeshores; golf or ski communities; friendly family neighborhoods; streets lined with stately Victorian mansions; and green acres graced with old farmhouses, rolling hills and cherry blossoms.[16]

In language that addresses head-on the harsh reality of industrial decline in places like Michigan, Daniel Pink, author of several books on the changing nature of work, asserts, "Jobs that depend on routine . . . [and] that you can essentially reduce to a recipe, which used to be a pathway to the middle class, are either being outsourced or automated." Given this, Pink suggests that a new economy is emerging wherein those who are "creators" or "empathizers" will have the greatest ability to excel. According to Pink, there is opportunity for those who are good storytellers and designers—people "who can fashion a compelling experience."[17] In this way, such boosters as these may be well positioned for an emerging economy through their storytelling skills and capacity for constructing compelling visions—even if there is reason to believe that the story may need to be reworked to fit a shifting cultural, social, and economic landscape.

At the time that I was beginning my research in Michigan, such place promoters spoke directly to emerging demographic trends and deliberately linked would-be part-time or full-time residents to larger social phenomenon taking place.

In Northwest Michigan, as in other sections of the nation, the migration of baby boomers to lake and resort communities is rapidly changing the character of the real estate market. Boomers are flocking in unprecedented numbers from Detroit, Chicago and northern Indiana metropolises to enjoy our sweet air, clean waters, and easy northern living. . . . [I]f it's finally time to make your Great Northern Dream come true . . . we're confident you'll find what you dream of in our corner of Michigan. Welcome home.[18]

Literal and figurative brokers of place, both real and imagined, these agents act to facilitate place-consumption choices. The idea of personal fulfillment in their *therapeutic ideal* is potentially conflicted, however, torn as it may be in a perceived choice between practical, material, and economic demands placed on the individual, on the one hand, and the emotional, spiritual, and moral needs of the person on the other.[19] Central to this book is the question of how people choose to respond to everyday struggles between contending obligations and visions of the good life. What are the particular challenges facing contemporary American families in a rapidly changing social and economic climate? Where do people find moral orientation at a time of instable social and cultural categories and diminished importance in traditional sources of shared meaning?

With parallels to long-standing, if now typically marginalized, American traditions of pursuing the "simple life" and getting "back to basics," lifestyle migration often involves seeking places believed by migrants to sustain commitments to "put family first" and to create a greater sense of control in their lives. As MacGregor noticed in Viroqua, I was struck by the degree to which participants in my project felt it necessary or at least highly desirable to attempt to bring their life into a kind of *resonance* with a set of larger goals and commitments. I began to wonder how this impulse might eventually lessen the weight or even supplant expected markers of social belonging such as ethnic background or social class. Through their act of relocation and distinct sense of the moral value of individual deliberation and choice, lifestyle migrants attempt to reposition themselves within persistent, culturally informed notions of the good life.

As an economic recession in the United States deepened in the later part of 2008, themes of "simplicity," "thrift," and "starting over" burst into public discourse and soon splashed the covers of such popular magazines as *Time*, whose April 6, 2009, issue was dramatically titled "The End of Excess." Consistent with a widespread yearning to find an upside to the economic downturn, its cover includes the tagline "Why this crisis is good for America" and features a large, red "reset" button. The notion of a kind of national reset whereby citizens collectively plot their reinvention in accordance to idealized visions, here of a leaner, greener America, parallels the stories of many lifestyle migrants and suggests a deeper longing.

Might the proliferation of consumer movements, such as "slow food," be part of a turn toward simplification? Maggie Jackson, author and journalist whose popular "Balancing Acts" column appeared for several years in the *Boston Globe*, suggests that for many families in America slowing down means disengagement from dependence on complex consumer and cultural value systems.[20] Lifestyle migration should be considered a meaningful part of a heightened public dialog on what constitutes *the good* in light of recent economic upheaval.

Critical Regionalism

Living and working now in West Virginia, some ten hours' drive from my old haunts in Northern Michigan, I have found unexpected connections between the two places. I began to find these connections in my exploration of migration out of West Virginia, which generally has been losing population since at least the mid-twentieth century. The flight of families by what has come to be known as "hillbilly highways," such as US Route 23 nearby my new home, led to the creation of enclaves of Appalachian expatriates throughout the Michigan and other midwestern cities to which I have already referred. The existence of these areas is commonly, mockingly acknowledged through use of colloquialisms such as "Ypsitucky" for the city of Ypsilanti, Michigan, which lies just off Route 23 within a couple hundred miles of its northern terminus.

As I heard back in Ypsilanti, among those in West Virginia who came of age in an earlier era of exodus from the state, people intone an informal slogan for the Appalachian diaspora—an essential lesson of generations past and ironic take on the standard "3 Rs" referred to as "Readin,' 'Ritin,' and Route 23 North."[21] In recent research, I have talked with those who sought work in the burgeoning factories of a postwar boom in the automobile industry of Michigan—at least some of them ending up as far north as Saginaw. Today, their children may find jobs in this industry, but opportunities are few for an upwardly mobile, middle-class lifestyle through employment in this line of work. It is quite unlike the heyday of unionized auto industry labor. Today, Ford and other automobile factories and parts suppliers have a workforce essentially divided between the old-timers and newcomers hired with entirely different compensation in what is now a two-tiered wage system.[22]

In reading the work of scholars of Appalachia, of which West Virginia is considered a virtual heart as it lies wholly within recognized federal limits, I have found inspiration for how I might think about the concept of *region*. For example, when applied to a wide-ranging collection of counties across several states from New York to Mississippi, Douglas Powell suggests that we think of Appalachia as a kind of "container" for a tangled, often temperamental history.[23] It is in the spirit of such a *critical* regionalism that I attempt to treat the region of Northern Michigan referred to colloquially as "Up North" in the state—not as a found thing but as an ongoing construction.

Evoking a region to describe or define places and people geographically situated is necessarily purposive—even intentionally persuasive. To what ends is this term employed and in who's interest? For my part, I employ reference to the region Up North analytically not to set it apart methodologically from other places, even while setting it apart is very much the intent of those that invoke it in everyday usage, but rather as a way of establishing consideration of a distinct set of relationships among different, potentially distant geographic locations. My intent is not only to recognize a term that has local meaning but also, analytically, to emphasize the relational and transitional qualities between local and larger social systems, structures of political, economic, and other forms of power, and patterns of meaning.

As a way of providing thorough grounding in the particulars of the local, its regional connections to places beyond, and a useful context to later, more abstract considerations of the analytic categories basic to this research, I would like to share an intriguing early twentieth century tourism brochure that describes what we can easily characterize as a travel story. Writing nearly a century ago, the authors clearly designed the tale as a way of defining Up North as region, physical destination, and structure of feeling. As a literary genre and icon for the American way of life, *travel narratives* like this early example are central expressions and sources for collective ideals of freedom and opportunity in the United States—they inform models *for* reality, notions of how things should be, and our images of the good life. In a manner akin to the moral foundations of a cowboy economy, such narratives resonate with an enduring belief that one can remake his or herself and redefine the course of an individual life through force of will. As we have already seen, Simon and Garfunkel's song "America"—itself a travel narrative—becomes a national hymn of wanderlust and faith in the ability to start over on the open road.

Fashioning "Up North" as Region of Refuge

Self-promotion of Grand Traverse as destination first kicked into high gear in the early 1900s. In 1924, a fledging organization known as the Leelanau County Association of Commerce was set up to advance the county in the hearts and minds of those residing well outside. In that year, they produced a compelling story of personal transformation through discovery of what is described as the "spirit of place." The original brochure that I examined in the Leelanau Historical Museum—archived as a cultural artifact of local significance—appears published with cooperation from what was known as the Michigan Transit Company. Now defunct, the company's original niche was operating steamships built to carry goods and crew between rising industrial cities of southern Lake Michigan such as Chicago and still prosperous northern lumber and fishing towns. However, as a timber operation became increasingly less profitable and stands of desirable species in the North neared exhaustion, the business was sold to a wealthy Chicago judge in 1919. After struggling into the late 1920s, it was sold again and became bankrupt in 1931, when all operations were finally abandoned.[24]

Today, we recognize this Michigan business's tale as a familiar story of a company—even an entire industry—bending to the winds of changing cultural, social, and economic conditions. The imperative is simple: reinvent or die. It is ironic that a steamship company coproduced a brochure that in the act of marketing local place to would-be tourists simultaneously tells the tale of an over*land* voyage by way of the increasingly ubiquitous and relatively reliable automobile traveling over improving state highways on which the auto became an instrument of creative destruction. It is in this way, however, that the booklet becomes a very early entry to the modern genre of American travel stories centered on *driving* places—of hitting the open road behind the wheel of a car.

Before its insolvency in the early years of the Great Depression, during the 1920s Michigan Transit Company heads were looking to recover lost business as industries based on resource extraction—the foundation of their operations—became less important to local economies because of dwindling stocks of lumber and fish. Local business and civic leaders focused attention on another of the region's assets, tourism, which seemed the best means to attract new capital. Given what social scientists would describe as "natural amenities" throughout the region in the form of plentiful inland lakes, abundant rivers, towering dunes, and miles of coastline, the potential for attracting visitors was high.

Unlike contemporary tourist brochures of few words but many pictures, this brochure is nothing less than a complete travel narrative. It is a carefully crafted account of a midwestern family's journey, in abbreviated form. Beyond being an account of the family's physical expedition, it is meant to convey an unanticipated personal transformation wherein an early industrialist uncovers what we are encouraged as readers to believe is a more authentic self through substantial alteration of everyday routine facilitated by a change of place. The account carries the somewhat dramatic title "The Captives: Being the Story of a Family's Vacation in Leelanau County (Michigan), the Land of Delight," which appears to capitalize on the romance and cachet of imagined frontier passage to a place that today con-

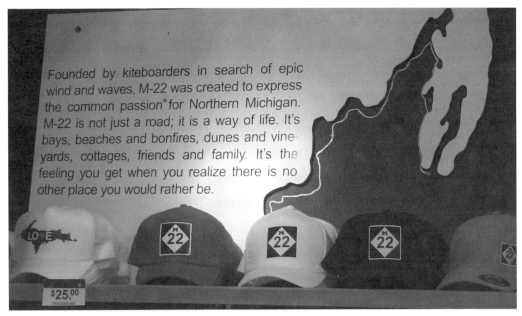

A sign inside the M-22 store in Glen Arbor that illustrates the attempt to
brand a sense and spirit of place through association to Michigan Route 22,
which follows the shore of Leelanau Peninsula. Photo by Brian Hoey

tinues to be home to Native Americans.[25] In apparent contribution to an emergent
discourse at that time about the potentially pathogenic nature of modernity itself,
the tale seeks value through what could otherwise been considered a liability aris-
ing from the region's isolation. Here that potential liability is skillfully converted
into an asset—in a manner akin to how this separation would later be branded by
the Traverse City Convention and Visitors Bureau as "A World Apart."

The name *Leelanau*, and its meaning, "Land of Delight," originate with the
nineteenth-century cultural anthropologist Henry Rowe Schoolcraft, who worked
for decades among Native Americans of the Great Lakes region as a federal Indian
commissioner and Michigan's superintendent of Indian affairs. Although Schoolcraft's story of "Leelinau" was attributed to indigenous peoples of Michigan's
northern peninsula, this tale's spirit was appropriated by boosters in the county for
use in their account as well as in contemporary local notions of the power of Leelanau to enchant people through arousing an inner, personal passion for place.[26]

In the wake of widespread disruptions in traditional life precipitated by the
Industrial Revolution and its impact on the social and cultural world of the United
States in the late nineteenth and early twentieth centuries, public interest for a personal quest in order to in some manner reenchant the world generated an industry.
By the 1920s, this emergent industry sought to cater to travel for retreat.[27] Thus,
like the Great Northern Dream of today, the region was then marketed as refuge
to a growing middle class eager to seek quiet retreat from hectic life in an urbanizing America by journeying to places of great natural beauty and real or imagined
remoteness. For this illustrative family, the personal quest begins as follows: "The
Cyrus Howards were burning up Michigan's Trunk Line Eleven, which follows the

lake along the state's western boundary. For three days the motor had been roaring, the car swaying, the trailer following like a kite tail as they sped from their sweltering Corn Belt home to the cool Northland."

Immediately, "Northland" is established and set dramatically apart not only from the reach of sweltering heat—before home air conditioning became feasible—but also from less tangible undesirables to the south. Referred to as Northland here, today the region is known as Up North. Importantly, the reference is meant to set a region apart as a state of being, as a way of locating oneself, as much as a distinct geographic location. Specifically, the term is used to distinguish the region from both the geographic location and the condition of being in the heavily urban and suburbanized "Downstate," as areas to the south are called by those living in and identifying with the northern parts of Michigan.

Cyrus is a prosperous industrialist from a then booming midwestern city in what would one day be known as the "Rust Belt," home to places like Saginaw, Flint, and Detroit. Like any good upwardly mobile cowboy capitalist, he has not allowed himself a moment of true, recreative rest in all his adult life, we are lead to believe. Even in this unfolding story, when supposedly taking time for leisure with his family on vacation, Cyrus cannot let go of a persistent and self-consuming drive to get ahead—wherever that might be. "Cyrus sat at the wheel, brows drawn, jaw set, driving as though fire and water rushed savagely in his wake. The siren wailed, the car ahead edged over and bellowing through the dust cloud they swung into the left and swept past. Mother spoke: 'Oh Cy, *why* such a rush? For thirty years we've rushed like this!' Mother went on. 'You've burned yourself up to get to where we are. Now there's enough to educate the children, enough for us to live on.'" For this story to work as a promotion for Leelanau County, the Howards need to end up there. Cyrus, however, is dogged in his determination to reach the Straits of Mackinaw, where Lake Huron and Lake Michigan meet at Michigan's southern peninsula's tip and an area established as destination for the Midwest's well-to-do and aspiring classes. Only after frequent and fervent pleadings by his exhausted family does he begrudgingly alter course toward the proximate Grand Traverse region: "At a fork in the road, a huge sign board told them that the turn to the left meant Leelanau County. To the right cars sped in an endless river of seekers after quiet and cool country; to the left the inviting road was uncongested."

Aside from illustrating what was presumably a plausible story allowing would-be vacationers to imagine better selves through seeking a kind of personal refuge in this place, the brochure's story is intended to recast the region as civilized nature—safe and accessible while also distant from the troubles of urban life. After taking a turn down what amounts to the proverbial road less traveled, the Howard family find themselves on a thoroughfare that was "as good a highway as the excellent pike they had deserted." Further, they were now in a place where "green country rolled away, farms, orchards, wooded hills, meadows in bloom." While watching her husband continue in his relentless pursuit of "getting there," regardless of where *there* was, Mrs. Howard glances into the back seat at her "spindly" son Ted. Surely this boy needs to partake in the physically, if not morally, fortifying lifestyle of the country! This is the way life *should* be.

Obsessed with the possibility of being taken advantage of as relatively well-heeled city folk, Cyrus worries over how to deal with car trouble as the motor begins to sputter and fail. He is not at all certain one could even find reliable service in what he still perceives as a veritable wilderness, so far off the beaten path. With characteristic cynicism, he bellows: "Up here off the main line with nobody but hay-makers in garages, fat chance of getting repairs!" Unexpectedly, they find a man who directs them to what proves an outstanding service station. For purposes of the tale, the character of this kindly man is meant to embody characteristics of what the author(s) wish to convey about this place as still frontier rough but possessed of a fresh and rejuvenating hardy health and authentic, childlike goodness and innocence: "He was neither old nor frowsy. His hair and beard were gray but his eyes were as blue as the lake itself and in them was friendliness and tolerance. His hands were browned and hardened but they were clean. He was a rugged fellow with many years on his shoulders but he had the smile of a boy and his voice was like a fresh wind blowing."

As the story continues, we learn that wherever they go, this old-young man appears when they need him. On one of their leisurely rambles through the countryside, they spot the man: "Oh, Neighbor!" called Cyrus, using the term of address he had by then adopted for him. "What're you doing up here?" While responding to Cyrus's query, the man provides a kind of folksy history of the area. His account is spun in such a way that the Howards become part of a long line of seekers who are responding not only to more predictable attractions of economic opportunity in exploitation of region's natural resources but also higher personal callings for seeking some sort of refuge in this place.

> "[I've been] waiting for you to come and get close to the Almighty . . . now you've got a start at a sunburn and are ready to rest in the Land of Delight. That's what Leelanau means in Injun," he explained to Mother. "They lived here and hunted and fished and was happy. Father Marquette and those other old fellers was here a lot and history showed they liked it. The fur traders come and our grandfathers followed them and in the late forties [1840s] commenced to build their homes. Folks've been comin' ever since to settle and now city folks've found out that we've got better roads and we're off the beaten trail and they've come to find contentment . . . like you have, friend."

He continues by saying, "There's rewards up here. We worked hard to whittle our homes out of the forest, but see what we've got. . . . And we can make cross men happy!" Foreshadowing today's weekend commutes made in some middle-class working families who continue to rely on salaries from work in midwestern cities like Chicago to subsidize Up North lifestyles, the man tells them of how city folks manage to live here and work elsewhere while plugging the services of the Michigan Transit Company at the same time. Of course, at the time of this narrative, men might leave their families for a work week during which wives would be expected to look after children rather than pursue their own careers. "They've got cottages around here. They leave Chicago Friday night and get here next morning; first stop. They're with their families until Sunday night when the boat takes 'em back again, ready for the job. Great for 'em!" Apparently, Cyrus begins to really warm to the place. In the end, he struggles to express his newfound sense of self and place at the moment they consider moving on again. He finally blurts out his feelings:

> "Mother," went on Cy, "I dunno. I s'pose there *are* other places, but what's the rush? We can take the road back and stay awhile. I'd like to see the woods in fall . . . and this farming thing might be the making of Ted. . . . Gee, we might as well *live* as just have a house and lot and. . . . Funny"— brushing a hand across his eyes—"I feel funny! Like something was pulling at me here,"—gesturing to his breast. "So do I," murmured Mother, her eyes misted.

So the story goes with the region now established as civilized nature possessing a sense of community and engendering an enduring sense of belonging. As a promotion, it hopes to attract educated, up-market tourists and possibly to convert them to full-time residents. At its close, the Howards finally find the true nature of their friend, Neighbor, as the embodiment of the character of place when he declares, "I'm what you'd call the Spirit of Leelanau. I'm old but I'm young. I'm a son of the Frontier but I've got over being rough." His dualistic makeup is precisely what place marketing in this illuminating brochure is aimed to illustrate. The pitch targets consumers who search for adventure even as they seek wholesome goodness and refuge in a place where a family can find themselves.

Today, this kind of refuge continues to be sought in the realm of the Rural, both real and imagined, as in places like Leelanau County, as the presumed cultural repository of authenticity, community, and nature. As people seek this refuge, they engage in reproducing certain understandings contained in culturally informed notions of community, of the iconic small town, as models *of* and models *for* reality that prevail in American society. At the same time, these refuge seekers are also actively constructing themselves as persons through this reproduction.

Social Construction of the Self

My own understanding of personhood—or what we might call, simply, the condition of being a person and especially of attaining those qualities that confer discrete individuality—rests on an appreciation of the individual self as *dialogical*. The self emerges from the fact that frameworks for self-interpretation and behavior are shaped by culture in constant exchange between individuals and other persons in a social and physical world in a process that social scientists may refer to as dialogical in order to emphasize that the person is engaged in a continuously meaningful give-and-take, or "dialog," with others.[28] Such a sense of the self depends on a deep appreciation for culture as public. As suggested earlier, it is through examining dominant symbols—such as community—as a medium of expressing a culture that we can come to know it as researchers. These powerfully meaningful symbols shape the way people see, feel, and think about the world. They also contribute to the existential "flavor" of a place and its people as a potentially generalizable and fundamental *character* or ethos.

In this way, I am particularly interested with how *key symbols* in American society, as essential *symbolic resources* such as those that figured prominently in the
Howards' story, including "the Frontier" and "the Rural," are maintained or transformed over time.[29] Anthropological opinion varies regarding where we should
locate forces that shape this process of social reproduction or change. Should structural relations be the primary focus where culture plays an ideological role in le-
gitimizing an existing order? Or should culture itself be the focus as the essential
source of meaning? I prefer an integrated approach that considers how individuals
negotiate actualities of structural relations—the patterned social arrangements in
a society—while making culturally meaningful decisions in the context of those
relationships. This focus on social action asks from where the system of social and
structural relations has come and how it either continues or is changed through re-
productive or transformative behaviors on the part of real people engaged in making meaning in and through the conduct of everyday lives.

Here culture gives shape and guidance to social action in ordinary life as both
a necessary and enabling resource for meaning-making activity. At the same time,
culture serves as a potential force of constraint and restriction on the sense people
have of the range of possible choices. We begin to see how knowing the varying abilities of particular segments of society—such as may be defined by social
class—to impart their own particular "spin" on the flow of ideas and symbols
within a cultural system is important for understanding the different degrees to
which a particular order is either enabling or constraining. People are in a constant
process of negotiating their own life's path by alternatively finding meaning either
in certain culturally provided, "ready-made" strategies or in those that must be individually fashioned. It should be noted that these strategies are themselves shaped
by the context within which people make meaning and take action. In this way,
understanding culture involves knowing how social action can be both *structuring*
as well as *structured*.[30]

Looking at culture from the bottom up in social action means starting where
people live and work—it means appreciating why people make the choices that
they do. What motivates individual behavior? An integrated and morally sensitive view of motivation considers those factors that point not only to how people
may choose to maximize well-being in economic and material terms but also to
how they strive for personal fulfillment. What is their image of the good life and
how does this relate to culturally defining symbols? Such a view must also consider a world of complex structural relations and potentially conflicting obligations
through which the person must navigate in an attempt to find practical and meaningful solutions to the everyday challenges and opportunities that they find as individuals. For lifestyle migrants at least, personal fulfillment depends on a quest to
identify inner selves and on living a life, or designing a lifestyle, resonant with that
imagined inner self.

Therefore, I have taken an integrated and morally sensitive view of motivation
where my approach to the moral may be compared to that of humanist-philosopher
Charles Taylor.[31] For Taylor, the moral encompasses not only questions about individual obligations and relationships with others but also visions of the good, which
entail questions of what gives meaning, fulfillment, and a sense of dignity and self-

respect to persons. For this reason, identity and morality are deeply intertwined in the unfolding *narrative* account of a person's life as a kind of quest to find a sense to that life.[32] As a matter of clarification, it is important to understand that narrative is not the story itself, but rather the *process* of telling the story. While a story may be thought of as a sequence of events, narrative entails the creative act of recounting those events wherein some occurrences may be purposefully left out while others are emphasized. The quest is thus accomplished by finding a meaningful orientation to the good in a self-defining narrative—as we saw Cyrus Howard struggling to negotiate—as a means of measuring the worth of one's life.

CHAPTER 3

Moral Horizons

Four hoarse blasts of a ship's whistle still raise the hair on my neck and set my feet to tapping. The sound of a jet, an engine warming up, even the clopping of shod hooves on pavement brings on the ancient shudder, the dry mouth and vacant eye, the hot palms and the churn of stomach high up under the rib cage. . . . I fear this disease incurable. I set this matter down not to instruct others but to inform myself. . . . A journey is a person in itself; no two are alike. And all plans, safeguards, policing, and coercion are fruitless. We find after years of struggle that we do not take a trip; a trip takes us.

—John Steinbeck, *Travels with Charley: In Search of America*

Lifestyle migrants look for something more enduring than an increasingly ephemeral source of identity provided through a particular job. A lifestyle commitment guides choices about work and family. For many this requires leaving established careers. For some this may mean dramatic defections from corporate America. For those just starting out in the world of work it may mean foregoing what many would consider a traditional career path. A lifestyle decision requires reconsidering the role of work and rethinking potentially conflicting obligations. The characteristic that distinguishes lifestyle migrants from those who may make similar choices regarding work and family is that their decisions are thought to *necessitate* relocation. Though there is evidence, discussed later, that lifestyle migration is not a uniquely urban to rural or small-town pattern, the study presented in this book focused on this particular form.

Demographers Kenneth Johnson and Calvin Beale note how through decades of exodus during this century—much of it more a matter of economic necessity than of real choice—from the rural communities that have in many ways embodied our national identity for generations, many Americans have retained a strong attachment to the Rural ideal.[1] This enduring theme of American cultural history is the need to live a life motivated by what might be called the spiritual itself grounded in an appreciation of "simplicity." Popular notions have typically associated the idea with some kind of unadorned country living. In American traditions, the simple life is often equated with the good life.

For the political scientist David Shi, whose work explores American ideas of simplicity over time, the simple life represents an approach that self-consciously subordinates material questions to the ideal and moral realms.[2] Simplicity demands judgments between what is necessary and what is unessential when measured against particular notions of the good. Shi recognizes that the term "simplicity" is itself anything but simple. As a label, it has been used to variously refer to concern for family nurture and community cohesion, hostility toward luxury and suspicion of wealth, a belief that the primary reward of work should be well-being, desire for maximum personal self-reliance and creative leisure, nostalgia for supposed un-complicatedness of the past and anxiety about present or future technological and bureaucratic complexities, a taste for the unadorned and functional, a reverence for nature and preference for country living, and a sense of responsibility for the proper use of the world's resources. According to Shi, there is no simple life that can be universally prescribed or adopted, "only an array of different patterns of living that in their own context are considered 'simpler' than other ways of life."[3] For lifestyle migrants, "vows of simplicity," however fashioned, may offer a way of regaining a sense of control over their lives—freed in some perhaps small or even wholly imagined measure from demands of the market and workplace.

Lifestyle migrants are either willing to challenge themselves to live differ-ently—if not more simply—by relocation to a new place, which is to say that they are *risk takers*; or they are effectively unwilling to challenge themselves by looking for or making it where they were, which is to say that they are *risk averse*. Either way, we can say that they are seeking to fulfill a particular lifestyle commitment somewhere else—through the option of elsewhere. As noted in Chapter 1, faith that we can remake ourselves through sheer force of will may be an essential part of a distinctly American character entwined with our predominant economic ide-ology. It is historically grounded in the history of America as a nation swept by waves of migration and countless individual acts of starting over in the unique circumstances of its social and geographic development as a nation. Recognizing the essential importance of the idea of the Frontier to the American mind and as the basis of an American ethos, in 1893 historian Frederick Jackson Turner reacted to the 1890 census report that asserted that settlement was over. Turner believed that the unique history of the development of the United States—of continually moving into a what was understood as a frontier zone—had shaped and would long continue to give form to a distinctly American character. He felt that our na-tional development had consisted of a perennial rebirth that would encourage last-ing fluidity and an incessant search for new opportunity in other places and social arrangements.[4]

Clearly, the economist Kenneth Boulding had this in mind when he used the expression *cowboy economy* to describe an American frontier ethic gone wild in the economic sphere with the destructive potential to use up one place in order to seek creative opportunity beyond the horizon. In his time, Turner believed that frontier had become an essential part not only of our nationhood but also of personhood in America.[5] While now we may not have the physical frontier, it is reasonable to argue that there is a lingering and powerfully motivating sense of geographic mobility offering possibilities for personal growth and renewal together with the simple but captivating allure of new places.

Lifestyle migrants with whom I worked made explicit comparisons between places left behind and those to which they moved. The sociologist Michael Bell has commented on the importance of such a contrast between places in his study of a small town in the hinterlands of London that he called Childerley—difference that was self-consciously used as a source of self-identity for newcomers and longtime residents alike.[6] Similarly, Lee Cuba's study of the construction of community and identity in Alaska identifies how contrast between places of origin and destination may be actively employed by migrants to intensify their identification with destination communities—just as a compelling notion of the Frontier found saliency and staying power from the juxtaposition of prevailing cultural images of nature and civilization. Drawing on work regarding the formation of subcultures in urban contexts by Claude Fischer in the 1970s, Cuba explores on the Alaskan "frontier" how geographic mobility that defines the experience of the majority of residents there—rather than diminishing the role of place in formation of individual and collective identity—intensifies a self-conscious, deliberate identification with place. As Cuba notes, "Mobility, and the concomitant opportunities it brings for interaction and comparison, provides the context for how residents acquire and how others attribute to them an identity as Alaskans."[7]

Lifestyle migrants in my study typically left behind urban and suburban areas, tending to seek places—and enhanced opportunities for interaction and comparison—that came with movement to rural and small-town places. Their own travel narratives track what we might describe in many cases as an escape from perceived ills of a given physical and social environment or from a life that offered only unacceptable compromise in some basic vision of self. As noted by the historian David Jacobson in his book on belonging in American history, *place* "has a distinctly moral element, containing as it does notions of belonging, of one's rightful place in the world, locating individuals and peoples geographically and historically and orienting them in the cosmos."[8] In his study of the community of Childerley, Bell found such moral thinking in identification with place where, "in a world where so many traditionally accepted sources of identity and motivation have come to be sharply questioned," people have sought an "alternative source of social self . . . as a legitimate basis for motivation" in what he calls a "natural conscience" that is believed, by those who identify with it, to be free from the morally ambiguous realm of social interests expressed in such categories as class.[9] In this way, a person's *sense of place* can be made to contain notions of belonging and one's rightful place in the world. Such a sense then serves to locate people and orient them—in a manner akin to Charles Taylor's understanding of the moral—to the greater world.

Beyond any simple dichotomy between particular places, such as among urban and small-town life, is the importance of actual experience. Lifestyle migrants recognize how place is essential in shaping them as persons. They seek the kinds of experiences that they believe a new place can offer them for starting over. Their recurrent use of words from a vocabulary of healing is remarkable. Running throughout their stories is language inspired by a therapeutic ideal. My informants have spoken of having been "scarred" or "contaminated" by past events and of needing "cleansing," "nourishment," or a "cure" in order to "heal" themselves—often by getting into what they described as better "balance."

In this way, relocating to the study area may be seen as an act of self-help. Many felt that they had lost control of their lives and passionately believed that they could wrest some back. Appearing to understand that we are shaped as persons by both the social and material worlds that we inhabit, they sought control by changing their place of residence and proactively selecting qualities of life found in a particular social and physical environment that would then contribute to them as persons. In this way, their desire for control at the personal level echoes in some measure interest among so-called *positive environmentalists*—such as the famed late nineteenth century landscape architect Frederick Law Olmstead—for exerting social control through changing behavior and fostering particular communal forms in the purposeful selection and manipulation of elements of the physical environment.[10] Interestingly, in their writings and work, these designers laid a foundation that justified government and private investment in developing the early suburban landscape.[11] American community planners and health reformers of the day pointed to the ability of such controlled environments to exert a powerful, restorative influence on the physical and "moral" self—as reformers of the period referred to the person in its nonphysical dimension.[12]

To place key themes such as these into some meaningful framework for understanding lifestyle migration, we need to consider how they are at play in the stories of real people. Speaking methodologically, this involves listening to and thinking about how people construct *narratives* of self. As the ethicist Alasdair MacIntyre explains, "stories are lived before they are told."[13] Narrative embodies the inescapable temporality of life experience. Our stories grow out of everyday practice and our literal as well as figurative movement through time and space. As previously suggested, they are naturally stories of travel. Like Richard Sennett, who speaks of the integrity of personal *character* contained in sustainable narratives of self, MacIntyre finds that to the extent that there is harmony in a person's life and continuity in sense of self, these reside "in the unity of narrative which links birth to life to death as narrative beginning to middle to end."[14]

Focusing on narrative calls our attention to lived experience not only in its temporal but also spatial aspects. Structures of the narratives of individuals, according to the philosopher Michel de Certeau, "have the status of spatial syntaxes" such that "every story is a travel story—a spatial practice."[15] The linguistic anthropologist Barbara Johnstone notes that people's sense of self and place is "rooted in narration" and that "there is a basic connection between stories and places." In human experience, she explains, places themselves "are narrative constructions and stories are suggested by places."[16] Autobiographies are intimately connected with places as individuals, regardless of circumstance, create and hold onto their own landscapes. Key symbols in place representations like Up North provide organization for building a sense of identity. These can become "precincts of charged meaning that we will never forget [as they] become the spinal column of our autobiographical structure."[17]

According to Charles Taylor, our identity is defined "by the commitments and identifications that provide the frame or horizon within which [we] can try to determine from case to case what is good, or valuable, or what ought to be done, or what [we] endorse or oppose. In other words, it is the *horizon* within which [we are] capable of taking a stand."[18] To lack such a frame or horizon is to lack a way through which things take on stable significance and with which individuals are able to weigh possibilities as good or bad, meaningful or superfluous. It is a question of orientation. An essential part of selfhood is that the person is situated not only in a physical world but also a moral space within which we can then know who we are. This orientation is not only within a space of questions about what is worth doing and not, it is also a part of how we find our bearings and locate ourselves in a moral, social, and material landscape. To speak of "orientation" then, is more than mere metaphor. We are in fact only selves as we seek and eventually find our own personal orientation to the good. It is a necessary feature of being human and of our participation in social and cultural life.

As I suggested in my analysis of the Howards' story of finding themselves in travel to Leelanau, I find interesting connections between the experiences of lifestyle migrants and stories told through travel writing. As in so many travel stories, lifestyle migrants understand their lives as a kind of quest. Although satisfying a basic penchant for glimpsing the previously unknown is clearly one goal, in the literature of what are variously referred to as travelogues, travel narratives, or travel journals, we typically locate something beyond mere descriptions of new people and places to fascinate our curiosity.

In a nation involved in a love affair with the auto and the open road, it is not surprising that many of the well-known examples of the genre of travelogues here in the United States involve unfolding maps, getting behind the wheel of a motor vehicle, and driving off to meet whatever destiny comes over a broadening horizon. As was the case in the tale of Cyrus Howard and family, the classic American travel story is spun around a quest for finding or rediscovering the essential nature or character of America through a journey of miles that weaves through small towns and close-knit communities along back roads away from the relative anonymity of cities and interstates. Well-known books include John Steinbeck's classic *Travels with Charley*. William Least Heat-Moon's personal odyssey on and through the back roads recounted in *Blue Highways* became a best seller that lead to a popular sequel (this time he traveled by boat through America's waterways). More recent illustrations include Brad Herzog's *States of Mind*. Herzog's book is literally the description of an on-the-road search for presumed elements of authentic American character such as harmony, unity, honor, and freedom fully lived as everyday attributes in little towns that have these as their actual place names. This is how the tiny town of Honor, Michigan, a community within my study area, earned a visit from Herzog on his coast-to-coast journey.[19]

The protagonists in these travel stories have typically hit the road in the wake of a personal crisis of faith about the direction of their life, the meaning of work, family, and community, and the promise of American dreams. In the process of connecting or reconnecting with intimate places, there is an inward journey as well—one of personal growth and discovery, discovering or rediscovering one's own essential nature or character. It is a search not merely for distinct places, but for particular experiences *enabled by* these places. While these are stories that find their narrative drive through the arc of roads and broad sweep of miles across the American landscape, their central tension resounds as well with cultural images of the potential for self-discovery in an inner-city setting.

In her research on urban gentrification, Brown-Saracino comments on the (perhaps all too harsh) characterization typical of both popular and academic writings on those who seek to in some measure *reclaim* the urban landscape. In particular she describes how their actions are often likened to settlers of America's home-steading past and their imaginings to imperialist fantasies about recolonization where the urban slum becomes analogous to the continental frontier—complete with potentially hostile natives. Even while her research finds that most gentrifiers in sites of her study do not attempt to extirpate "natives" or erase historical evidence of their presence, Brown-Saracino recognizes that the prospect of personal transformation through the experience of selective and cautious alteration of place of residence in order to build a home in their chosen environment is a strong motivation. At least a significant number of these migrants seek to discover something essential about themselves through attachment to and transformation of place through what they believe to be rediscovery of the authentic nature of the places that they choose to inhabit. Like the *social homesteaders* described in her study, many lifestyle migrants "appreciate authenticity," which like these homesteaders they associate with the built or natural environment where "gentrification's cost for longtime residents are not their central concern."[20]

Lifestyle migrants often relocate at seemingly pivotal points in their lives. Watershed events can open up the possibility of reconsidering who they are or might become and where they are or might go. Such possibilities may take the form of more obvious and perhaps negative changes such as loss of a job, divorce, or a death in the family. Less obvious, however, are when people have received promotions in their careers, retired, or had some kind of physical injury. These are all significant contributors, if not the cause, of personal crises. Whether or not we might think of them objectively as "good" or "bad" as life events, they are junctures where people experience what I call "time out of time." In this distinct experience of time, there is a chance to see oneself in a new fashion.

Vacationing may offer such "time out of time" and, for some, an opportunity to find temporary refuge from the habits of everyday life in large part defined by routines of work. Vacations sometimes serve as a brief but meaningful break, an opportunity to "step outside" of one's ordinary life. The historian Cindy Aron's study of domestic tourism in the United States *Working at Play* sheds light not only on the cultural history of ideas of work and leisure within and across social class, but also on the importance of rural places in this history. Aron explains that those places with unique natural beauty typically found in the countryside have long become some of America's most sacred places. Embarking on a trip as a tourist to spend time in one of these places becomes a secular form of pilgrimage.[21] By the end of the nineteenth century, at a time when the urban seemed increasingly less civil and humane, the rural parts of the country were already being construed as somehow more "authentic" and even as potentially civilized retreat from the ills and potential brutality of city life. It was this presumed character of the Rural that literally came to life as the Spirit of Leelanau in the Howards' travel story. For members of an emerging middle class, vacationing out of metropolitan areas was a way of seeking short-term respite and refuge.[22]

Finding or believing in a place of refuge or asylum can be essential to people at turning points in the life course. Vacations may provide short-term time out of normal time as they serve up opportunities to imagine other life possibilities. As evidenced by tourism research, people may experience other dimensions of self as they engage in new and different activities while vacationing within physical and social settings a world apart from their everyday lives.[23] It follows that more lasting refuge in relocation to these places should offer the time and place not only for reimagining and envisioning new directions but also taking action on newfound alternatives. That is the fundamental assumption of lifestyle migration.

Lifestyle migrants describe experiencing a kind of personal sanctuary and a sense of well-being derived from feelings of rootedness or connectedness to particular places. In their accounts, however, we see a tension between two simultaneous tendencies—much like the diametrically opposed centrifugal and centripetal leanings to which I referred previously. On the one hand, they exhibit a clear desire for retreat in the need to find personal refuge in order to "take back" their lives. On the other hand, however, we find desire for engagement with the world expressed through longing to experience intimate connections to place and a need to feel that they belong, in a personally meaningful way, to what so many describe plainly as "something bigger than themselves."

CHAPTER 4

Place

As I have endeavored to make clear, it is less the place itself and more the *idea* of place that is of critical importance to understanding lifestyle migration. So far, we have examined how actual place is converted into virtual commodity whose signs or meanings and their consumption are ultimately as important as the physical place itself. This speaks to concerns of such social theorists as Jean Baudrillard, whose analysis of contemporary society describes a shift in emphasis from production to consumption wherein things or places become objects of consumption by being made signs so that they may then stand for something else. In this process, they can become personalized such that the "commodity-as-sign" is then associated with lifestyle and integrated with the social life of persons.[1] Yet, despite this turn, it is still necessary to *locate* these particular stories of relocation. There is a physical and cultural geography to relate. It is also not as if this specific place and its unique history are unimportant to the story. I could go on about the idea of place being more important than any particular place, but that does not change the fact that for these lifestyle migrants it is ultimately *this* place—and all its more or less tangible qualities—that they have chosen. If nothing else, when we tell a story, people like to know its setting. A story must take place somewhere. For these migrants, that place is Up North—a place both real and imagined.

As noted in Chapter 2, since the dawn of the local tourism industry the Grand Traverse region has been marketed as retreat from the enervating effects of the urban and industrial world. Being here was understood to be somehow rejuvenating. To the masses living in rapidly urbanizing midwestern industrial towns, the Grand Traverse area became a welcome retreat. It was an Up North frontier without the danger of being mauled by a hungry pack of wolves or attacked by restive natives.

The four counties of my study area have long attracted tourists and seasonal residents. The lure of natural beauty and the mystique of a pioneer history have kept families coming back. In reference to the original, modest camps and places of family retreat, second homes are typically referred to as "cottages." The older, quite simple second homes may be passed down for generations. Over the years, however, they may go through a metamorphosis as families grow and gatherings push the limits of accommodation—sometimes transforming a genuine cottage into something much grander indeed.[2]

Although I barely knew of the area during the initial few months of my time in graduate school in Ann Arbor, four hours to the south of the region and forty minutes from Detroit, I already felt that I needed it. I had picked up a tourist brochure in the Michigan welcome center off Route 23 coming out of Ohio the day that my wife and I first came rattling into the state in our lumbering U-Haul truck. The glossy pamphlet remained tucked away among piles of books and papers that were accumulating to lofty heights. In a moment of inspiration our first Thanksgiving—or was it desperation—I dug toward the heap's bottom and eventually pulled out a modern equivalent of the Howards' story. I allowed my eyes and imagination to wonder over captivating photos and appealing descriptions of endless beaches, towering dunes, quiet country roads, and deep forests dotted with crystalline lakes. I felt the pull, as was intended. Like Cyrus Howard, I set a course northward. We spent that first holiday in Michigan staying in an all but deserted lodging in Leelanau County.

Crossing the Line

Not long after moving to the area to begin my research in early 2000, I began to recognize and feel a certain connection to being Up North and knew what local residents meant when they would talk about "crossing the line" when they headed north on Interstate 75 in Michigan after spending time Downstate. This highway runs out of the heart of the often-bleak urban landscape of Detroit and meanders through rambling suburbs that year after year progressively encroach on dwindling agricultural land. After less than an hour, I-75 plows through the depressed industrial centers of Flint and Saginaw—the fates of which I spoke earlier—on its journey northward. Out of Ann Arbor, US 23 joins the interstate south of Flint. The early reaches of this route are inevitably busy with traffic. As the major north-south connection for the state, it has a steady stream of trucks. The highway links the urban cores of the South with the distant hinterlands of the Upper Peninsula on the other side of the massive Mackinaw Bridge, which since the 1950s has spanned the Straits of Mackinaw between the state's two massive peninsulas surrounded by Lakes Superior, Michigan, and Huron. Pockets of industry, like sprawling General Motors plants—both operational and shuttered—and a variety of automotive parts manufacturers, are interspersed with vast acres of farms, equally industrialized for mass production of monocrop corn, sugar beets, or soybeans. North of Bay City, farms dominate the largely flat landscape as it reaches outward to the horizon. For some thirty miles, the highway follows the edge of Saginaw Bay, which lies just out of sight.

Where US 23 splits off from I-75 to skirt the western shore of Lake Huron through sleepy lakeside communities, the scenery abruptly changes. That first time I went Up North I did not take notice of any change. Today, however, it has become a palpable transition for me. At the tiny town of Standish, somewhere just off the interstate and approximately 120 miles from downtown Detroit, the traveler crosses a discernible line and with this crossing passes from the imagined realm of Downstate to Up North. The civic and business leaders of Standish seem to recognize the significantly liminal location of their little hamlet in proclaiming via one of the final billboards that Standish is "Gateway to Michigan's Sunrise Side." Although specifically orienting themselves to the area accessed from US Route 23, Standish recognizes itself as a kind of place of passage from one world to another. It is at this point that weathered barns, reminders of an agricultural past, together with their sheet metal modern counterparts and giant silos, make a near total retreat as trees close in on both sides on the interstate. Ubiquitous billboards that had solicited business for over a hundred miles—first for outlet malls and roadside cafés and then increasingly for ammunition and beef jerky—dwindle in number.

Some line has been crossed.[3] Surely, this is a kind of *ecotone*—a transition between two distinct ecosystems. To the south, geologic and climatic conditions have favored modern agriculture. Economies of scale and distance have also helped establish the conditions for this noticeable transition. To the north, forests have been steadily recovering from the heyday of logging that helped build midwestern cities and some small fortunes. Now these stands spread out in white and red pine, spruce, poplar, and birch. The terrain begins to gradually undulate. Here the highway cuts inland away from Lake Huron, at the twin lakes of Higgins and Houghton, which lie roughly at the center of northern Lower Michigan. Interstate 75 makes a solo traverse to the Mackinaw Bridge, the lone highway from here northward. Now that I have made the trip many, many times, I feel that I know the transition.

The line exists for the ecological and economic reasons I suggest, but it has been imbued with personal meaning for those who make the trip to "get away," either temporarily or permanently. It is both real and imagined. While its reality may have practical reasons, it has wholly imagined status as the point of passage to Up North refuge. Numerous lifestyle migrants have described a feeling of relaxation that comes with the sense of growing distance from chaotic urban places they now only visit but cannot see themselves ever again calling "home." Travelers bound for the Grand Traverse region, nearly two hundred miles from Detroit, must leave the highway at Grayling. Exiting gives further sense of separation and distance from the reach of the urban. As residents in the study area have put it to me so often, this place is not "on the way to anywhere"; you have to want to come here. From Grayling, it is another hour over rambling Michigan 72 until you reach Traverse City, some fifty miles to the west at the base of the Grand Traverse Bay.

As the regional hub, Traverse City and the immediate area have the heaviest concentration of stores and services, virtually all of which operate throughout the year unlike other places more dependent on seasonal business. On the weekends, stores are typically jammed as people crowd in from smaller outlying communities to take care of weekly shopping. Checkout lines can grow particularly long in spring as people stock up bare shelves, plan for summer parties, and prepare for seemingly endless streams of visitors. Beginning in mid-April, increasingly crowded roads and stores mark the first step in gearing-up for summer. Many new faces in the crowds are seniors returning from winter habitats to the south. They participate in a circular migratory pattern alternating between Northern Michigan and points south that lends them the name "Snowbirds." As weather improves and

slowly grows warmer, trailers start rumbling around town as people go about rituals of moving around, tinkering with, and eventually placing their boats in one of
many inland lakes. Year-round residents and their part-time neighbors have almost
settled into a comfortable arrangement for another summer season when suddenly
tourists begin to arrive en masse, piled into SUVs and campers loaded down with
coolers, beach chairs, and bikes. With determination akin to Cyrus on his journey,
they sit at the wheel, with their "brows drawn, jaw set, driving as though fire and
water rushed savagely in their wake" and hurtle toward a thousand different destinations in hotels, motels, campgrounds, and cabins.

The area attracts tourists mainly from the Midwest, but its reputation is ex-
tending further every year. There are now a decent number of tourists visiting
from abroad to see the great inland seas of America.[4] During a pleasant dinner one
balmy summer evening as the sun set over Lake Michigan and the fishing boats of
the tiny town of Leland's historic "Fishtown," my wife and I were asked to smile
for a photo that would appear in the periodical *Stern*, as part of an article on the
area's potential appeal to German tourists.

Memorial Day weekend is early for the tourist season, but by this time the
spring crop of "For Sale" signs are in bloom in yards, woodlots, and remaining
shorefront holdings around the entire area. The intent is to attract the attention of
visiting dreamers and thus the prices are jacked up every spring to reflect "tourist
prices," with prices dropping every fall. As schools let out around the state and
region in late June, the number of visitors climbs dramatically. These numbers are
quickly pushed beyond any reasonable figure as hundreds of thousands attend the
annual Cherry Festival in downtown Traverse City, the self-proclaimed "Cherry
Capital," during the first week of July. Experiencing anticipatory anxiety, loudly
complaining about the onslaught, and even making plans to leave town during
the event have become significant markers of local identity. It is not until after
Labor Day that crowds diminish. Families are the first to leave as children return
to school, and finally, sometime late in autumn, Snowbirds fly away to warmer
climes once again.

This is not the place for everyone—at least not on a year-round basis. Winters
are long and cold and feature abundant amounts of "lake effect" snow that can
come out of the clear blue skies before you have had a chance to ready yourself for
another fast-falling foot. There have been enormous changes on the retail front in
the last twenty years with the arrival of two malls with enough "big box" stores to
nearly decimate the everyday-needs stores of the historic downtown. Despite this,
it was not that long ago that people relied primarily on mail order or day trips to
Grand Rapids—over two hours distant—to do much of their shopping for cloth-
ing and specialty goods. Longtime residents still recall sharing catalogs and ar-
ranging seasonal trips Downstate to make purchases of those things either locally
unattainable or unreasonably priced. Acres of shopping malls now form a perime-
ter around Traverse City that should satisfy everyone's tastes but probably do not.
At the same time, revitalization efforts breathe new economic life into the city's
downtown with trendy retail shopping and posh condos even as the largest retailer,
a holdout from the pre-mall era, closes its doors for good.

Boomtown

The landscape of the Grand Traverse region is defined by proximity to a long, deep bay of the same name running north-south for over twenty miles. Dug by glaciers that retreated as geologically recently as twelve thousand years ago, the bay is bisected by a long, hilly peninsula left by those glaciers. Named for an Indian mission once located there, Old Mission Peninsula stretches out from its base at Traverse City. With its rolling, vineyard-covered hills and panoramic views of the Grand Traverse Bay, it includes some of the area's most prime real estate. As the region produces roughly 70 percent of the nation's tart cherries, it is still widely covered in gnarled trees. Despite their place in local identity, the trees are being cut on many older farms to make way for ostentatious homes built for people whose incomes have little to do with the local economy—though forward-thinking planning has gradually helped to shore-up the agricultural heritage and character of the landscape.

The land beyond Traverse City is thickly forested over wide tracts of secondary and tertiary growth after the near total deforestation of the "Big Cut" during the lumber boom of the late nineteenth century. Most of the area not under regeneration as forest is either active or idle farmland. Although small areas of typical midwestern crops like corn, soybeans, and cereal grains can be found, the area is mostly known for its fruit. Although cherry orchards have dominated the landscape for over seventy-five years, the area is now increasingly known for its grapes or, more precisely, what is being made from those grapes. According to the program manager for the Michigan Grape and Wine Industry Council, "wineries and tasting rooms are an important segment of agricultural tourism in the state, hosting at least half a million visitors annually. People feel a special connection to the country [and] winemakers help them to take some of that feeling home in a bottle."[5]

Just as the dot-com bubble seemed poised to burst, the owner of Chateau Chantal—one of the local wineries—had a go at going public with an initial public offering (IPO) of stock. I got to know the owner, Robert Begin, a former Catholic priest and owner of construction companies in southern Michigan, while working with him (in order to earn some extra income) to place phone calls to those on his winery contact list. Coming up here and starting a winery was a lifestyle choice for him. When we talked about the meaning of the IPO, he joked how this was not like investing in a dot-com, which at the time were already on pretty shaky ground. He hoped that people would see that participating in his stock offering was an opportunity to invest in the land and the buildings, in *real* things. More poignantly, however, it was for him an opportunity for others to invest in a *way of life*. For people who could not do what he was doing, it was a chance, as he put it, to "partake" of the Up North dream just as Downstate people may feel that they do by sharing in the region's wine. Indeed, the IPO was christened "Partake."

I couldn't help—talking with Bob about this notion—but think about the French concept of *terroir*. Originally applied by the French to agricultural products ranging from wine to coffee, the term was meant to speak to distinct characteristics that geography, geology, and climate bestow on these products thus giving them a unique, place-dependent character. Thus, the idea of terroir, now used to talk about the unique properties of wines produced in the Grand Traverse region, is much like the notion of "sense of place" that is a major part of my discussion of lifestyle migration.

While tourism is now considered the principal local "industry," the region had a truly industrial past founded first in resource extraction and developed later in heavy manufacturing. In the second half of the nineteenth century, the region supported a thriving lumber business. In addition to vast forests of pine, numerous rivers and lakes made the area attractive to lumbermen as water transport and power for milling. The local industry began in 1847 when the appropriately named Harry Boardman bought land at the base of Grand Traverse Bay to build a sawmill. The first house constructed was a log cabin built by his sons at the foot of what is now Boardman Lake in Traverse City. Only a few years later, Boardman sold his sawmill to a new partnership of Chicago businessmen, Perry Hannah, Albert Lay, and James Morgan. Hannah, Lay, and Company would propel the lumber business into full swing.

The first visit to the region by these entrepreneurs in the spring of 1851 was by way of a Great Lakes schooner—the area's only regular connection to the outside world at that time. This would have been much like the replica constructed by volunteers of the Maritime Heritage Alliance based in Traverse City on which I eventually served as mate during my years in the area. I know from experience sailing on *Madeline* that Hannah's account of coming into safe harbor after three rough days on Lake Michigan from Chicago is an accurate account of the special appeal that land holds for one after weathering the lake's tumult. Whether shaped by days on this inland sea or not, Perry Hannah's account conveys an early vision of the area's enchanting charm.

> We rounded Old Mission harbor, just as the sun was going down behind the tops of the tall maples that stood on the ridge in the center of the peninsula. It was one of those serene and beautiful evenings, with the southerly breeze not more than half a mile per hour as we entered the harbor and on the banks of the western side sat perhaps forty or fifty old Indian hunters. I could see with my glass that each one had his pipe in his mouth, and they were sitting on the bank, watching the movement of our ship, chatting and talking, as happy as one ever could imagine. To the rear of them were perhaps forty or fifty nice whitewashed wigwams and further up, in among the tall maples, could be seen the large white mansion of Rev. Peter Dougherty. Further up beyond that, the Indian ponies, with bells on their necks were jumping from place to place, looking for their last meal for the night. A more beautiful picture I never saw in my life.[6]

By 1862, Traverse City was a growing lumber town. Morgan Bates, who founded the *Grand Traverse Herald* newspaper, arrived in town for the first time and stated, "It was a perfect 'Traverse' day. The air was tempered by a faint north wind and laden with the spicy odor of pines. We landed at the dock and crawled through the piles of lumber to the sawdusted highway. The Traverse City I then saw was composed of a dozen or so buildings."[7] Hannah, Lay and Company had by then built a larger steam mill on the bay. Between 1851 and 1886, this mill would harvest more than four hundred million feet of pine lumber in what is now known as the Boardman River valley, which was shipped primarily to Chicago in the company's own vessels. Some of this lumber rebuilt Chicago after the Great Fire of 1871.

The first road connecting the area to population centers to the south was the Northport-Newaygo state road, which opened in 1864. It was not until the arrival of the Grand Rapids and Indiana in 1872 as the first of what would be three railroads into the area that local people truly felt that they had emerged from the seclusion of wilderness. Until that time, the only regular contact with the world beyond was by way of schooner or steamer on Lake Michigan—contact that would cease for up to five months a year during long, icy winters. When the first train pulled into Traverse City, whistles blew, and church bells rang out, and people danced in the streets. Marking the historic and momentous occasion, the Grand Rapids and Indiana announced in banner headlines, "Out of the Woods at Last!" The railroad definitively ended what had been a local expression of the region's isolation and began a period of significant in-migration. Until that time, one spoke of "going outside" when planning a trip away from Traverse City.

By 1895 the great forests of the North were steadily becoming a memory. Lucrative white and red pine timber had been completely depleted. Nevertheless, the years 1880 to 1990 saw local population and economic growth at a rate that would not be seen again until the 1970s. City population during this period nearly quadrupled, from 2,663 to 9,407. Homes and buildings of lasting significance were built and still stand today. The first two decades of the twentieth century would bring change. Although growth continued, it had nearly leveled off by this time. By 1915 the area had been essentially cleared of all its large timber, both softwoods and hardwoods. Now largely denuded, the land was in danger of serious environmental damage from heavy erosion of the area's mostly shallow, sandy soils. As the state of Michigan's land-grant school, Michigan State University began looking into the risk. Widespread replanting through tree farming and furthering acreage under fruit-tree agriculture were encouraged as a way of halting further soil loss.

Cherries and apples tend to grow well in the hilly terrain near the water where Lake Michigan moderates climatic conditions. The earliest European settlers to the region recognized the area's potential for fruit cultivation. The Reverend Dougherty, mentioned in Perry Hannah's recollections of his arrival to the area by ship, planted several varieties of fruit trees not long after he arrived and founded the Indian settlement at Old Mission in 1839. By the 1850s, his was the first large orchard. While many farmers enjoyed the fruit for their families, selling surplus for profit when possible, it was not until the 1880s that local farmers began shipping considerable quantities out of area. One of the earliest orchards of truly commercial size was planted in 1900 on 110 acres near Traverse City. Fruit farming continued to grow with the first major cannery being built in 1902. Cherries surpassed apples in total production by 1914. By 1920, Traverse City had proclaimed itself "Cherry Capital of the World."[8] The same lake-moderated climate that nurtured the cherry now attracts vineyards, which are more lucrative. Grapes fetch an increasingly higher price per ton than both cherries and apples. As noted earlier, the wine industry also fits well with the area's appeal as a lifestyle destination marketed as possessing a well-balanced, even sophisticated, blend of both nature and culture.

Around the same time that local land reclamation began, industry was booming in Downstate Michigan and elsewhere in the Midwest. This growth, together with the expanding wealth of a large segment of the population, enabled and encouraged many families to seek quiet refuge from the noise and filth of burgeoning cities. Before widespread use of automobiles and the creation of decent roads and travel facilities, they came in large numbers by ship from Chicago and points south to ports throughout the region—including Traverse City. Ships and ports once used for the lumbering trade now catered to tourism. As we have seen, much of the promotion came in the form of pamphlets, like the 1924 brochure that told the Cyrus Howards' story, first produced by shipping companies looking for revenue lost as the timber dwindled. From approximately 1920 to 1950 the area saw population growth at 15 percent per decade.

In the 1970s, oil and gas were discovered in the northwestern portion of Lower Michigan. During that decade, the region grew at seven times the rate the rest of the state of Michigan. Not since the lumber era had it held the promise of great wealth. As in that period a hundred years before, there was a boomtown mentality as the economy again focused on extractive industry. The boom fostered rapid growth in population and with it commercial and residential construction. The 1970s also brought the oil embargo and widespread fuel shortages and anger over US dependence on foreign oil. This helped to further fuel the social unrest in America cities that had begun during the civil rights and antiwar movements of the 1960s. As noted previously, a significant portion of the region's growth was no doubt the result of families fleeing midwestern cities in favor of the relative safety and even racial purity of the area. Today the population in Grand Traverse County is still less than 5 percent white. During this spurt of in-migration, some counties saw their rate of growth jump dramatically. Kalkaska County, at the center of the burgeoning oil industry, more than doubled in population in less than a decade. Young workers and families looking for a place to raise kids contributed to a growth of nearly 100 percent in persons aged twenty to thirty-four.

Much as documented by demographers in other parts of the country, the rural rebound seen locally in the 1970s seemed to reverse itself as the 1980s began. In-migration slowed dramatically. Population loss was evident in certain age groups, especially in those aged twenty to thirty-four, whose ranks had so quickly swelled during the previous decade. This is the group we would expect to be most affected by economic fluctuations and labor market shifts, and to seek work elsewhere. While young people fled, the oldest segment, aged sixty and over, continued to grow. Compared with those still in their active working years, this older segment of the population were less affected by the changing fortunes of the local labor market. Older persons continued to seek a rural or small-town lifestyle. As the bubble of the oil boom gradually deflated and shed excess, many of the recent in-migrants from manufacturing regions who had committed to staying in the area for their own lifestyle choices explored the option of literally setting up shop Up North. In so doing, they utilized skills learned in their various trades in another

Sign erected along M-22 by Glen Arbor Township. Photo by Brian Hoey

life and contributed to the area's high number of small specialty machine shops, many of which would supply the state's main auto industry to the south.

Mirroring national trends, in-migration was again on the rise during the 1990s. At a rate of 20 percent for the decade, the region had grown at an even greater rate than the period of steady growth that began in the 1920s. According to the region's Realtors, relocating urbanites account for as much as 50 percent of all recent transactions. This demand drove astronomical property value increases. For example, in 1997, the area around Traverse City was noted by industry experts as having one of the country's largest increases in property value with appreciation in a single year of over 30 percent.[9] More recently, property values have declined in response to a nationwide housing crisis and recession—although those properties closest to Traverse City have seen, on average, a decline from 2008 to 2012 of around 2 percent.[10]

One lifestyle migrant, who relocated here from Detroit in the early 1970s and has watched the area steadily develop, expressed his dismay over what seemed to be rampant speculation. He remembers the lyrics of a song decrying local gentrification. The words lead him to his story:

> [This recording artist] has a great song called "Boomtown." It's from the stand point that now we're all living in trailers on the edge of town while some people are drinking café mochas. Once I had occasion to be at a meeting of a consortium of insurance companies. There was a local insurance company involved. The CEO of the local company gets up and says "Have you all seen everything around here? Have you seen the Bay and have you taken a drive? Well, I've only got three things to say. Buy. Buy. Buy." Wow!

This is what it is. This is an area—talk about rich for harvesting. For people with a lot of money, this is a place to double it.[11]

During the same period of dramatic increases in property values, Traverse City's own Cherry Capital Airport was the fastest growing airport in the country, with a five-year growth rate from 1990 to 1995 of over 300 percent. This growth has made it more convenient both to get there and to live there while continuing to have work connections well outside Traverse City and the surrounding area. While the 1970s saw a great deal of migration led by employment opportunity, during the 1990s in-migration to the Grand Traverse region became primarily one of lifestyle choice. In the 1970s those that came for reasons other than employment were driven by factors that effectively pushed them out of their previous places, with white flight being one significant influence.

Local growth after the 1980s was based solidly on local quality of life and natural amenities rather than the area's natural resources. In the 1990s marketing of place became much more sophisticated as suggested by the Traverse City Convention and Visitors Bureau's decision to contract the multinational Landor Associates for a comprehensive brand strategy. Rather than just being a reaction to the in-migration-induced changes, promotion and planning were more organized in the effort to attract capital—both economic and social—and to profit from the lifestyle choices of in-migrants. It was also a period for more organized efforts to preserve and protect the region's natural, historical, and cultural resources.

In the early 1990s, *Outside Magazine* named Traverse City one of the top ten places to live in the United States. This is not the only list that Traverse City has made it on to. Based on votes of viewers, ABC's *Good Morning America* recently proclaimed Sleeping Bear Dunes National Lakeshore "the Most Beautiful Place in America." It hasn't all been about the out-of-doors, however. A trade magazine known as *Site Selection* circulates to over fifty thousand corporate decision makers for plant and facility development among the nation's businesses. An article entitled "Small Towns, Big Opportunities" in the March 2000 edition ranked Traverse City seventh out of one hundred small towns with populations under fifty thousand people around the country for corporate facilities development. The article explains that while many decision makers looking to relocate to promising sites "are dealing with metros that can't rid themselves of the dirty little 's' word (i.e., sprawl), others are finding the pleasures of a small-town existence much more to their liking. With Baby Boomers and New Economy labor wanting better quality of life, small towns have made a huge comeback."[12]

Throughout this period, the trend was for many large corporations to move to smaller towns for benefits realized from lower costs and better quality of life for their employees. And sprawl is more than just an aggravation; it can prove expensive for doing business. Although challenged by rapid retail development, Traverse City is spared much of the sprawl by virtue of the fact that it is not a "satellite" community to a larger metropolitan area nor is it located on a major interstate highway. In both respects, Traverse City was unique among all the other top-ten communities in the *Site Selection* ranking.

PART II

Patterns of Migration

CHAPTER 5

A Story of Lifestyle Migration

On a warm and breezy day in May of 2000, I began regular conversations with a voluntary corporate refugee who became the man that many in the state of Michigan and beyond have come to know simply as "the Pie Guy." Mike acquired the moniker after leaving his job as an engineer turned midlevel executive for a major defense contractor. He left this job just two years earlier in order to move to the study area and start a family business making pies in a town that claims the title "Cherry Capital" for being at the center of the nation's largest source of tart cherries. Not a bad place to give pie making a go.

We are in his prosperous shop across from county offices and the city fire department on a busy street through Traverse City's revitalizing downtown of stately brick buildings and attractive Victorian-era homes. A mere two blocks away the cool water of Lake Michigan laps at an inviting, sandy shore in a ribbon of city parkland. In a well-coordinated local plan of "smart growth," public open space reclaims what were once unsightly processing areas for vast timber operations into the first quarter of the twentieth century and more recently the fruit-packing industry that replaced them. On this beach one may gaze down the long, cerulean-blue arm of Grand Traverse Bay, which reaches northward, skirted by rolling hills of old orchards—increasingly supplanted by vineyards—for twenty-odd miles until it rejoins the inland sea.

Smiling comfortably as he takes off an apron—decorated with the splatter of his early morning labor with such fruits as cherries, apples, and blueberries—Mike emerges from behind the long glass counter. Beyond him several large racks stand filled with picture-perfect cooling pies, each bubbled over slightly in its sturdy tin. The shelves are labeled with inviting names like "Old Mission Cherry," "Lakeshore Berry," "Farmer's Market Peach," and "Autumn Harvest Pecan"—names that evoke memories of beloved local places and community events. With hands dusted in flour, he presents me my cup. We are surrounded by a thick, moist air rich with smells of brewing coffee, baking fruit, and browning crust. After a lingering winter of cold and snow, the relative warmth of this spring afternoon seems to promise redemption through long summer days. Basking in the warm glow of sunshine through nearby windows, a thoughtful expression on his face as we grip our steaming drinks, Mike begins outlining his narrative of relocation. His voice carries the unmistakable confidence of a man proven right in a critical, life-changing choice. He speaks with telltale conviction of the converted. Like other lifestyle migrants, Mike reached a breaking point and lost faith in the promises of a corporate career.

This is when he began his plan of striking out on his own with all the exhilaration that kind of risk entails. At the same time, his tone suggests a humility that I would later understand comes from knowing how his success has depended not only on detailed planning and a good business sense but also on a leap of faith.

Mike's tale is of a young man who grew up in Michigan's state capital of Lansing in the 1960s and 1970s. In 1980 he graduated from Michigan State University in East Lansing looking to find a job in an economy staggered by the oil crisis and wide-reaching impact of accelerating deindustrialization and a more heavily globalized market. The city of Lansing lies in a wide band of industrial areas that spans south and central Michigan from the east in Detroit to the shores of Lake Michigan at Muskegon to the west—an area largely dominated by the "Big Three" auto manufacturers of Ford, Chrysler, and General Motors. This swath of places in Michigan that includes both Saginaw and Flint is part of a vast archipelago of industrial areas scattered across the northern tier of the midwestern and northeastern states that collectively make up "the Rust Belt"—a term used to conjure images of decaying industrial places from another economic era. As I have already described, Michigan—the prominent buckle on this ragged belt—has thrashed very publically in its decline over the first decade of the twenty-first century because of the impact of deindustrialization and declining opportunity on job markets and population numbers.

Although parts of these industrial landscapes have attempted various forms of local renaissance in recent years, in the early 1980s the harsh reality that former glory had now become a bygone era was sinking in for most. As with all places in the Rust Belt, the Lansing area has had to deal with economic restructuring. Like many of his peers, Mike anticipated work in the automobile industry that continued to define much of Downstate Michigan when he began his studies years ago at a time when the mid-1970s recession had only just begun. In the end, he earned a degree in engineering. Thinking back to that time, he said:

> There was not much going on in the Midwest in terms of growth. The auto industry was down. Not a lot of opportunity. California was booming, and I had a certain amount of just "'Hey, I lived twenty years here." One of my friends went to work at Oldsmobile [based in Lansing]. Being an auto town, through the generations they just get into Olds and that's *it*. You're done. Man . . . I couldn't think of that. I'm going to get into this job and that's the rest of my life, you know? Career was generation to generation and these guys would just go in on that line—the ones that went to college really didn't so much—but they'd go to work for the state of Michigan, or they'd work for another fairly set company, and that's it.

While drawn by the same golden promise that had long helped swell the West Coast's population at the expense of other areas throughout the 1970s and into the 1980s, Mike figured he would be back home after riding out a midwestern slump and enjoying a few wild years in sunny Southern California as a young single guy. Ties to a college relationship with a girl back home, however, remained. Eventually they married. Rather than returning to Michigan, Denise joined him in California, where by now he was comfortably settled into a pattern of work that began to define a seemingly lasting career path. Soon they began a family. Mike embarked on a high-powered corporate trajectory with a major defense contractor in San Diego. Before the end of the cold war during the Reagan years, this industry saw tremendous growth. Despite a good run through these years, by the early 1990s there were major changes. Already, there were indications that if Mike had any chance of staying on with this company, he'd be looking at a life fashioned to be much like those described in *New York Times* reporter Peter Kilborn's book about the normalization of corporate job relocation and the creation of a class of workers forced to live an itinerant life, who are known as "Relos."[1] He was not going there.

Although he made a good salary and enjoyed full benefits and stock options, Mike started questioning his working life. Where was it all going? He questioned a life where he put himself so fully into projects that had started getting axed by corporate decision makers and where the division he worked for was moved around in an elaborate game of chess only to be sold off according to an economic calculus seemingly immune to the concerns of working families. He explained:

> So tons of hard work and years of hard work and, you know, smart people are moved to Hammond, Louisiana—I resisted that one. They wanted to move me down there . . . but that's where the future of our division was. And it's a good thing because all those folks ended up having to either move back or they just lost their jobs because three years into the program . . . no [government] funding. I just kind of got really turned off on that whole thing—how these decisions can just mess up everything. [Later] the company lost interest in our little group and we were sold. We were just kind of a tag-along group. So we got sold. This is not what I perceived as a stable future in this job. [Meanwhile] San Diego had somewhat of a recession when the company was shedding facilities. When I started working there, they had twenty thousand employees in the city, and now there are maybe three hundred.

As Mike suggested was the case for San Diego, such corporate downsizing has real consequences not only for individuals and families but also places. As I previously noted, in a society increasingly engaged with the representation of things, with image and imagination, the idea of community is something bought and sold. Though places have long been marketed to attract residents and/or investments, today they are literally branded akin to any modern consumer good. The human geographer Mike Goodwin notes that "the emergence of style as identity and consumption as a form of self-definition has gone hand-in-hand with an increasingly reflexive and aesthetic appreciation hastened by the proliferation of visual images and electronic media."[2] Thus, the selling of lifestyle as part of a place's identity "becomes part and parcel of an increasingly sophisticated commodification of everyday life in which images and myths are relentlessly packaged and presented."[3]

The desire of families for community, for a sense of belonging, is driving places to market themselves in new ways within an economy that demands a new kind of place-based economic competitiveness. Becoming savvier through the necessity of economic survival, many places are opting to forego a kind of smokestack chasing that characterized past strategy for a greater focus on enhancing quality of life and livability. As noted previously, livability became a core political concern in Michigan as community leaders attempt to banish tarnished, rusty images of decline. Concerns over quality of life make up what is being called "soft infrastructure" to emphasize that they lie outside more tangible, "hard" infrastructural matters including roads and utilities.[4]

Frequent magazine articles feature "top" places to live for quality of life defined in ways that suit their own target audiences. *Ladies Home Journal* rates locations with an emphasis on their advocacy for woman's issues. The most hip locales for teenagers are a predictable concern for *Seventeen*. *Outside* focuses on places that are fun, friendly, and outdoorsy for the recreationally active. These articles attempt to provide simple roadmaps or how-to manuals for pursuing lifestyles likely to be idealized by their particular readership. The popularity of place-ranking articles suggests that many middle-class families in the United States have become sophisticated consumers of place where sense of place becomes part of a self-conscious construction of identity through lifestyle choices.

Mike's story continues as the economic restructuring of the early 1990s marched onward, taking with it most of what was left of the implicit contract between corporation and employee that was enjoyed by his father's generation. Reacting to feelings of increasing anxiety as seismic shifts in corporate America set the ground in motion beneath his feet, Mike became savvier, shrewder, and more pragmatic in his thoughts about work. He began thinking of his present job as training for something else down the road where he could have greater personal control. What remained in the way of loyalty to the corporation dissolved as it became clear that there was no guarantee of reward for being faithful to a company looking out for its own interests and fully prepared to sacrifice its workers to fulfill the demands of swelling ranks of shareholders. It now became a question of timing for him. It was about staying in it only so long as it worked for him and he felt that he is getting something useful. He noted: "So, in the process I'm getting good training. This is like graduate school to me now. I'm not loyal to the company, I'll do what they ask but I'll work through the process and learn business."

At this point, Mike saw himself gaining important skills at the company's expense. He knew they believed that they owed him nothing. He was acting with what amounts to enlightened self-interest. All the while, he was rethinking where he was and where he was going. He was taking stock and looking for a way out that made sense to him and was likely to be best for his young family. He continued with his story: "So there are several things happening. I don't want to do this for the rest of my life. So that's another factor—you kind of assess. I think everybody does at a certain age. Is this a livelihood? You know? I want to get into something more simple that I can get my hands around, and I want to get something where I can *control* my own destiny instead of just sort of floating with this company."

While still with the company, at this point Mike was on the brink of reaching a kind of breaking point. He had already experienced a breach in the implicit contract, of trust and faith between employer and employee born of repeated examples of corporate indifference to the personal needs of workers. He and his wife started scribbling in legal pads. The yellow pads began to fill with detailed lists of pros and cons of leaving the known reality of their present life weighed against speculation in starting over in a new, yet unknown place. This new place was one that they hoped would better *resonate* with a lifestyle choice of a simpler, more integrated and balanced life where family comes first. Michael Bell speaks of this resonance in the context of his work in Childerley, noting that "there is a kind of intuitive pleasure, an intellectual state of ease, which comes from achieving the adjustments in understanding that bring out a resonance in life" between thought, action, and context.[5] For the participants in both our studies, it is about finding that "right" place and making decisions that harmonize with a kind of moral orientation. Mike described how he used popular self-help books to aid them in the process of working through the decision to relocate and to find greater resonance: "We sat down with the *Places Rated Almanac* and *What Color Is Your Parachute* books and did some exercises. The engineering part of me is trying to take the emotion out of it, but then you have to factor it back in. You can't completely ignore that, but we did go through and say, okay, this isn't it so what should we do?"

They did this *weighing* over the period of two years, all the while factoring in new information and concerns as these were realized or somehow came into play in the course of their everyday life. After this two-year weighing period, they decided on a place in northern Lower Michigan that is well outside any metropolitan area, although it qualifies as a micropolitan location. Traverse City appealed to them because it is close to what had been home for Mike down in Lansing, a three-hour drive to the south, and a place that they both see as smaller scale, slower paced, and more family oriented. Consistent with Mike and Denise's expectations, it is a place actively marketed as "A World Apart."[6] From the perspective of would-be small business owners, they also recognized the area as one that attracts people with some measure of disposable income. Using the *Places Rated Almanac*, they determined that seasonal influxes of vacationers and sizeable in-migration of yearlong residents boded well for a number of possible service-oriented businesses. Although they enjoyed Southern California, lived in a good neighborhood, and had many friends, with their sights on the promise of greater personal fulfillment in the option of elsewhere, they packed up and moved out.

For Mike and Denise, having decided on a place that had the potential to fulfill their lifestyle goals, the question then became "Okay, what can we do there to make ends meet?" Based on some pleasant days they enjoyed while experiencing their own time out of time during a vacation to a quiet mountain town in California, they began to seriously explore the option of starting their own business. A small pie shop thrived in that town by virtue of its excellent pies and a steady stream of tourists seeking an experience of quiet and quality. In the temporary refuge afforded by vacationing away from their daily routines, they envisioned other possible selves. After deciding where they would seek these alternative selves, Mike decided to make pies in a parallel situation to that model pie company in Traverse City. I am taken by the meaningfulness of this choice, for it is perhaps not coincidental that in an increasingly uncertain and tumultuous world, a homemade pie becomes an especially powerful symbol—perhaps even a summarizing, *key symbol* for a putative American culture—of goodness and simplicity. Quite simply, it is an edible icon of the good life itself.

Mike attacked the problem of building this new vision like the engineer he was trained to be, thus putting into service skills gleaned from another work life in order to construct a new one. He put together what he believed was a sound business plan. While the enormous task of creating a business wholly from scratch presented a real threat to their goal of achieving a balanced work and family life, this new venture embodied a guiding philosophy born out of the lifestyle choice they have made. Restraint was important. Mike continued: "Yeah. I don't want to jump back to what I *was*. At that time it was 'God, I just want to work in a pie shop and enjoy the simple life.' I read this book, I think it was called *The Simple Life* or something like that, and that was his philosophy. What you really need to do is reconnect with community, you know? You need to reconnect with your families and get rid of this big company stress stuff."

An uncertainty lingered about setting out on his own. Would there be a way out of this course of action? What would they do if the dream fails? "So, okay, I've made it and supported a family in the corporate world, but can I make it on my own—flat out on my own? You can't hide behind the corporate identity, you know? I didn't think there'd be an *out* here in Traverse City. I see people who come here and try something, and it won't work, and then you see them doing some other very menial job because there aren't a lot of jobs that are high paying. So my out would have to be leaving, which would be kind of rough on the family . . . but we were ready to do that." Recognizing that basic and heretofore taken-for-granted cultural models about work and family life are being actively reworked, the question we must ask is from what sources are people acquiring the raw materials or—thinking pies—the *ingredients* to use when creating fresh definitions of the good life? Important works that document historical changes in the meaning of family, such as the cultural historian John Gillis's *A World of Their Own Making*, or of shifts in civic engagement, such as Robert Putnam's *Bowling Alone*, explain the nature and scope of the relative decline in importance of social institutions in shaping how people in the United States find meaning and purpose in their lives.[7] These works further document a shift in finding meaning from the sphere of production and work to an orientation that more heavily depends on insight derived from the realm of consumption and leisure.

While defining oneself by way of a job might have been something embraced by William Whyte's "Organization Man" of the post–World War II economic boom—who not only worked for but also affectively *belonged* to the company— today's workers are increasingly savvy to the fact that there is no guarantee of stability in the world of work as a source for self-definition.[8] Research by sociologist Stephen Sweet on issues related to a changing economy, lessened job security, and individually perceived risk, provides a greater context within which to evaluate the decisions of lifestyle migrants like Mike and Denise to relocate and make significant career changes in the process. As noted by Sweet, "there is a growing interest in the ways in which workers adapt to what is now a normative situation—employment in jobs that offer only limited security. This can have an impact on expectations toward jobs, careers, employers, communities, and the fabric of society."⁹ The study of lifestyle migration may provide some insight into one way that people like Mike attempt to adjust to, or possibly take advantage of, a changing economic order and who thus create potential for further change.

Indeed, adjustment is the name of the game. Accordingly, "flexibility" is a valued quality expected of today's worker. Departing from the ideal of a standardized industrial world, today's worker must be malleable and forever learning. Through his research on the dynamics of work and family in Silicon Valley, anthropologist Charles Darrah documents how today's workers are expected to see themselves as a set of disembedded skills rather than as a complete and integrated individual with a particular, discrete job.¹⁰ This worker becomes what I call the "person as portfolio." Gillis suggests that we are now living in an era where people of all ages are encouraged "to think of themselves in a perpetual state of becoming . . . [and where we] are asked to retrain, re-educate, and recycle."¹¹

Given an imperative to constantly remake of oneself, the notion of an "identity crisis" may no longer be an exclusive descriptor for culturally constructed "midlife" exigencies. Rather, the *midlife crisis* has become a metaphor for life at all its stages as those in societies shaped by similar imperatives must attempt to organize their lives around states of ongoing instability.¹² While such ambiguity is not new, sociologist Richard Sennett explains that, when compared with any other time in history, present-day uncertainty is peculiar by virtue of the fact that it "is woven now into the everyday practices of a vigorous capitalism. It is meant to be normal."¹³

In the twenty-first-century working world, workers increasingly feel that they have to deliberately and actively chart their own career paths. By both voluntary (as seen in "downshifting") and involuntary means (as in when "downsized"), increasing numbers of workers in contemporary society are becoming *free agents*.¹⁴ In the world of sports, a free agent is a player whose contract with a particular team has ended and who is now free to sign with a team of their choosing. In the world of work, the term free agent may be used to characterize a growing number of workers who are in some manner working for themselves and living lives like those documented by Fast Company executive Daniel Pink in his *Free Agent Nation: The Future of Working for Yourself*.¹⁵

That employers view employees as "free agents responsible for their own employability" is evidenced in findings of the Families and Work Institute.¹⁶ Work and family scholars such as Jill Paine have provided considerable depth to our understanding of a younger generation of workers' relationship to employers and their apparent proclivity toward higher levels of job (and perhaps geographic) mobility when compared with earlier generations.¹⁷ Today's lifestyle migrant may be a product of the simultaneously enabling and challenging flexibility, mobility, and potentially superficial connectivity of contemporary life. As individuals, migrants in this study attempt to use opportunities presented by these changes even as they, incongruously, search for roots in particular places they come to see as comfortable eddies in global flows—potential anchorage for the unmoored.

Theirs is an "adaptable sense of fixity" comparable to that found by Bell in his study of the people in the community of Childerley outside London, who like others have had to look to find alternative "moorings of self" through self-conscious identification with place and, specifically, with what in his own study he calls a "pastoral natural conscience."[18] While we should recognize their simplification of complex patterns of motivation, sociologists Arthur Vidich and Joseph Bensman argued in their landmark 1950s book *Small Town in Mass Society* that idealization of the small town in America expressed a need to displace resentment against both personal and collective dependence on "mass society," that is, social relations that characterize the modern, centralized state and widespread consumption of commercial media—both of which can have a homogenizing effect.[19]

A Moral Story

As suggested earlier, the account of lifestyle migration that this book provides is a moral story. Lifestyle migrants are searching for what Charles Taylor simply calls *the good*.[20] In order to understand what it is to be a person or a self in a particular society, it is necessary to understand a prevailing notion of the good within the dominant culture. Selfhood and the good, which Taylor uses interchangeably with morality, are inseparable. Taylor's is a broad understanding of morality that includes not only those issues we normally associate with the term, such as questions of right behavior, the principles or standards that guide action and tell us what we should do, but also what it is good *to be*. Answering these questions entails determining what has intrinsic value and leads the person to a sense of dignity and self-respect. Similarly, my own understanding of the moral goes beyond a focus on what is right to do to include the nature of the good life, that is, what underlies notions of a life that is fulfilling. In this way, my position is consistent with that of virtue ethicist Alasdair MacIntyre, who criticizes a general reduction of the moral in academic and public discourse to questions of negative sanctions and control. The moral must include consideration of the basic questions concerning what makes a life worth living and confers meaning on individual lives.

As a key symbol and normative statement in the United States, an American Dream has served as a moral framework embedded in fundamental cultural understandings of how the world works. Originating in part in the historical particulars of a frontier nation and the philosophical underpinnings of the Declaration of Independence, the dream both depends on and contributes to a particular notion of the good. As moral framework, it encourages people to work hard by giving them hope that their labor will not be simply compensated but rather *rewarded*. What sociologist Robert Wuthnow considers simplistic understandings have made the American Dream out to be little more than "a materialistic value system, holding forth the prospect of a high paying job, a comfortable home in the suburbs, and opportunities for one's children."[21] Wuthnow suggests that closer consideration shows it to be much more than materially defined. The American Dream as a moral framework—or, as previously described, a model *for* the world—has served to shape the emerging economy of the past century by providing a set of assumptions about work and money and giving people a reason to toil long and hard with the expectation of just compensation and reward.

It lives on in popular conceptions and, as key symbol, continues to legitimate hard work while providing a still partly convincing link between work and money and other aims and aspirations, though the housing crisis has fundamentally challenged our assumptions about a cornerstone of the American Dream. At least since the United States government's "Own Your Own Home" campaign, ownership of one's home has been viewed as an unquestioned virtue. Launched in 1918 by the US Department of Labor and a cabal of industry groups—including the National Association of Real Estate Boards and National Federation of Construction Industries—the campaign began during a period of labor strikes and social unrest following World War I with the objective of restoring political stability by encouraging dispossessed urban workers to become home owners. The platforms of presidents from Herbert Hoover and Franklin Roosevelt to Bill Clinton and George W. Bush have all taken it as a foregone conclusion that home ownership was the sine qua non of middle-class membership.

Although many Americans would no doubt say that the work that many do at least in part to own and maintain a home is at least partly meaningful and even in some respects fulfilling, they might also feel pressured, dissatisfied, and uncertain about how they can fit this work with the rest of their lives. Despite possibly misleading statistics indicating greater leisure time as well as rising average family incomes, most people do not feel as though they have more discretionary income or more time on their hands. Just the opposite, they have felt increasingly rushed and squeezed. If people do indeed have greater material abundance, then they are relatively unable to consistently put together the time necessary to think about how they might render this economic success into meaningful, qualitative improvements in their lives.[22]

Many Americans appear perhaps unwitting members of what former secretary of labor Robert Reich calls a new "anxious class." This contemporary manifestation of the middle class is composed of people frantically trying to piece together two or more paychecks in order to meet widening gaps in income, health care, and pensions.[23] These pronounced cracks hasten an apparent disintegration of the middle class as historically defined. As the recent Great Recession has made even more apparent than the economic slow-down taking place while I began fieldwork with lifestyle migrants in Northern Michigan, downsizing, part-timing, and a loss of benefits have become a way of life for America.

In this emergent economic order, the relationship between economic life and a quest for deeper human values, the goal of simple living already discussed, has become increasingly problematic. Although the work that people do and the money that they make, which allows them to buy things, remain at the center of striving for and achieving "success," these economic commitments increasingly seem to impede the individual and collective pursuit of other vital human needs. These are needs that individuals feel originate from an inner self, from their very person. To follow these needs is an act that, in itself, fulfills an essential quest for "the higher," for simplicity in a commitment to personal truth. They include the need to develop and cherish more intimate relationships with family, a desire to feel belonging as part of a caring community, and a fundamental longing to better know oneself and to see and experience personal growth. The result is an internal tension between the material side of our lives and something of the human spirit. For some, this tension may be little more than a nagging doubt about choices.

For others, however, a full-blown conflict demands complete attention and leads them to question the footings of their lives, their very commitments. Ultimately, it is a question of whether economic success—as it has generally been defined—is enough.

People approach this crisis in different ways. As I have seen in the accounts of lifestyle migrants, some gradually attempt to divide themselves in an attempt to balance competing pressures by compartmentalizing their lives and thus creating distinct work and family selves. They may then hold entirely different definitions for success that they apply independently to these different selves, often in conflict with each other. Others may attempt a different course where the emphasis is less on forcing oneself to *adapt* to external conditions and more on rather trying to *change* those conditions. Lifestyle migrants concentrate on relocation as a way of forcing or perhaps focusing this change and as an expression of their commitment to certain lifestyle choices in an attempt to reprioritize and integrate their lives. The act of relocation becomes a means of realizing some degree of personal control in a quest for more fully integrated spheres of community, work, family, and individual life.

The lifestyle migrant identifies him or herself with an emphasis on quality of life rooted in a very personal sense of their "true" self. This emphasis gives them a feeling of empowerment against potentially fragmenting pressures of the world of work. It is what makes this a moral story. As Taylor explains, how we choose is an essential part of morality. When individuals and families struggle to decide *how* to live their lives, it is not simply an economic question, although this is a central part. The search for meaning and the process of decision making about the fundamental choice of how to live a life is a moral question involving basic values.

Guided by their own moral compass, constructed itself out of a concern for quality of life, lifestyle migrants define the good life. When people speak about quality of life, they necessarily begin setting standards by which they will judge the relative value of different aspects of living. They include such tangible features as the physical environment (both natural and built), the variety of stores and restaurants, the frequency of so-called cultural events, the reputation of local schools and hospitals. They also take in intangibles of soft infrastructure, like the sense people get from a place, whether they feel connected or that they belong, how people appear to treat each other in the street and in places of business, or the apparent "pace" of life.

As noted by Bell, "to the extent that people can truly choose where they live, a person's choice of residence depends as well on . . . [a] 'symbolic ecology,' the cultural meaning of places. Thus, to account for the great overall increase in enthusiasm for country living [as in both our studies], new cultural factors must be taken into account."[24] Migrants who choose their place of residence on the basis of such considerations are making a moral judgment on the status quo way of life where your job dictates not only *where* but also *how* you live. People choose places that they feel offer a quality of life that is consistent or resonant with a lifestyle commitment. Whether or not there was any possibility of making adjustments to a life lived where they were and before relocation in order to achieve the standards of their own emerging sense of the good is seldom clear. What is clear, however, is that they have made the decision to exercise their right to move on and (hopefully) achieve these new measures of the good life in the option of elsewhere.

An engineer turned pie maker, Mike chose to reorient his priorities from pursuing a career where he made daily sacrifices of time and energy for an ever more uncertain future payoff to one focused more completely on a sense of control in the present together with greater everyday devotion to family. His decision, moral though it is in nature, is wholly individual. The question is not one of right or wrong, but rather of whether this course of action is going to work in a cost-benefit analysis between pluses and minuses expressed in terms of trade-offs. It is a matter of self-reliance. The good in this basic practice of the contemporary self depends on questions of individual preference and, finally, a lifestyle choice.

Among distinct aspects of modern identity is a sense of inwardness and uniqueness. The concern is with authenticity where people feel that they must aspire to be true to their inner selves. The increase in this concern comes as established orders of cultural meaning gradually loose power and significance in people's lives. We are encouraged by new and progressively more secular messages to explore inwardly for meaning and to find our moral source. Consistent with this, Taylor finds that "the higher is to be found not outside of but as a *manner of living* ordinary life."[25] What matters then is not so much *what* we do as *how* we do it. In this way it is much like David Shi's ideas of simple living as more a state of mind than standard of living. Each person must decide for him- or herself what being true to self means and in what manner to live life. Personal fulfillment depends on an individual quest to identify inner selves and on living a life, designing a lifestyle, resonant with that self.

Freedom and "the Good"

The ability to engage in this personal quest, in a manner idealized in the travel narratives of American literature—to which I have previously referred—is part of the freedom that we value and celebrate as a nation. In many ways, it is this freedom that defines a prevailing idea of the good rather than some abstract notion of rights. The good is a real, lived experience of being able to pursue one's own dreams and make one's own choices. Though less acknowledged, it is also then a freedom to make one's own mistakes and accept responsibility for them. It is the freedom to construct one's life in a way one sees as best. It is freedom as well from infringement by the beliefs and standards of others. The only constraint on freedom is that individuals should avoid interfering with others. In this basic relativism, the primary edict is that, if in doubt, one should always aim to be true to him- or herself.

As individuals, we are ever more dependent on finding a sense to life by framing our own meaningful expressions. What meaning there is for us in the world depends, at least in part, on our powers of expression as our ability to find a framework is interwoven with inventing. In this way, we may say that meaning is found, in part, through our consumption and lifestyle choices. The capacity for self-expression is so important that Taylor finds that our "contemporary notions of what it is to respect people's integrity includes that of protecting their expressive freedom to express and develop their own opinions, to define their own life conceptions, to draw up their own life-plans."[26] Thus, as I will examine in greater detail in Chapter 9, the symbolic resources for this expressive power are essential.

In one of our conversations, a former Towncar-driving soft-drink company executive turned pickup truck driving landlord wonders about how one identifies what should constitute the good life. As for so many, Alan ultimately feels that success is equivalent to freedom. Or rather, freedom *allows* one to live the kind of good life that should define what it means to be successful. But he might not always have felt that way.

> Do you get told what the good life is or do you figure it out for yourself? I did in corporate America—I started getting told. I was told what the good life was: a four-bedroom colonial house in the suburbs and working for a main company, dressing in a suit every day, going to the job, weekends off and getting to go someplace . . . the ability to go someplace on the weekend. And where did I go on the weekend? I went to Traverse City. But I wasn't happy. I just didn't know it. I drove down the road [a tree-lined road in the country just outside Traverse City] and I thought, why would I leave all this? I thought success was living in the big city. But really success is being able to afford to live in a little town and being able to go back to the city when you want to. Instead of living in the big city and going to the town to have a good time. Let's live here all the time, and then when you need a touch of the city, go back.

Alan suggested that we need to figure out as individuals what the good life really is. We might be told what it is, but that does not mean we should embrace that interpretation as our own. Alan also explained that even believing that we are living the good life needs some kind of affirmation. How can we be sure we are not just making ourselves believe it in order to be comfortable, as he had done, either before or even after breaking from the corporate vision to one based more on a lifestyle and concerned with finding a work/family balance?

> So many times people, once they get up here, start saying, "Well this is the good life. I was wrong all the time." Do people start rationalizing their situation to become comfortable? So the real test for me was when I started getting signals, feedback, from others. Feedback from others tells you something about yourself. Like when a friend said, "You've got to take up golf so you can stress like the rest of us." And I thought that's pretty damn funny. Or "You're smiling a lot more now." Or "you're a lot more laid-back."

Normative cultural traditions define the meaning of achievement and the purpose of human life in ways that have left the individual in a kind of terrible isolation. The ultimate goals of a good life are matters of personal choice where the ability to choose is believed to be realized through economic progress alone. Freedom defines the good in both personal and political life. This is the freedom to construct one's own life as one best sees fit. It is essentially the same sense we have of freedom as the right to be left alone by others that encourages development of so-called gated communities or "lifestyle enclaves," which serve the need for perceived protection from diversity and difference. It is about not having other people's values, ideas, or styles of life forced upon oneself. As Alan explained, "Success is being able to live the life you want the way you want to."

For participants in my project, being free went beyond being left alone. Being free meant being able to become your own person in the sense that you feel that you have defined who you are and have determined what you want out of life. Freedom is also "freedom from," understood as the capacity to have some degree of control of one's life—even if at the cost of being alone in a world of other individuals seeking the same freedom from each other. This was something recognized by the young Frenchman Alexis de Tocqueville in his seminal *Democracy in America*, written in the 1830s. In his examination of culture in the early United States, Tocqueville found that the nascent American middle class were people who had already formed a habit of thinking of themselves as individuals in isolation from the greater world of social relations. He saw that they imagined the whole of their lives as being a matter of personal choice, utterly in their hands to make happen, and as individuals forever thrown back on themselves alone.

This sense of the self-made individual, usually expressed in terms of economic achievement, was firmly established in the rise of great individual wealth among captains of American industry during the Industrial Revolution. Today, these enduring ideals are enhanced and furthered by modern psychological principles and espoused in ideologies of personal fulfillment. They serve as larder for modern-day personal success manuals that have flourished over the past few decades. These are born of a therapeutic ideal—to which Robert Bellah refers—that "posits an individual who is able to be the source of his [*sic*] standards, to love himself before he asks for love from others, and to rely on his own judgment without deferring to others."[27]

One consequence of these freedoms is that it is clearly now the more or less exclusive burden of the individual to find satisfactory ways of allocating time and energy among the various realms of an ordinary life—work, family, community, and self—in a way that is most personally fulfilling. Notwithstanding the sense of limitlessness that is inherent in our cultural notions of individual freedom and the potential for economic success, our economic commitments are embedded in moral frameworks that continue to exert some degree of restraint on our economic behavior. People recognize limits and know when they are asked to go well beyond them in terms of the amount or kinds of work they are asked to do. While they may not always resist or take action, people sense that moral codes in the framework can be violated. The role of moral orientations with regard to economic life is not to restrict behavior, making this realm less meaningful to the individual, but rather to set limits around its meanings and show that they are bounded, thereby making judgment possible.

A moral discourse does not necessarily provide justifiable reasons to cut back or to restrain one's economic activity through shorter hours or downshifting, but it does help by providing a means of *weighing*. As MacGregor found in her study of community and identity, it provides a "logic of commitment" that serves as a basis for ordering life priorities and evaluating everyday options. As we saw in Mike and Denise's story, weighing according to such a commitment allows people an opportunity to understand whether hours spent at work are, in fact, contributing to more than the bottom line. Are they also contributing to the realization of one's innermost goals and personal identity? As an outward expression of moral orientation, weighing provides a way of traversing between one set of meanings and other valuations. But where exactly do people find encouragement to downshift, to reign in commitments to work, to set limits, and to allow for greater awareness of inner goals for personal growth? Where indeed, we might ask, when the dominant messages in our culture are to work hard, play by the rules, and earn as much money as possible? Choosing not to devote oneself to economic achievement and material wealth goes against the predominant grain of society and can even be a source of personal shame. That there is erosion in the strength and capacity for influence from traditional sources or models of self-control is evident in the fact that many people appear to go well beyond conventional boundaries of moral restraint in pursuit of greater economic success and material abundance.

The idea of an individual "having discretion" once connoted the caution or prudence suggested by self-restraint. Today the meaning is redefined in practice to stand for the exercise of personal choice. This important change suggests that the idea has become a fundamental part of economic life. This idea of discretion as freedom of choice parallels the idea of "flexibility" in the new economy. Flexibility is an essential part of the story. Robert Wuthnow notes that in the workplace, the rise of individual discretion means greater emphasis on autonomous decision making, "with fewer tasks being mandated specifically by someone in authority. The choice of careers themselves and decisions about particular places of employment have increasingly become matters of personal discretion." In the absence of guiding constraint, discretionary behavior for many has become "the domain in which economic influences are permitted to reign with virtually unlimited authority."[28] The idea of moral limits, of restraint, is relegated to areas that lie almost entirely outside economic concerns. Morality as a whole today is seen as having relevance in discussions of sexuality, for example, but is substantially lacking in any consideration of what should be the nature of the good life. Lifestyle migrants variously challenge this absence.

CHAPTER 6

Locating the "Fifth Migration"

When Manhattanites start moving into the Midwestern backwaters, into a nowhere northern Michigan peninsula like the Leelanau, you know something's happening to the country's demographics. It's too soon to say what, but the feeling you have watching it is similar to seeing geese flying north in November: it's not what you expect. . . . The desire for freedom and opportunity, to live a vision of a better life, which brings people to America in the first place, seems to keep them moving once they get here, and the seductive beauty of the Leelanau Peninsula has lured more than one couple away from economically secure urban lives.

—Kathleen Stocking, *Letters from the Leelanau*

Lifestyle migration runs against the grain of what are generally identified as the most significant migration patterns in the world today in terms of both the impact and numbers seen in labor migration and the movement of refugees. Although a search for better quality of life is fundamental to voluntary migration in virtually all forms, lifestyle migration has not received as much attention given other migratory forms. Emphasizing elements of leisure, the term *lifestyle* migration is used to identify migration of relatively affluent individuals and families who relocate in search of what they feel will improve personal quality of life. In the case of the lifestyle migration documented in this book, this generally involves chosen relocation away from metropolitan areas in favor of rural or "micropolitan" locales. The demographer Kevin Heubusch defines such micropolitan places as distinct small cities located beyond much larger and urban metropolitan areas. He describes the most livable of these places as offering amenities normally associated with the big cities on a more "manageable scale—community without the crush, services without the stress. . . . [Where they] are large enough to support jobs, restaurants, diversions, and community organizations, but small enough to sidestep the traffic jams, high crime rates, and high property taxes often associated with highly urbanized areas."[1]

Lifestyle migrants have the apparent luxury to relocate to places that they believe will support a desire to simplify their lives—among other motivations that I explore. Given that they do not move to pursue place-dependent opportunities for work, unlike most voluntary migrants, they cannot be characterized as labor migrants. Rather, work becomes a calculated means to an end, something to permit lifestyle migrants to be in a geographic place that is personally meaningful to them and that they believe will fulfill commitments to a particular lifestyle—much like what MacGregor observed in her study where particular ideas about obligation and agency, and specifically the extent to which it was worthy to bring one's life into resonance with a set of larger goals, both motivated individuals to action and defined personal identity.

Outside of the field of studies on lifestyle migration, research on this comparatively privileged demographic has been limited to such groups as professional expatriates, to a focus on international flows of skilled, tech-oriented laborers, or to the international migration of well-heeled retirees.[2] In research on the career and retirement choices of these sorts of migrants, we begin to see the kinds of connections that I will make between studies of lifestyle migration and research into work and family issues, most especially the area of "work and family balance," as a critical aspect of individual and familial identity processes.

The range of migratory forms that might be categorized as lifestyle migration is broad and international. It is generally the case that migration such as that documented in this book has not been described as lifestyle migration in the United States but is more commonly known as "noneconomic" or "amenity" migration. Demographically and behaviorally similar migration in Europe uses the term "lifestyle" as evidenced by a range of recent publications such as an edited volume by sociologists Michaela Benson and Karen O'Reilly.[3] Although referred to as lifestyle migration in Australia, particulars of geography and popular culture in that country have led to popular use of the term "sea change," from the title of an Australian Broadcasting Company miniseries *SeaChange*, about such relocation, for much of the migration involving relocation from urban centers to largely rural, coastal areas of the country.[4] Recent migration patterns in Australia appear as well to suggest what many are now calling a "tree change" in the decision of many seeking alternative lifestyles through relocating away from cities to pastoral environments away from the coasts.[5]

Turnaround Migration

According to census data, during the 1970s population in the rural United States suddenly jumped 14 percent. While heralded by a media as a "mass return to the land," many scholars were skeptical that in-migration from urban and suburban areas could bring dramatic reversal to a nearly century-long trend of declining rural population. Many dismissed figures as fluke or aberration. Data in the 1980s seemed to confirm their suspicion when, perhaps exacerbated by a pronounced economic downturn, most rural areas again experienced a net loss of population. Initiated at least in part by the farm crisis of that decade, the 1980s could be seen as a temporary setback in early stages of a longer trend. Population in many rural counties had grown by 1995 at a rate three times greater than in 1980s. This was not fueled by births but rather by net in-migration from both urban centers and surrounding metropolitan areas.

This apparent alteration in patterns of migration from rural to urban areas is important not only as behavior with real consequences for the physical and social landscape of America but also as a catalyst for bringing about change in prevailing theories of migration behavior. Prior to the early 1970s, migration models had relied more or less exclusively on economic perceptions of motivation to explain migration behavior. There is still a bias toward an economic understanding in many of today's models. Economic explanations of migration are part of an orientation in social theory that assumes that individuals are rational actors. In this context, theorized rational actors are thought to sensibly select a place of residence in an area that optimizes their economic potential. This conscious maximization of financial good constitutes the paramount of rational behavior defined in these economic terms. The demonstration of seemingly deviant and economically irrational behavior on the part of migrants to rural areas—still in their productive working years—challenged the dominance of economic explanations for migration behavior.

With established assumptions, what appeared as a "sudden preference" of people for a rural lifestyle understandably shocked many social scientists as rural areas were thought to be a major economic disadvantage for individuals when compared with metropolitan centers. The persistent belief was that people move where they do in order to maximize their potential as wage earners. Challenged by other possibilities suggested by the shift, researchers began to seriously consider and explore other motivations for migration behavior. At the most basic level, researchers of migration had not been asking the right questions in order to determine the emotional dimensions of motivation behind observed behavior.

The data available from census and other sources allows for an examination of *net* migration. This is nothing more than the balance after out-migration is weighed against in-migration. Because the value for net migration necessarily conflates personal decisions about leaving a place as well as those for moving in, the implications for behavior on the individual level cannot be easily deduced. For example, the apparent 1980s reversal of the turnaround in rural-urban migration observed in the prior decade could be interpreted in two very different ways. On the one hand, it may be seen as a return to higher out-migration in age groups sensitive to the plight of more agriculturally dependent economies during a period especially hard on farms. On the other hand, the reversal can also be interpreted as further shift in preferences or concerns of would-be migrants who opted not to relocate to nonmetropolitan areas in greater numbers than the decade before. Without individual-level data on behaviors and motives, analysis of existing data has necessarily been based to some extent on speculation established from consideration of certain structural changes and county-level differences with regard to these changes as well as preexisting characteristics such as quantity and quality of *amenities* associated, for example, with geographic location such as access to outdoor recreational opportunities.

Recognizing important demographic and economic changes in the post-WWII period such as the growth of early paid retirement, longer life expectancies, increased mobility due to transportation and communication improvements, and an increasingly service-based economy, the geographer Edward Ullman was among the first to suggest that these amenities, including climate and geography as well as the charm of small towns and availability of recreational opportunities instead of what he described as "narrowly defined economic advantages," would generate population growth in largely nonmetropolitan areas of United States.[6] Giving support to Ullman's early projection, research beginning forty years later in the mid-1990s by David McGranahan at the US Department of Agriculture found that rather than related to urban proximity, population density, or economic type, county population and employment change since the early 1970s has been more closely related to amenities such as varied topography and proximity to surface water such as ponds, lakes, and shorelines.[7] It was through such findings that the term "noneconomic" emerged as a way to depict migration patterns in which a significant number of migrants in their productive working years voluntarily relocated to areas well outside centers of business and recognized forms of economic opportunity. Referring to this as noneconomic was meant to distinguish it from the expected pattern of voluntary migration where economic opportunity should be the primary motivating force for presumed rational actors.[8] As I suggested earlier, this is akin to the reason for using the term "lifestyle" more recently to refer to a broad range of such migration behavior.

Speaking in the context of his long-term study of noneconomic migration in the Gallatin Valley area of southwestern Montana, centered in Bozeman, Patrick Jobes found it not at all coincidental that a "paradigmatic shift" in migration theory began during this period when motives among migrants seemed to shift to a more conscious valuing of noneconomic factors.[9] Jobes offers interesting analysis based on his observations since the 1970s of the changing social and physical ecology of the rural West. He notes that the 1970s turnaround suggested that idealization of rural living by utopian writers such as Helen and Scott Nearing had gained more widespread appeal. Their books promised rewards from pursuit of "voluntary simplicity" or living by choice, not necessity.[10] Some inhabitants of America's materially decaying and emotionally alienating urban and suburban areas embraced the Nearings' teachings, which espoused an approach to living founded on the reduction of material desires.

For many, the Nearings' message conveyed a desire for communities that people might truly grasp. There was a desire for a smaller scale than that experienced in rapidly growing and often-fractious metropolitan areas. Where people felt they could not find adequate community, as a lived experience, a few endeavored to create this from scratch in the form of *intentional* communities. There were many extremes, but the fundamental interest of migrants in what has been called the "back-to-the-land" movement was to change lifestyle and by so doing, to improve quality of life on individual and collective levels. It is possible to identify distinct periods within a back-to-the-land movement after frontier homesteading subsidized by the federal government ended in the early twentieth century. The first period occurred in the 1930s, partly as a response to tumult of the Great Depression. The Nearings document this period through their own life stories. Similarly born of uncertainty and strife, the second period was part of broader countercultural trends born of the civil rights movements and protests against the Vietnam War in the late 1960s and early 1970s with urban-to-rural migrants leaving cities in search of a life such as that described by the Nearings. We continue to see migration that can be characterized as back to the land, not so obviously the product of turmoil, but rather alongside a consumerist-simplicity movement characterized largely by middle-class families moving to rural areas—families who we could characterize as among the varieties of lifestyle migrants.

As a subset of the broader counterculture of the 1960s and 1970s, the back-to-the-land movement shares a primary concern for quality of life with lifestyle and other forms of so-called noneconomic migration. A sociologist who studied the movement, Jeffery Jacob calls contemporary back-to-the-landers "new pioneers" in order to suggest their apparent return to a model for living characteristic of the American pioneer past but enacted in, and variously altered by, a novel context born of an increasingly postindustrial society and a hegemonic consumerism. These new pioneers return—as it were—to small-town and rural America motivated by visions of a simple life modeled after an idealized frontier life, such as raising livestock and cultivating fields in order to provide their own food. But most must live with incongruities imposed by continued dependence on the mainstream economy, given that these households typically need at least one person to hold a wage-earning job, and by their own ambivalence over how to fulfill their practical and moral commitments to a normative simple life when weighing, for example, the decision of whether or not to use various forms of technology or how to educate their children.[11]

A range of so-called quality-of-life studies attempts to explain such forms of motivation. One of the first comprehensive studies on the salience of quality of life was produced by the EPA Office of Research and Monitoring in the early 1970s. In their foreword to this work, the authors describe a then emergent notion of quality of life as "an indefinable measure of society's determination and desire to improve or at least not permit further degradation of its condition; . . . it represents a yearning of people for something which they feel they have lost or are losing, or have been denied, and which to some extent they wish to regain or acquire; . . . it is a new name for an old notion. In the context of this document, it refers to the well-being of people . . . as well as to the 'well-being' of the environment in which these people live."[12] By this definition, one should have no problem defining the migrants of studies such as Jacob's as *quality of life*, or indeed, *lifestyle* migrants.

As I have already suggested, explanations have varied for both a 1970s turnaround in urban-to-rural migration and what later became characterized as a "rebound" to the apparent slump or "reversal" of the 1980s during the 1990s. Three explanatory models are worth discussing in greater detail. The *period-effects* model refers to influences specific to particular points in time—effects thought to be unique economic or demographic circumstances to which any observable fluctuations in population growth or decline may be attributed. The *regional-restructuring* model holds that this trend may be an expression of a shift from a more concentrated industrial economy to a more diverse structure of employment characteristic of a postindustrial, service- and information-based economy furthered by advancements in transportation and communication. The *deconcentration* model points to an apparent shift toward more dispersed settlement patterns that may result from increasingly important noneconomic factors in migration decision making on the level of both individuals and corporations.

Importantly, the period-effects model attributes the 1970s turnaround to a unique confluence of circumstances whereas, to different degrees, the other two explanatory models see the turnaround as part of essentially "evolutionary" re-distribution patterns or even "revolutionary" tendencies in American social and cultural life. The 1970s growth in nonmetropolitan areas is explained through consideration of the focused influence of economic and demographic factors particular to that historical period. These factors included an oil crisis and subsequent recession. The 1970s recession led to or furthered declines in manufacturing at the same time that heavy industries, which had been the foundation of an American way of life for the better part of a century, were already becoming less labor intensive through gains in automation. The net result was significant loss in production-sector jobs. The race riots that ripped through American cities like Detroit are also seen as a key precipitating factor—at least as regional sources of period effects on migratory behavior, including a wave of in-migration to the study area that happened to coincide with an early natural gas boom. Demographic forces such as coming of age of the baby boom cohort are also seen as having played a significant role. Many Baby Boomers, having attended schools in smaller college towns, are seen as having opted for work in these areas outside declining labor markets within traditional, urban centers of business and industry. At the same time, large cohorts of those born in the first two decades of the century contributed to growth in smaller-sized retirement communities throughout the country.

Like period effects, the regional-restructuring model attributes change in population distribution to significant economic shifts specific to that period but is less dependent on this circumscribed effect for explaining events. More important to the model are fundamental changes in the organization of production activities characteristic of an ongoing process of deindustrialization and globalization. Most specific to this view is the suggestion that a functional differentiation in parts of the United States is developing whereby some areas will continue to prosper or even become centers of regional, national, and/or global economies along broad functional lines at the expense of other areas. The importance of these centers of growth will depend on their emergent roles within an economic order where certain areas gain through a tendency toward agglomeration while others only lose relative status and population. This perspective holds that the apparent turnaround of the 1970s was the realization of a long-term trend made more dramatic by period-based influences, most particularly the mid-1970s recession. Once the shakeout of deindustrialization was more or less complete, certain metropolitan areas would again grow in response to the new order of a postindustrial economy.

Based on the work of sociologists and geographers in the tradition of human ecology, a deconcentration model gives particular attention to residential preferences as a form of *consumptive* behavior. While emphasizing consumption patterns and individual behavior, enthusiasts of this perspective continue to recognize the significance of structural and technological changes and their impact on production activities. The understanding that emerges from this position is that long-standing preferences toward lower-density, high-amenity locations are less constrained both spatially and socially when compared to historical periods prior to the 1960s. Certain facilitating factors, such as transportation and communication advances, the spread of services, and the changing distribution of employment, have allowed more people to realize preexisting cultural aspirations or fulfill such latent American ideals as rural living.[13] Deconcentration theorists hold that the turnaround of the 1970s was the beginning of a long-term shift and fundamental redistribution of US population.[14]

Of these three main interpretations of the turnaround, the deconcentration perspective took a more "revolutionary" as opposed to "evolutionary" approach. Those most convinced that the 1970s represented a true turning point suggested that a "clean break" had been made with past migratory trends. They emphasized that observed changes were more than a temporary fluctuation and certainly anything but an aberration or anomaly.[15] Proponents of the deconcentration view asserted that urban-to-rural migration was an expression characteristic of fundamental predispositions in American culture. At the least, this migration was seen as a reassertion of tendencies that were pushed into the recesses of collective American psyche by the ongoing process of industrialization and urban concentration beginning in the second half of the nineteenth century and continuing through World War II. These include an appreciation for freedom of mobility and a desire to be closer to nature—even to seek the Frontier.[16]

Explanations for urban-to-rural migration from these three perspectives, and all points in-between, fall out along two basic lines: one emphasizing *production* and another emphasizing *consumption*. Interpretations on the production side rely on appreciating the inherent logic of capitalism where both individuals and organizations exploit opportunities created by shifting economic conditions resulting, in this case, from ongoing deindustrialization and capital decentralization in different locations. Production-side explanations center on economic and structural factors and tend to emphasize consideration of rational, calculating social actors. In contrast, consumption-side explanations focus on decision making in terms of consumption choices and, at least so far as individuals are concerned, what consequences these choices have for the constitution of identity.

While I recognize the explanatory power of both lines of reasoning, my concern with lifestyle migration leads me to highlight contributions on the consumption side. At the same time, I have explored meanings of the changing economy and world of work for lifestyle migrants as individuals and the choices that they make in response to these structural changes. An *integrated* approach to explaining lifestyle migration seems most reasonable. Understanding migration trends depends on being able to separate out a variety of factors ranging from possible changes in the propensity for Americans to relocate, greater salience of certain preferences in determining place of residence, and both structural and cultural changes that serve either to enable or constrain action.

A Fifth Migration?

The stories of lifestyle migrants told in this book may be contextualized within a history of distinct patterns of migration, each of which has contributed to shaping the physical and social landscape of America. Some researchers who have looked at historical trends in American migration refer to today's most significant pattern of internal migration in the United States as the "fifth migration."[17] The renowned urban historian Lewis Mumford may be credited with establishing this numeration through describing the emerging conditions for what he termed a Fourth Migration.[18] Writing in the 1920s, Mumford described how the United States to that point had seen three important migratory periods. In his reckoning, these began with clearing of the continent through pioneer settlement, leading to eventual relocation from rural areas to emerging industrial towns together with immigration from Europe, and lastly to the growth of great metropolitan centers of commerce and finance at the expense of these industrial towns. For Mumford, the Fourth Migration would become the pattern to dominate the twentieth century. Coming from what we would now describe as a deconcentration perspective, he provided what he understood to be the sources for a "radical decentralization" of the functions of the city that would redistribute population through entire regions in what we now refer to as "suburbanization."

In his time, Mumford saw remarkable advances in transportation, including most especially the rise of the automobile, together with communications, including telephone and radio, and widespread electrical transmission as being all profoundly distributive and decentralizing agents. These changes allowed both individuals and companies greater freedom with regards to decisions about where to locate and with whom they would need to interact—ultimately making a traditional, largely rural interdependence with others based on geographic proximity basically unnecessary. Although his emphasis was, on the one hand, focused on the technological and structural conditions for emergence of the suburb on a mass scale, more generally Mumford recognized that these periods of "flow," as he called them (in a manner remarkably sensitive to concerns that would later preoccupy postmodern theorists), were ultimately caused by "new wants and necessities, and new ideals of life."[19] For Mumford, periods of flow provided an opportunity for people to "remold" themselves and their institutions as "great tides of population . . . unloosed all the old bonds."[20]

Mumford was gravely concerned that, as seen in earlier flows, the Fourth Migration might materialize without the thoughtful planning that he deemed necessary to avoid broadening and deepening a host of mounting social and environmental problems. He considered the period in which he was writing crucial for enacting the kinds of policies that today we might term "smart growth." Here we see how Mumford lamented—in what appears a direct attack on the *cowboy economy*—the missed opportunities that lead to profound costs through disorderly growth in earlier periods, driven by what could be described as a frontier spirit that callously cut down and wasted both natural and human resources: "Homes blocked and crowded by factories; rivers polluted; factories and railway yards seizing sites that should have been preserved for recreation; inadequate homes, thrown together anyhow, for sale anyhow, inhabited anyhow. The result was called prosperity in the Census reports, but that was because no one tried to strike a balance between the private gains and the social losses."[21]

Relocation of families from the cities into suburban areas was a significant period and one that most Americans would closely associate with the idea of an American Dream that is rooted in the notion that home ownership is an essential achievement in the course of one's life and for membership in the middle class. Coming home from the Korean War, my father used the GI Bill to obtain his MBA and eventually a corporate job with IBM. After having grown up in a crowded Brooklyn tenement as a son of Irish immigrants, he was able to take his family to the suburbs and, thus, to fulfill a dream sustained by daily commutes to newly sprouted suburban office parks. This prosperous postwar period made mass-scale suburbia possible. In turn, suburbia made possible the naturalization of particular kinds of work and family culture that people have since largely taken for granted but now struggle to reconcile with changing economic realities by slowly constructing new work and family arrangements and goals.[22] That is one important contribution of the study of such phenomenon as lifestyle migration to our understanding of contemporary life in the United States and elsewhere—to explore the means by which people attempt to negotiate this disconnect between an established moral order and changing economic conditions. Writing about "the" American family for a sociological audience in the immediate aftermath of World War II, the anthropologist Margaret Mead recognized the corrosive potential of a tension born of this disconnect when she asserted that "a large part of the disorganization of family life today, the frequency of divorce, the incidence of neurosis and disease, may be laid to the discrepancies and contradictions between the expectations learned in childhood and the actualities of the present time."[23]

In some respects, we might characterize postwar suburbanization as less a distinct migratory pattern than a reorientation within the overall industrialization and urbanization of the twentieth century.[24] When compared with earlier migrations, rather than seeking economic opportunity elsewhere, at first young families sought to realize and display an achieved status made possible by work still tied in important ways to the urban areas that they had left behind. Later, fueled in large part by rising racial tensions in the late 1960s and early 1970s, large number of families fled economically declining metropolitan areas to greener pastures of the urban hinterland in what for places like Detroit can realistically be described as an exodus. Large numbers of families abandoned cities in a wave of out-migration now expressively called "white flight." This was the attempt by increasingly mobile middle-class whites to escape declining property values, failing schools, rising crime, and higher taxes—as well as what may be called "racial tension." In the case of Detroit, even before the notorious race riots of 1967, the white population of 1950s Detroit had declined by 23 percent over the 1950s. while the proportion of nonwhites rose from 16 to 29 percent.[25] Virtually all of the forty fastest-growing counties in the 1990s were at least 70 percent white, and most were more than 85 percent white.[26]

Some of the older participants in my project recall this unsettled period. Although some of them admit that social unrest helped push them out of Detroit and other urban areas of the Midwest, they say so apologetically. Patrick, who moved to the study area in 1977, thought about how there might be clusters of migrants related to such period effects on migration patterns. He explains: "They would be of different eras, so there would be the early '70s migrants out of Detroit. Two things would be bussing [of black school children to predominately white schools] and the riots. I was just talking to relatives about that. I realized that I had forgotten the enormous impact this had on the city. Some people moved to Livonia [a growing suburb], and other people packed up and came here. So, there'd be an early '70s wake, and then there would be the late '70s wake, which I would be a part [of]." Many lifestyle migrants offered their sense that a lack of ethnic diversity in the Grand Traverse region was a detriment and worried about the impact this might have on their children's sense of the world. For example, Mark relates that before he moved his family from a relatively diverse community in Southern California that "the one thing that I really didn't check out . . . didn't factor it in very heavily, was the racial purity of this area. It's incredible. And I don't mean positively. We're missing something by not having more diversity here for the kids."

Though both the urban historian Robert Fishman and the land economist Jack Lessinger describe four distinct migratory patterns leading up to the present period—including the suburbanization that I describe and that is at least partly foreseen by Mumford—they come to completely opposing conclusions about *where* migrants of a fifth great demographic shift in US history are likely to be going. In short, Lessinger believes that our next most significant migratory period will be migration from urban and suburban areas to those places on the outermost fringes of the metropolitan in what is generally described as *exurban*. Conversely, Fishman describes what he feels will be a period of *reurbanization*. Importantly, they ascribe very similar motivations to their would-be migrants—regardless of where they may want to go.

Though Lessinger's scheme does not match Mumford's, they both recognized the same basic patterns. Lessinger's primary concern was to establish reasons for emergence of what he first termed the "Fifth Migration"—although without acknowledgement of Mumford's earlier work.[27] His work builds on those—discussed later—who attempted to explain demographic data that suggested rising demand for rural and small-town living in the 1970s in a manner contrary to prevailing outmigration from these areas during most of the twentieth century. In examining this "rural renaissance," as it was sometimes called, Lessinger concluded that the suburbs were now likely to see an outmigration akin to that previously experienced by the central city because "a new kind of real estate consumer is emerging . . . [who] prefers the simple yet cosmopolitan lifestyle found in many nonmetropolitan areas."[28] Lessinger provides a typology—here based on an amalgamated character that represents each migratory period. For this fifth migration to exurban America, Lessinger suggests that we will see a "caring conserver" emerge who will be born of dissatisfaction with status quo values that define the fragmenting relationships of work, family, and community characteristic of suburbia. In his view, the suburb will fall to "penturbia," as he brands the exurbs, through the force (again) of changing consumer tastes. "Caring conservers save and guard their resources. They will do this by law, by propaganda, and by appeal to conscience. The will to conserve extends to savings, investments, energy, clean air, and water. It extends to cultural artifacts like historic buildings, parks, all forms of art, and people. Caring conservers see women, minorities, the elderly, and the handicapped as underused resources."[29] According to Lessinger's projections—provided in the late 1980s—the caring conservers who he expected to participate in this penturban migration would demand the kind of judicious regional planning that Mumford so desperately wanted for the earlier suburban migration. They would seek quality of life, effectively guarding livability in the communities to which they relocate through protection of open space and in efforts at historic preservation—mixing nature appreciation with a postindustrial ideal. Lessinger's enthusiasm for the transformative potential of this new middle-class consumer lead to an essentially utopian view that did little to address apparent contradiction in behavior that simultaneously demonstrated a conviction for what we may call a personal "place attachment" even while these consumers severed other attachments.[30] That is, they uproot themselves from places of origin and, while in destination communities, drive up land values and taxes thus fueling trends toward closure of historically communal access points to natural areas—all of which could severe the place attachments of longtime residents leading to what is often called *displacement* to suggest the unsettling quality of losing these affective ties with personally significant places. A growing tension in the study area over such access is captured in an August 2000 front-page headline of the Traverse City *Record-Eagle*: "Public site or privacy right? Lawsuits erupt over road end access sites on lakes."

Much like Mumford, who saw a nascent conservation movement and early attempts at coordination among municipalities through regional planning—both of which were regularly overwhelmed by exuberant growth in the second half of the twentieth century—as progressive reactions to the impact of wasteful and destructive periods of earlier migratory flows, urban historian Robert Fishman holds that the unsustainable nature of suburbanization has led to a set of countertrends. In his view, these countertrends will contribute to a multiracial and largely immigrant-driven reurbanization of America's inner cities in what we can now see being called a "back-to-the-city" movement that has prompted discussion over the potential for reinvestment in the urban sphere. While Mumford declared urban density obsolete and urban decline essentially inevitable in a world made hyperconnected by advances in transportation and communications, Fishman finds reason to believe that that same density is desirable again for a variety of reasons both consistent with preindustrial time and also reflective of a shift in consumer values (again) that now may be of postindustrial origin. Fishman's fifth migration primarily entails not further decentralization by way of an emerging penturbia, but rather rediscovery and/or re-creation of traditional urbanism. Specifically, Fishman notes, "In a strange alchemy, precisely the disadvantages of inner-city districts in the age of the fourth migration—pedestrian scale, resistance to the automobile, aging housing stock, 'obsolete' retail and manufacturing facilities, reliance on mass transit, minority and immigrant populations—are turning into advantages for the fifth migration."[31]

In essence, migration in this period of flow is thus understood as the result of "feedback" from the fourth migration and, in particular, broad opposition to suburban sprawl fueled as in earlier migrations by a frenzied rush for maximum growth and individual profit together with a desire for personal quality of life and collective livability. As Mumford noted, the impact of great periods of migratory flow on American society came not by way of population redistribution in and of itself but rather from materialization of the predominant *lifestyle* that migrants in each period pursued and the prevailing cultural ideals that these expressed. In this fifth migration, we see people seeking—either in small-town/rural or urban landscapes—a quality of experience seldom effectively duplicated in suburbia (although this has been the aim of more recent new urbanist development).

Though Fishman's assertions concerning the prospects for reurbanism are restrained when compared with than those of Lessinger regarding penturbia—which could be called positively boosterish—we might be inclined to discount his vision as similarly idealistic were it not for studies such as that of Brown-Saracino on urban and small-town gentrification. As she notes, in virtually all literature on both urban and rural gentrification there is an overwhelming expectation for gentrifiers who are of a "frontier" mentality—inclined to value these places more for what they might become than what they either are now or had been in the past.[32] That is to say, most writings on the topic of gentrification have seen these migrants as inclined to use the opportunity of lower-cost housing to build financial capital and status through a transformative processes of reclamation from longtime residents and, potentially, deterioration from some earlier form—thus necessarily creating a relationship of distance and conflict between newcomers and longtime residents.

Taking a more ethnographic approach uncommon for such studies, Brown-Saracino's work suggests that the on-the-ground reality is not so simple. She finds no straightforward relationship between the socioeconomic status of newcomers and their ideological stance regarding their role in destination communities. Of particular interest is that fact that she identifies a category of gentrifier (the majority of those in her four sites) that she calls the "social preservationist" and whom she finds in some ways analogous to environmentalists, stating that "like environmentalists who seek to preserve nature, social preservationists—those who adhere to the preservation ideology and engage in related practices—work to preserve the local social ecology."[33]

Akin, perhaps, to Lessinger's largely theorized "caring conservers" and certainly like the real-life lifestyle migrants in my own study, Brown-Saracino finds that most newcomers in her study share concern for fostering a sense of place, community, and authenticity that stands in self-conscious opposition to the callous frontier-minded invader of largely negative, popularized notions of the urban, small-town, and rural gentrifier. Similarly, Fishman asserts that the reurbanism that he heralds "means the end, or at least the softening, of the gentrification era."[34] As with my own work on lifestyle migration, Brown-Saracino finds that ultimately while there is much scholarship on the outcomes of such in-migration, there is comparatively little known about the motivations, beliefs, and daily practices of the migrants. In a manner that seems at least to partly accept Lessinger's characterization of an emerging consumer—the caring conserver who acts to guard a particular quality of life—Brown-Saracino suggests that foremost among the desires of these preservationists, who act in apparent response to the rapid change, uncertainty, and invasive market forces of globalization is "a desire to preserve the authentic and fragile, whether a dilapidated Victorian home, a two-hundred-year-old landscape, or the faces, voices, and everyday presence of people seemingly detached from the mechanism of change that many gentrifiers have come to associate with themselves."[35]

Taken together these studies suggest that what I am calling lifestyle migration may be a response to "feedback" from earlier migratory flows and the wants, necessities, and ideals of life—the models *of* and *for* the world—that we can associate with these periods. Today's response may lead to a fifth migration that entails *both* exurbanization and reurbanization through shared interest in quality of life fostered in the deliberate cultivation of a sense of place, community, and authenticity in both largely rural and urban landscapes.

Lifestyle Migration

Who exactly are the migrants to small-town and rural areas? As already suggested, they tend to be mostly white middle-class professionals and young families. They are often people who have worked a number of years in relatively well-paid jobs. In his study of in-migration in the rural West, Jobes found that in-migrants had a range of shared characteristics. They were of primarily of middle- or upper-middle-class status. Most were young or early-middle-aged and married adults who were likely better educated and what Jobes described as more "ambitious" than the general population. The in-migrants were also likely to have professional, managerial, or trade skills but to be living after their relocation with incomes significantly lower than might be expected given their level of education. In addition, they were likely to undergo an occupational change because of moving. Jobes found that most were nonagrarian in their lifestyle after relocation. They were not moving back to a way of life in which they had been raised. Finally, the majority of migrants could be described as experienced movers who moved either as children or adults and who tended to originate in metropolitan areas immediately prior to their relocation to Jobes's study area.[36]

High in-migration from metropolitan areas and the reality of lower income potential in the Grand Traverse region prompted coining of the much-invoked phrase "A view of the Bay is half the pay." Lifestyle migrants usually offer the idiomatic expression not with frustration but rather as a measure of personal pride. Use of this saying appears to be a way of both declaring membership in the local by these newcomers as well as a means of emphasizing the nature of a lifestyle choice motivated primarily by *noneconomic* considerations. Consistent with the quest for something more meaningful in their lives—as with Brown-Saracino's social preservationists—for lifestyle migrants it appears to emphasize the choice to live more in tune with the ideals of a search for something more personally fulfilling outside of material gain. Nevertheless, this choice can have difficult consequences as we shall see later. In other areas of the country, correlation between natural beauty of rural places and low salaries has been wittily referred to as "poverty with a view."[37] During a visit with a longtime resident at his home, I was presented with a T-shirt that he had purchased at least ten years earlier in a downtown shop. My host laughed as I gripped the shirt and spread it out so that I could clearly read the emblazoned slogan "Drain the Bay, Double my Pay."

Many lifestyle migrants acknowledge that their relocation might constitute sacrifice on some level. Specifically, many speak of "letting go" of predominant means of defining success and of the need to be open to taking risk. At least in some respects, the lifestyle migrants in my research are akin to a broad category of newcomers in MacGregor's study site ("Alternatives" in her typology) who—due in large part to the depth of their sense of agency—are able to take the risk of moving to a place where they do not know anyone with the faith that they can either find or *make* what they were looking for and carve out lives and livelihoods that balance economic necessity with broader personal goals while finding personal fulfillment together with like-minded people. Both groups hold a deliberate, goal-oriented ethic of agency paired to a logic of commitment that is ironically tied less to a sense of obligation to particular place—in the strictest sense—than to personal goals and values that motivated their relocation.

So often we think of relocation as associated with career. Often one's job quite literally depends on following the whims of an employer who may shift a department to another area of the country—a move that Mark refused to make. During the rapid development of the postwar years, many families were relocated as corporations grew and expanded their reach into new territories. For most of these families, there was little opposition to going along with the plan laid out for them by their employers. It was all part of the arrangement, an oft-unspoken contract, between paternalistic firms and workers, who give up a little freedom, self-reliance, and control today so that their families could depend on the employer being there for them in retirement.

In his 1972 book, *A Nation of Strangers*, sociologist Vance Packard identified what he suggested would be a growing contingent of peripatetic corporate workers moving in and out of communities comprised largely of houses built on speculation. I know something of this life, as my father was moved by IBM all around the metropolitan New York region while I was growing up. At company picnics, he and his coworkers would joke that IBM stood, in fact, for "I've Been Moved." Peter Kilborn, a reporter for the *New York Times*, documents normalization of corporate relocation as a way of life in his book *Next Stop, Reloville: Life inside America's New Rootless Professional Class*. Kilborn's book contains stories of modern-day company nomads, "Relos," who as midlevel executives for a range of corporations like IBM, live lives that depend on their readiness to uproot families in pursuit of professional success and who, together, may constitute a new social class of people who are comparatively well-off financially but fundamentally insecure in their material success.[38]

Unlike Relos, lifestyle migrants are not moving to further (or even to keep) particular careers. They do not, like Relos, move with the understanding that their destination community is only a brief, temporary step that should allow them to maintain a given career trajectory. By moving—either into the outer reaches or even beyond easy access to corporate world—they are not positioning themselves for climbing its long-promised ladder of financial wealth and social status. At least as a fundamental part of personal narrative, lifestyle migrants often put emotional attachment to geographic places (something seemingly impossible for a Relo) above the job. For many, cuts in salary and benefits are not only possible; they seem to be the order of the day.

Despite the reality for many executives detailed in Kilborn's book, articles in human resource magazines in the 1990s began to urge companies to be aware of the needs of employees before, during, and after job-related relocation. For example, in a late-1990s edition of *HRMagazine*, a human resource publication aimed at corporate managers, the president of an organization that specializes in relocation services stated simply, Relos aside, that "employees are no longer willing to lead a nomadic life for a corporation."[39]

That some people may no longer be willing to lead an itinerant life for corporations may be because workers no longer expect to be with a given company for the long term. Perhaps it is simply a lack of trust as the old contract, or what the sociologist Phyllis Moen refers to as an implicit understanding of "the often informal trade off of awarding security to workers with seniority in return for their commitment."[40] In today's economic climate, many companies have opted to shed senior employees from their payrolls while hiring less expensive, younger, and often part-time staff, instead of rewarding seniority as they did in the past. People recognize the need to take care of themselves because they cannot expect their corporate employer to be there for them in the long term. This represents a significant change in orientation, in expectations, in strategy, and ultimately in priorities and values.

While employers may deem relocation necessary, employees may seek alternatives when they feel such moves might degrade quality of life. Importantly, resistance appeared as employees became increasingly unsure if they could depend on the implicit contract of old. Throughout the relatively prosperous 1990s, corporations worked harder to counsel employees and their spouses about relocations and to provide more of what has been called "transition support services" in order to help meet varied family concerns. Otherwise, the request to relocate might lead to the loss of a valued employee who would be expensive to replace in a tight labor market.

Increased attention to employee quality of life was enabled by a surging economy at the end of the 1990s fueled in large part by a veritable explosion in the technology sector of the American economy. For much of this period, a shortage of qualified labor put many workers in the driver's seat when it came time for negotiation with employers. In the present climate of widespread layoffs and bankruptcies, however, the perceived necessity to take the path of least resistance out of gratitude for being kept in the ranks of the employed might change people's willingness to resist an employer's request for relocation. Thus, Reloville may be alive and well as the need to care for employee quality of life fades. People do not have the same confidence about abundant alternatives in a receding economy, the early signs of which were visible when the rapidly expanding bubble of the tech sector began to deflate at the time that my research began. Nevertheless, I am confident that any retreat from taking a more self-confident stand against undesirable relocation on the part of employees, or from being more humane in the consideration of quality of life on the part of employers, will rebound in better economic times.

PART III

Searching for Meaning

Overleaf: Sign at the end of driveway on Old Mission Peninsula.
Photo by Brian Hoey

CHAPTER 7

Place of Work

> The object of living is work, experience, and happiness. There is joy in work. All that money can do is buy us someone else's work in exchange for our own. There is no happiness except in the realization that we have accomplished something.
>
> —Henry Ford, quoted in *Forbes*, January 1, 1963

Despite significant changes in the nature of work, it remains a central part of the working person's life. It reaches outward and influences other spheres of our lives at the same time that it also reaches inward and shapes who we are and how we think about ourselves. It is not merely earning a livelihood; it inevitably contributes to our personal development—albeit at times in ways or in directions we might not consciously choose. Work has always allowed people to find a place in the world as well as to be placed in the world by others. In simple terms, work can establish a role or purpose for the individual within a community or network of social relations composed of such roles.

Although some may try to separate and compartmentalize their means of livelihood as distinct from personal lives, these cannot be practically separated because it is through work that people create not only individual lives but also—through collective action—the very conditions of social existence. Work may serve as a source of "ego boundaries," the limits and outlines of personal and social identity.[1] Work establishes a coherent set of expectations for the particular rhythm, direction, and definition of our lives.

Like so many social categories, "the job" has been taken for granted as a thing of lasting value and dependable stability. The idea of having a job, however, is founded on a distinct cultural history in the West. In the Western world, at least, it has come to be taken as a given—a fundamental part of being human. We can trace the origins of this particular notion of work to the Industrial Revolution. Although we may now shudder at the thought of a jobless world, the modern job was something fashioned to service the economic realities of the industrializing world in the nineteenth century. Many at that time saw the idea of discretely packaged vocations as a violation of people's basic freedoms, and it was met with no shortage of criticism. Nevertheless, the job as we know it was a response to the demands of the kinds of work and the particular workplace that the industrial economy of the 1800s spawned.

For at least the last century, jobs have been the building blocks of our understanding of society—the basis of a meaningful, purposeful, and stable life. We have been socialized to think in terms of "having a job." As the modern, industrial economy declines, conditions that formed our earlier notions of work are changing along with the nature, or even existence, of the job. When people are asked when they will "get a real job," it is likely they are working some kind of piecemeal arrangement cobbled together to sustain them, at least temporarily. The sentiment behind the comment reflects the bias of our society as to what constitutes a good job: a good job is one that "makes you somebody." Interestingly, however, the arrangement to which this derisive comment is directed more closely reflects the reality of today's world of work than it does the outdated, idealized image to which today's world is being compared.

It is indicative of our times that one of the country's largest private employers is not a giant of industry. It is neither from the old industrial order based on resource extraction and materials refinement nor born of today's high technology. Rather, this giant stands as a business that makes nothing and has no plants. It is in the booming business of selling discrete packets of labor. With well over a half-million workers by the early 1990s, Manpower Inc. became one of America's largest employers and the world's largest temporary employment agency.

Since that time, Manpower has continued to flourish as America's traditional giants continue to cut people from their own workforce. Today the Milwaukee-based company has more than forty-three hundred offices in seventy-two countries. To many, the country appears to be increasingly one made up of part-timers, freelancers, temps, and independent contractors, all of whom are part of a new "disposable" workforce. In 1993, the total number of temps (1.5 million) was already three times as large as it was just ten years earlier. One in every three workers in the United States had already become a member of what has been called the "contingent workforce."[2]

The term "contingent work" was coined by Audrey Freedman, an economist who had worked for both Manpower and the Bureau of Labor Statistics, to describe "conditional and transitory employment arrangements as initiated by a need for labor—usually because a company has an increased demand for a particular service or a product or technology, at a particular place, at a particular time."[3] Freedman's use in 1998 of the term "contingent workforce," before the Employment and Housing Subcommittee of the Committee on Government Operations of the U.S. House of Representatives, was meant to describe a management technique of employing workers only when there was an immediate and direct need for specific work to be done. The term has since been applied more widely to a range of employment practices that includes part-time work, contracted or outsourced workers, home-based work, and even self-employment. For some, the term applies to nearly any arrangement that deviates from the standard model of a full-time wage or salaried job.

In contrast to the idealized worker of the regular, industrialized world of last century, workers today are asked to be multitasking, adaptable, and forever learning. That is what it means to be part of the "just-in-time" business model—only now as the human resource equivalent to that developed for commodity inventory. It is about being conditional. When companies moved to just-in-time manufacturing during the 1980s, it was only a short step to apply this to workers. Employers today increasingly want what are variously referred to as "portfolio workers," "career gypsies," "project workers," "temps," and "task consultants" to do specific but transitional jobs. This is not the kind of long-term system on which workers relied for much of the twentieth century for the stability and sense of control necessary to build up a personally meaningful narrative of self through work. Today's workers increasingly do not have the relative security and protection provided by a lastingly defined job description.

A lifestyle migrant who gave up a high-status position in a major corporation, Alan recognized the importance of work in shaping a life and decided to embrace the fact, taking the chance to completely redefine his work and life through leaving a corporate job and relocating to Traverse City.

> Nowadays, you've got to put together your own life. So many times in the past when I decided to look for new jobs they were pretty specific. The objective was to keep the unions out and keep the morale up and we have to reduce the workforce. And the guy who was running the Midwest division picked me up, and he said, "I want a guy like you. I don't want a team player. I've got this problem . . ." And I remember, they said, "We don't care if you fire everybody because in nine months were going to close the plant. Including the plant manager, but we'll keep you if we like you." And nine months later, I was the only one kept.

Alan's work as a kind of corporate hit man, a hired gun, is iconic of the just-in-time workforce. His work was both shaped by and gave shape to the contingent workforce of the flexible economy. "They said raise hell with the unions. We had three walkouts, and every time I had the factory running again in fifteen minutes because I just went into the offices and said, 'Come on, we're going to run this thing.' I would have the [machines] making noise and stuff . . . and it got the union scared that we were going to run it without them. I would bring in temporary labor services. I was doing everything. It took them two years to clean up all the arbitrations I started. That's what I was hired to do." We came into the 1990s with a recession where jobless rates were up, and we came into next century within another downturn. With the coming of the Great Recession in late 2007, we saw tremendous job loss. Although we can dwell on the numbers of the latest economic bloodbath, the real story is not in the loss of jobs in quantitative terms, but rather the loss of the job itself. It is not a question of "jobs" simply but rather of the "Job" itself—job with a capital *J*. Like many lifestyle migrants, Alan knew this was happening. In his case, he was neck deep in the process.

The practice of defining oneself through the performance of a specific job and through association with a particular company was the model of my father's generation. Now there is neither a guarantee nor an expectation of the durability of such a definition because the world of work on which it is based is unstable and unpredictable, more fluid and boundless. Valued workers today are expected to exhibit these qualities. This is not your father's Oldsmobile. Oh yeah, by the way, Olds didn't make it in the new economy. The nearly hundred-year-old company, based in Lansing, Michigan, that Mike—the corporate refugee turned pie maker—had shunned, despite strong local tradition, for sunny California as a newly minted college graduate, was axed by its parent company, General Motors, in early 2001. Its apparent demise seems tied to the all-important issues of branding and image. People apparently couldn't let go of the old-geezer image of Olds, and so another giant of the old economy bit the dust.

Though the changes in work are widespread and profound, in the past decade the category of the job in common usage is only gradually shifting in meaning. The meaning that is emerging is much closer to the idea common before industrialization of people *doing* certain tasks as jobs rather than "having them." In yesterday's job paradigm, people were located at a particular level in a vertical hierarchy. They were also located horizontally in a functional unit responsible for some particular set of tasks. People were given a well-defined area of responsibility, which was formalized in a job description. Accordingly, people could see a fairly straight "career path"—as was the common notion—that they could aspire to follow, ladder-like, toward greater financial reward and status. While perhaps stifling, there was order and predictability in this arrangement.

Although this kind of set path—more common a generation ago—has become outmoded, in the immediate post-WWII years it was being strongly reinforced. As noted earlier, this was a boom time both in terms of economic and population growth. For nearly twenty solid years there was a sense that this growth was unlimited and required only sufficient labor to sustain it. Through the beginning of the 1970s, government and corporations could hardly find enough qualified people to fill managerial positions within a burgeoning economy. During the period, the economy grew at a comfortable average of over 3 percent annually while real earnings expanded, growing over 60 percent in the first ten years and nearly 50 percent over the following decade.

Workers needed little in the way of the pep talks and sessions on reinventing themselves that would become part of the climate of economic restructuring that characterized the 1980s. In the prosperous years following the war, there was substantial security in bringing home a steady paycheck from the same company week after week. There was security as well in knowing what it was that you would be doing for years down the road. Opportunity for advancement was available to those who demonstrated ambition and capability by devoting themselves more fully and completely and by putting in longer, more demanding hours.

As the Baby Boom generation grew and went on to earn advanced degrees to an extent previously unknown, a workforce emerged that was both highly educated and comparatively large in number to the preceding generation. With the economic downturn and recessions of the 1970s and 1980s, however, later Baby Boomers entered a job market where the story of their parents' generation had shifted from one of relative plenty for the loyal and dedicated worker to one of anxious competition and uncertainty. While the number of potential positions shrank, the numbers of highly qualified applicants had grown dramatically. People had to work not only harder to get in the game, but even harder to stay in it. This has been appropriately called "manic capitalism" by the medical anthropologist Emily Martin, whose work has shown that mania may be examined as a cultural phenomenon that plays a role in contemporary society including as inspiration for a robust capitalism as a potentially creative, driving force for successful entrepreneurs.[4]

While the struggle required in order to stay on that tenuous path of career had increased in the 1970s, so too did the tenacity of the professional to follow it onward and upward by scrambling up rungs of the corporate hierarchy and tenaciously clinging to an increasingly less relevant model. Movement "upward" with the financial reward and the status this conferred continued to largely define personal success. In order to achieve this success, one had to demonstrate the desire to advance in a clearly quantifiable way. This was all the more necessary now that the onus was so much more on the individual to achieve and prove worth. If there was a sense of getting something for next to nothing before, there was a sense now that only the fit would survive. But having molded and adapted themselves to the way of this world of work, people still believed in the career—in following a discrete path of jobs seamlessly connected by upward mobility. The climb was harder and might require greater competition with peers, but the way was still there.

Given the reality of the shifting economy it is frankly surprising how workers have hung on to a model that no longer represents actual structural conditions. But devotion to a compelling model of work and its standard definition of success—as to any system of beliefs—effectively frees the individual from having to question the status quo. So long as people believed that the system could deliver and they worked hard enough to prove themselves through their devotion, they were free from having to face the existential angst of feeling the ground drop out from under them. It is not at all surprising that an emphasis on "self-help" blossomed in the New Age phenomenon of the 1980s. While New Age is normally relegated to the realm of "alternative" approaches, its message of self-help was a basic part of the emergence of a "personal excellence" movement and what Amy Saltzman has called "evangelical entrepreneurialism."[5]

When people felt in danger of losing their footing on shaky economic ground, they could explore the reasons why they were not being productive enough, they could work on their time management and communication skills, on boosting their self-esteem, on trying to deal with their growing anxiety by embracing it and putting it to work for them. All of this while largely ignoring the voice that begged to question what was being asked of them as workers: to place their jobs before all else and to work with little expectation that there would be a job with the company down the road. Corporations realized that they could maximize worker efficiency by actively promoting the idea that career fulfillment was equivalent to personal fulfillment. Simultaneous with the demise of career as it was known for several generations, many older, larger corporations were working to eliminate tens of thousands of jobs at the same time that they exploited the individual drive to succeed by encouraging workers to put their professional lives before their personal ones. As a new economy took shape, novel communities of work emerged in places, like Silicon Valley, that centered on young companies with often quite young people at their helms. The leaders of these emergent communities, the movers and shakers, preached a kind of personal salvation through self-actualization in performing one's work. The masses of Baby Boomers, driven, highly educated, ready to strike it big, and keenly aware of the need to stand out and survive in an increasingly competitive workplace, were easily converted. These newfangled communities of work became a possible source of guidance at a time when traditional sources of meaning were declining in their capacity to influence and thus in their relative importance in people's everyday lives.

Numerous lifestyle migrants have described how they adhered to a system of beliefs, as they participated in work, with nearly religious qualities. For many, answers to historically religious questions could be sought in wholly secular activities and attachments as found in the workplace—including such basic questions as "Who am I?" and "Where is my life going?" People found meaning and purpose in work in a way that became practically religious in nature. Examples of devotion, even in today's increasingly suspicious atmosphere between workers and employers, were not uncommon.

Jim, a middle-aged lifestyle migrant who experienced a brutal and personally motivated layoff from a small but highly successful software company in southeastern Michigan began to share his compelling story with me over lunch. As his touring motorcycle was being worked on at a busy shop off a rural highway south of Traverse City, we met in a smoky roadside diner, whose décor, dark with its scant windows and stained paneling, suggested it had not seen remodeling since the 1970s. As we munched on our salads, he explained that at the time he worked for this company, his relationship to work was like that of a cult member: "I had been drinking the Kool-Aid. It was like the Jim Jones gang [a reference to what most people characterize as a cult]. I was drinking the corporate Kool-Aid [and] believing that this was the way. I mean, believing that this work was the way to an *honorable* life."

Given the necessity for believing in "the way," what amounts to a kind of dependency or forced addiction appears to have developed: "At a certain point in the corporation, you change your *worth*. You trade in your career capital to benefit the company. You're worth more to the company that you've been working for than you are on the street. You get up to *here* [*he raises his fork to eye level before me*], but if you were to go looking for another job you don't start there. That's just the way it works. I think that corporate America takes advantage of that. It's the 'golden handcuffs.' And you have to have faith." In similar fashion, an unmarried woman in her mid-thirties speaks of her experience in a software firm in Silicon Valley. Although Susan grew up in the Midwest, it was the West that—as with Mike—beckoned when in her early twenties she sought to find her working life and was drawn to the exciting industries of the tech boom in California, which promised not only financial reward but an elusive "something more" out of work. She felt strongly that the work she was doing was meaningful and she *believed* in the mission.[6] Speaking to this, Susan said "The company I worked for [was] in the throes of what's been going on the last ten years in Silicon Valley. It's pretty crazy. It's really exciting, high-energy . . . working hard, making a difference. We were doing GIS, geographic information system, software. All over the world it was being used for really incredible things and the application part of it was fun and important."

There came a point, however, when her faith shifted from beneath her as corporate profit seeking caused a divergence from the values that initially guided development of the company and attracted ideologically driven workers like her. Her context swings as the workplace is turned upside down by new priorities and economic imperatives. Susan enters a period of personal crisis and moral uncertainty that culminates in what can easily be characterized as a quest for more personally defined meaning *outside* the world of work. "All of the sudden, we bought a company bigger than we were and we are trying to go public, and there was all this politics involved. All of a sudden it's all about money and not the application. We were a bunch of young, you know, twenty-eight, thirty-year-olds . . . even the president of the company—the person that started it. I was asked to set up the whole inside sales team while we were trying to merge with this other company which had an outside sales force team, and it got really ugly." This is a point where the believer's conviction in "the Company" and its mission is severely tested. There is a crisis; here it is explicitly one of faith that leads to a kind of break and the eventual quest for new ways of finding meaning.

The idea that work might be used to provide a way toward finding greater fulfillment is not new. It was established in a fundamentally religious context during the Reformation with deep roots in the Protestant ethic of work. Luther said that one might live acceptably before God by devotion to one's secular "calling" as God's will. It was on this basic notion that the ethic of self-discipline, duty, asceticism, and a basic concern with achievement and personal betterment through work would be based. The true believer would come to have the conviction that work was worthwhile in its own right as an indirect way of rendering service to God and by developing one's own moral character. In the end, work would become the very core of moral life and thus—as the philosopher Charles Taylor suggests—a way of finding orientation in the world.

As the nature of work has been reformulated over time, so too has the work ethic. During the post-WWII period in America, the emphasis was one of delayed gratification fulfilled in the form of material things. In the short term, it becomes what the architect and social critic Witold Rybczynski called a routinized "living for the weekend."[7] It became a matter of working in order to achieve the time to devote to other things in the form of leisure activities—a point that takes us back to my earlier discussion of the rise of consumption over production activities as a source of meaning. In the long term, it is a promise of future reward through promotions and a sequentially higher standard of living together with the respect and admiration of one's peers and eventually a sponsored retirement. While severely eroded by the changes wrought by postindustrial economic restructuring and globalization, this view of the "giving-getting compact" persists in a kind of "structural lag" as the essential core of what we continue to understand as the American Dream.[8]

The late 1980s and early 1990s was a critical time for the meaning of work in American society. During this period, we find two parallel processes. One leads toward an even greater devotion to work while the other begins pushing people to question underlying assumptions of a system of delayed gratification. Both are responses to new realities of economic restructuring and deepening social changes. Those workers continuing to believe in and pursue an upward path of climbing the ladder toward greater fulfillment and reward embody what could be called the emergent *personal* work ethic. As in the Protestant work ethic, there is devotion, but the dedication here is to one's own work rather than to the workplace or company. It is making an investment in "Me, Inc." as the free agents to which I have previously referred.[9]

We saw this strategic self-interest in Mike's account of his attitude toward working for the old "Company" as he planned to set out on his own as a small business owner. Acquiring the knowledge and skills to stay alive and keep moving as the entire world of work shifts is the reward. Although loyalty is practically irrelevant, devotion remains the key to reward, only now that commitment is to oneself and the reward must be crafted under conditions where the individual is totally responsible for either achieving or failing to reach it. Workers are increasingly working without a safety net, or at least, work with a net of their own making. Today's 401K retirement plans, while offering greater flexibility and portability, are the employee's responsibility. We are entering a world where the preponderance of accountability for risk-related decisions such as concerning finances, insurance, and privacy will be shifted to the individual as companies as well as state and federal government agencies reign in support services and benefits as a means of cutting costs.

CHAPTER 8

Consumption of Place

Leisure is displacing work from the center of modern social arrangements. There is evidence in the movements of the 1960s that the world of work has played out its capacity for regeneration. Experimental forms of social organization are no longer emerging from the factories and offices as they did during the period of mechanization and unionization. Rather, new forms of organization are emerging from a broadly based framework of leisure activities. . . ." Lifestyle," a generic term for specific combinations of work and leisure, is replacing "occupation" as the basis of social relationship formation, social status and social action; . . . affirmation of basic social values is departing the world of work and seeking refuge in the realm of leisure.

—Dean MacCannell, *The Tourist: A New Theory of the Leisure Class*

As suggested in the statement above from sociologist and cultural critic Dean Mac-Cannell, in the contemporary world lifestyle has emerged as a powerful means of identity formation, and consumption as a manner of promoting a given lifestyle. Lifestyle may, in fact, now be of greater importance to people than work for providing and maintaining a coherent identity. Work may be defined in a web of social relations whereas consumption is inherently a more individual practice despite being shaped by social and cultural factors. Lifestyle migrants practice self-definition by relocation. This choice involves consumption—if not of physical things, then of the idea of a place or community that is shaped by an individual's perceptions and judgments. In his assessment of the literature on quality of life produced by social psychologists, David Hummon has summarized their basic argument as one where "a person's sense of well-being, whether family, work, community, or other facets of life, cannot be understood as a direct product of the material conditions in his or her life, but must be interpreted in light of the way that individual perceives and judges those circumstances."[1]

Small-town life may offer an alternative to lifestyle migrants who seek to break from a model of success, for example, that demands self-sacrifice for a possible future and a *potential self*. I have extended this idea from its original conception in the work of Arlie Hochschild, a sociologist who studied what she coined the "time bind" and dilemmas of work and family inherent to corporate America. In her study of workers at a company that she refers to as "Americo," Hochschild uses the idea of a potential self to talk about the harsh reality of everyday balancing between work and family obligations and economic challenges. She describes how as people make sacrifices in devotion of time to family, community, and self, they may hold on to the promise of an imagined self as a kind of wish for a better time to come. Unlike lifestyle migrants who were willing and able to act on this promise through a lifestyle commitment, in most cases Hochschild looked at, people evaded the time bind and attempted to adapt to existing conditions through the imaginary of potential selves.[2]

In a society where people are concerned with quality of experience and, in particular, personal growth, a feeling of well-being is an important life goal. American consumer culture appears shaped by an ideal that judges our personal relationships and commitments in terms of their ability to contribute to a sense of well-being. This is a therapeutic ideal. According to the sociologist Phillip Rieff, few things suited an emergent therapeutic ideal in the twentieth century better than a "prevalent American piety toward the self. This self, improved, is the ultimate concern of modern culture."[3] In this view, people are inclined to develop an individualist moral language based on media-influenced notions of what appears "right" and "good." The belief is that the individual can pick and choose from a free market of things to satisfy needs to construct and improve self-image. Increasing importance is given to lifestyle choices. In a report from the early 1990s, the editors of *Research Alert* projected that with the aging of the baby boom generation, the United States would experience a kind of national midlife crisis. An emergent value would be a "seeking of quality" represented not only in our evaluation of things but also in our choice of relationships.[4]

In a consumption-oriented culture, the product is the form for different manifestations of desire, the vehicle for engaging, satisfying, exploring, and creating further desires. The product need not be a material thing but may also take the form of a lifestyle. Often embodied in particular places, lifestyles such as that believed to characterize "Up North" are marketed and consumed in much the same manner as physical products. As people aspire to realize a more idealized vision of the self, the product becomes a means of taking action steps toward that goal. The most successful products are what might be called "empty." These products are more about possibilities and potentialities than actualities. The empty product, like the potential self, can be made into one's own hopes and dreams.

Although I focus primarily on the idea of place consumption, this must be examined within a more general understanding of the culture of consumption in America. American consumers can have extraordinary expectations about what products can do for their lives.[5] What is most central about this idea to my research is "placed" consumption or the consumption of lifestyle within which place plays a central role. Anthropological study has attempted to better understand American consumer culture through exploring materialist desire and what meaning it plays in the character of American lives.[6] Through the desire for and consumption of things, people seek to achieve a number of goals. These include aspiring to status by making desire into a way of becoming. When families aspire to a particular lifestyle, this desire motivates them to undergo often profound life changes. The act of consumption can also provide people with a valuable sense of control, even if only fleeting. Much of American advertising documents an enduring belief in the potential for self-mastery. This advertising reinforces our belief that we can choose to remake ourselves through concentrated effort and will alone. Consider, for example, the well-recognized ad campaign for Nike, "Just Do It." The very idea that people can "just do it" by moving Up North to live the good life is an expression of this faith in this capacity.

In *A Great Place to Raise Kids*, sociologist Kieran Bonner notes that "consumerism panders to a fantasy of paradise, and it is successful because it tells and retells us that the world can be arranged so as to satisfy private desires."[7] In these desires, or the fantasies born of them, there is always a desire for what is good. We see this desire in families seeking a good place to raise their kids or to plan a family. Lifestyle migrants have strategically drawn on the opportunities and resources characteristic of our present state of high fluidity in order to pursue and hopefully realize dreams of an abiding sense of place, community, and authenticity. This sense and opportunity to feel a degree of personal control by actively cultivating it is pursued and ultimately constructed as a kind of antidote or even as a form of resistance to the unbalancing and personally destabilizing forces of the contemporary world.

The popular press has led many Americans to think of economic commitments and family life as necessarily a trade-off. Frequent articles in newspapers and magazines describe what appears as a necessary dichotomy between to diametrically opposed spheres. A common illustration portrays people engaged in a kind of battle where individuals stand torn between work and family. Works such as historian and moralist Christopher Lasch's *Haven in a Heartless World* have no doubt contributed to widespread adoption of this view in popular discourse.[8] The dichotomy, however, is unrealistic as economic commitments are an essential part of how the family has been organized. Despite this history of mutual implication, in the United States we have come to regard family as a potential alternative or even as remedy to materialism of the other sphere. The perceived trade-off is indicative of a more basic shift in thinking about the American Dream. The nuclear family has functioned ideally as an emotional and psychological escape from the market economy in spite of the fact that it could never provide refuge against economic forces. As the nuclear family retreats further into itself in response to this unrealistic pressure, it is easily seen as weak or even "embattled." The family itself is sometimes viewed as a combatant faced with confronting overwhelming forces from the outside.[9]

It is not surprising that desire for distinctiveness and individual self-expression is strongly exhibited in the home. While vacations to beautiful places may celebrate the freedom to break from the everyday and escape to a world apart, home is ultimately a powerful means of asserting control over the nature of our experience. Americans are in the process of inventing a new domesticity in order to experience the meaning of home in new ways. As before, it is also a means of displaying the fact that they have "arrived." This desire to advertise one's good fortune is exhibited in the Grand Traverse region through ubiquitous signs posted at the end of long driveways winding out of thick woods that proclaim, for example, "Mission Accomplished." In this case, it is a clever play on words given that this particular home is located on the Old Mission Peninsula. Here the intended message is clearly one of consumption and lifestyle goals achieved. Others signs speak of a state of being simply "Up North," which is displayed together with the family name, as in "The Smith Family, Up North."

Place Marketing in the Consumptive Society

Given shifts in the economy as a result of restructuring, changing demographic patterns, and consumption choices, as well as new ways of manipulating ideas and images for the purpose of marketing and managing identity, what kinds of re-sponses by places are suggested? Due to slow workforce growth in the Midwest, a tight regional labor market was sustained through the 1990s. Policy makers and business leaders were faced with problems associated with labor-constrained growth rather than the underemployment experienced in prior years. In response, the state of Michigan launched a media campaign aimed at wooing workers from other midwestern states. One of many potential lifestyle migrants to the Grand Traverse region living in the urban centers of the Midwest who contacted me by e-mail was a single man in his forties from Chicago. He said this about the state's campaign:

> When I was up in Michigan a few months ago, I read an article in a local paper that there was a lot of concern about the aging of the population up there. They had statistics for each county. Young people were leaving, and the population was creeping up in age. Recently on our local TV stations there has been a saturation campaign promoting high-tech jobs in Michigan and referring viewers to the state's website. These commercials have been running four times an hour. They stress wonderful lifestyle available as a perk. They cut from images of computers and high-tech workers to a woodsman in the great outdoors—the lake and a lighthouse in the background.

As I suggested in the Introduction, the selling of place has become a sophisticated business that spans many areas from local government to real estate to mass media. As a consequence, geographers have given special focus to this particular phenome-non of "place promoting" and "place-based competitiveness" as objects of research. Chris Philo and Gerry Kearns's edited volume, *Selling Places*, provides a historical and contemporary overview to this important area of inquiry. In their own chap-ter, Philo and Kearns explain that the selling of places "entails the various ways in which public and private agencies—local authorities and local entrepreneurs, often working collaboratively—strive to 'sell' the image of a particular geographically defined 'place' . . . so as to make it attractive to economic enterprises, to tourists, and even to inhabitants of that place."[10]

Landor Associates is a huge, multinational marketing corporation that one would not normally associate with the likes of small towns like Traverse City. If you visit their website to find out more about the company, upon clicking on the "About Us" link you are told, simply that it is "21 Global Offices. 16 Countries. One Landor." What else do you need to know? A company that has massaged the public image and shaped the brand of such internationally ubiquitous companies as FedEx and Microsoft as well as prominent organizations such as the Olympic Games and government agencies including the US Department of Homeland Security, Landor aided in the branding efforts of such far-flung but ambitious places as Traverse City. In 1998, the Traverse City Convention and Visitors Bureau trademarked the logo and the slogan developed through Landor, "A World Apart," with the US Patent Office. Hayes Roth, then senior executive director for Landor, echoing the intent of the Cyrus Howard story in a tourism campaign seventy-five years earlier, asserted, "Your mantra now should be, 'A World Apart,' because that emerged from our studies of consumers. . . . They said it's different up there, special, that they really felt far away but really had a good time there."

According to a Landor press release, consumers are drawn to "belief brands." Alec Rattray, director of Landor's London office, asserts that belief brands "not only meet consumers' needs, but more importantly, they create them." Rattray holds that the "vision and resolve of the brand holder is critical to its success. In fact, they are more important than the functional characteristics of a brand." In the most telling statement, Charlie Wrench of Landor London says that today's belief brands are "a type of religion." Wrench feels that people "turn to them for meaning." In this climate, he finds that the brands that are succeeding are those with "strong beliefs and original ideas . . . [who have] the passion and energy to change the world and to *convert* people to their way of thinking through outstanding communications."[11]

The Traverse City Convention and Visitors Bureau sought the expertise of Landor to craft a slick marketing campaign. Deborah Knudsen, speaking as then president and CEO of the bureau, speaks with the conviction of a true believer with the will to convert others: "We are passionate about sharing the secret of our world with the people beyond our beautiful borders. You see, the uniqueness of the Traverse City experience is not found in a single detail, but in a collection of diverse experiences. A symphony of music in the open air, a walk through the woods, moving through snow on a sunny day and diving into water; big and blue, turquoise and crystal. Our lake, our land and the imagination they will inspire will transform each visit into a new experience."[12] Traverse City as belief brand is all about the possibility of finding something different from the ordinary, a place to rediscover oneself: "The Essence of Traverse City . . . A World Apart. . . . Is there even a word for it—that ineffable feeling that gives a place its unique essence, its . . . soul? It's easy to cheat with 'indescribable,' simple to hedge with 'indefinable.' It's much harder to pin down exactly what it is that draws people to one spot on the globe that feels exactly right."[13]

Particularly interesting are the abundant place rankings available in numerous magazines that feature the naming of top places to live all over America focusing on different issues and kinds of places, from rural and small-town to major cities, and using vastly different objective and subjective criteria. The extreme form of these rankings takes shape as the mammoth *Places Rated Almanac* produced by David Savageau.[14] Although criticized by demographers for sloppy research and questionable statistical analysis, including the measurement of various ill-defined "social indicators," these rankings sell plenty of magazines and books. The relocation narratives of lifestyle migrants frequently mention how these guides provided information that helped them to make decisions about where to live, work, and raise their families. Many lifestyle migrants, as we have seen in Mike's account in Chapter 5, recount stories about reading these articles and sitting down with pad and paper to come up with lists of their own priorities and rankings.

Reinvention of the Rural

Community is continuously reinvented in forms that derive from how it has been imagined in the past. This reinvention is exemplified in how a mobile middle class attempts to construct community in their desire to find stability and authenticity in particular places and to seek sanctuary in a tumultuous world by attempting to control or perhaps mitigate its influence on their lives. Even the basic idea of the Rural, for example, is subject to reinvention as changing, or perhaps rediscovered, aspirations lead to social practices such as lifestyle migration. As discussed earlier, in the Grand Traverse region this reinvention has continued for over one hundred years as the area has variously been defined as the source of abundant natural resources and potential wealth, as an agricultural center, or as a treasure trove of natural beauty and refuge for urban weary such as Cyrus Howard and family in the travel narrative cum tourist brochure of nearly a hundred years ago. Today these meanings of place are layered one on top of the other at times blending and at other times opposing, never wholly removed or obscured.

Of course, the capacity to participate in redefining and pursuing new aspirations is one facilitated or constrained by the realities of social class—a fact that I will explore in Chapter 13. The relative importance of the Rural as a space of cultural tensions where not only the hopes and dreams but also the prejudices of more privileged social classes are played out is, ironically, inversely proportional to its importance economically. In what can easily be applied to the American condition, Raymond Williams writes of Britain, where there has been a near "inverse proportion in the twentieth century between the relative importance of the working rural economy and the cultural importance of Rural ideas."[15] As the defining agricultural life and economic activity that has shaped a unique character of rural places for generations lose grip in the wake of revolutionary economic and structural change, they are ever more subject to the application of new interpretations and outside representations.

In a context of persistent nostalgia for such idealized ways of life, the practice of place marketing is ever more important. Central to these activities is deliberate manipulation of cultural meanings designed to enhance the appeal of places, particularly to a well-off and educated workforce as well as up-market tourists. According to Philo and Kearns this depends on "promoting traditions, lifestyles, and arts that are supposed to be *locally* rooted and, in this respect, the selling of places has what the humanistic geographers might call an 'authentic' quality spawned by the cultural life of the places themselves."[16] In the Grand Traverse region these traditions, lifestyles, and arts are lumped together and promoted as the hearty, woodsy, civilized yet laid-back Up North sensibility. This sensibility is akin to the character of "Neighbor," from the travel story of the Cyrus Howard family, who embodies this idealized blend of nature and culture. There is a local publication that dedicates itself to the "Way You Live Up North." In the March/April 2001 issue of *Northern Home*, the editor at large reflects:

> When I meet and interview Northern Michigan homeowners, I ask a favorite question: "How did you come to live Up North?" The stories that people share fascinate me. Collectively, the tales make up a patchwork. I think of them as the patchwork that makes up the fabric of life Up North. The details of their stories differ, but [they] share a common interest: They delight in living here. It is a refrain we at *Northern Home* hear from natives who have gone away and chosen to return, from young adults who are creating memories for themselves and their children, and from retirees who revel in having extra time to savor the region. The North offers a way of life we are proud to share.[17]

CHAPTER 9

Place for Personhood

I interpret the act of relocation among lifestyle migrants in this study as a strategy aimed at resolving tension between personal experience with material demands in pursuit of a livelihood in a "flexible" economy and prevailing moral meanings of—and cultural conventions for—the good life. Under current economic conditions and imperatives, people are expected to live in a perpetual state of becoming. This may lead to a crisis of individual identity not easily remedied by jobs in the contingent workforce. Relocating to personally meaningful geographic places may become the basis for defining self-identity within narratives essential to personhood. In this way, I have found that lifestyle migrants affirm an essential relationship between individual and local character. This chapter's central thread is my focus on the notion of "character" as applied to understanding both person and place—their mutually constituting characteristics.

Despite those who decry apparently willful placelessness in contemporary American life, place as both real and imagined continues to be an essential part of the intentional construction of individual identity. The anthropologist Setha Low states that "place is space made culturally meaningful" and that, further, it is "not just a setting for behavior but an integral part of social interaction and cultural processes."[1] Similarly, the folklorist Ken Ryden provides a definition closely tied to personhood in finding that as distinct, predictable, and culturally meaningful space, place is "an essential component of individual identity . . . [and] definition of self" where its "continued existence provides a reassuring sense of the world's continuity and stability."[2] This chapter discusses how a sense of place—manifest in personal attachment to real and imagined elements of particularity in specific locations (e.g., topographical forms, architectural features, local businesses, and climatic conditions), or manifest as what is commonly called *local character*—may support people in their ability to form autobiographical accounts expressed in moral narratives critical to personhood.

My use of the term personhood combines an appreciation for a *dialogical* self as well as material aspects of the person. A dialogical self arises from the fact that frameworks for self-interpretation and behavior—models *of* and models *for* the world—are shaped by culture in constant interaction and exchange between individuals and other persons in a social domain. In addition to this social dimension, materiality through embodiment is a basic ontological feature of the person—it has to do with the nature of being itself. Embodiment entails the way persons mediate, interpret, and interact with the social and physical environments of their everyday lives through their physicality.[3] The person is oriented in physical space, in part, by virtue of being embodied. Thus, materiality is as fundamental to being human as is our sociality. Stories of lifestyle migrants exemplify how some persons deliberately attempt to "root" their personal accounts—their moral narratives—through attachment to place. This appears an intentional reaction to the invasiveness of increasingly translocal market forces into the long-standing American practice of defining self through career and the emergence of a workplace increasingly reliant on commoditized notions of the worker.

A Question of Character:
The Case of Lifestyle Migration

A former soft-drink company executive from southeastern Michigan, Alan would have been considered successful by widely accepted social standards for having a generous salary and benefits and for living a seemingly comfortable and well-appointed suburban life. In his account of relocation, Alan returned routinely to his sense that he had been merely "struggling along" as a person before his decision to break with his former life. He felt unable to experience states of personal integration and fulfillment—an idea to which I will return later in this chapter. Alan spoke of how choices made in his job position brought him to where he felt that his "value system was being destroyed." He concluded that continuing on this path would only "tear him down," as he put it, literally *dis*-integrating him. Alan described finding himself being in no less than a disorienting crisis of deeply moral dimensions that violated his fundamental values and what he described as his "true self." Among the lifestyle migrants who I worked with, Alan was far from alone in this sentiment—even if he was especially articulate in conveying his feelings. For all these people, including Alan, getting out of this vein was a question of character. In the first place, it was one of what we might call "individual character," but then it became very much as well one of "local character." Alan felt that he needed to live a life defined on his own terms. This might allow him to orient himself to an inward sense of the good—a kind of moral horizon—and to construct a narrative consistent with an idealized vision of self.

> One day they told me, "You know you have to fire that guy. His wife has got a serious illness, and the insurance is costing us a fortune." There's nothing wrong with the guy. "Well, you'll have to find something." It was an inhumane decision. One guy got prostate cancer, and the president of the company said, "Well, he's a goner. We don't have to worry about him anymore." That's corporate America. I was trading away my value system for the job and in support of the company. You are brought up with certain morals, ethics, and values, and then you find yourself in a system that is not allowing you to live your life properly. All I was doing was tearing myself down.

When we were having out conversations in Northern Michigan, Alan described acting after his move Up North in ways that could be considered sharply incompatible with what would have been expected from him before relocation. His decision making reflected perhaps not so much a change in character but rather a desire to be true to an inner self.

> But now I can make decisions based on income or I can make decisions based on people. I'm people oriented now. I can decide not to raise this guy's rent. There is this handicapped guy living in one of my units, and he's got his little thirteen-inch TV. He doesn't have much of life outside that TV, so I went and picked up a big twenty-five-inch TV for a hundred bucks and went over and gave it to him and told him somebody left it in one of the units and that he could have it. I needed to do that for myself. There's decisions that you do based on your faith . . . your religious faith which has got a lot stronger for me. That's saying that I've gotten happy with it. Is there a God? Yeah, there's a God. There are some things in life that you can't explain. It's got a lot stronger since I've been up here. I got a lot more faith. Some of those decisions are about what's the right thing to do. A lot of that is a people-related process too, but in the corporate world it is a black-and-white process—it's numbers.

Alan came to see the cost he was paying to maintain that former self as very high indeed. By not being true to himself, he felt that he was losing what amounted to his very soul, and to a dream that was, in fact, never really his. He explains how even the dream itself is something you find yourself stumbling into and adopting.

> The old American Dream was to buy a house—or is it a dream of having a job, a career, and all of things you receive because of that? If the definition of the American Dream is having a career, a job, a future, I didn't have a whole lot of career focus or direction throughout my growing up. I stumbled into a lot of stuff that I did. You start on a path, and then you realize maybe this is a good path, maybe this is the dream. I developed the American Dream, a good job . . . a house in the suburbs and all those trappings. Then it became the dream. This was all coming from outside of me. Because of the circumstances I fell into, it became "this is the direction you should go." It was the logic of where I was.

Given how he was trading his value system for the job, how important was this to Alan's sense of self? What does having left this life mean now? For Alan it is about being able to define himself according to his own moral narrative. It is about finding personal integration and balance. Success is about living life on your own terms without having to sacrifice yourself to a dream that is not really your own but rather only something borrowed.

> I would say that working in corporate America was extremely important to my identity at that time. It really defined me. It really defined me for my daughter, for my family. You could see that in the way that she reacted when

> I left [my job]. I was a failure. Now, to say that what I'm doing now defines me . . . hmm, does it define me? I keep asking myself if I have a job title. A job title is a definition of a person. What am I? I call myself a landlord. But [my wife] cringes at that. She says to call myself a property manager. She's trying to find a better term or more acceptable or palatable term for what I am doing. But that's become the definition. To this day I don't know how to define myself.

Leaving that other life meant rediscovering some essential part of himself and being true.

> I never went looking to rediscover myself . . . but I think I did. Now looking back, the way I was reacting I was trading away my value system for the *job* and support of the company. My value system was being destroyed, and I didn't know it. You are brought up with certain morals, ethics, and values, and then you find yourself in a system that is not allowing you to live your life properly. This is on your mind whether it's conscious or subconscious, and it manifests in behavior. Looking back it is easy for me to analyze it. It was manifesting itself in behavior that I was not proud of. I was tearing myself down. It was a violation.

Alan jokes about how he used to say that Democrats became Republican when they grew up. Now he finds himself, a Republican, becoming sympathetic to the little people. Although he is not ready to embrace a social agenda more characteristic of the party that supports the unions he once worked to antagonize, he recognizes changes that he has undergone and embraces them. He blames not only corporations for the hardened and heartless attitude of his prior self, but also the urban environment in which he was working. In his mind, these cultures are closely intertwined in a brutal, "jungle"-like world that reduces people to basic instincts and that strips them of their humanity. Getting free of these things required being clear of that world completely both in practice and in place. In this way, his story resonates with a long history in America of holding up a rural or small-town idyll against the perceived ills of the urban.

> I think the problem was the big-city environment. When I go back there, people act differently. For me to get my personality back to where I trusted people and I liked people, I had to get *away* from the environment where you don't trust people. You become hardened in the city. I noted things in my personality . . . my language deteriorated. I yelled a lot [because] that's what people reacted to. Is this the right way to treat a human being? No. But that's how you got things done. That becomes your whole life. Pretty soon you're screaming at your wife and you're screaming at your kids.

Alan now feels that the decision to give up his corporate career and follow his wife's decision to relocate to Traverse City has become what he refers to as his "second chance." Here, again, we have a notion common to many lifestyle migrants and a definitive expression of the American ideal of starting over. He intends to do it right, this time. After breaking from a commitment to the corporate career that came to largely define not only the routines of his everyday life but his very sense of self, Alan sought a physical place in the world that he believed possessed qualities of local character necessary to support his decision to start over, including commonly stated associations with "slower pace," "simple," "nurturing," "community," or "traditional values." Starting over for migrants like Alan entails pursuing a potential self through lifestyle commitment to a way of life summed up in an imagined, future self that would be consistent with "core values" essential to individual character.

Like Alan, many lifestyle migrants describe feeling "torn down" and violated, without time either for self-creation or to connect with family or community. Combining what I earlier conveyed regarding the author William Leach's attempt to document the "demolition" of local place in America with the sociologist Richard Sennett's concern for the world of work and what he described as the "corrosion" of individual character in an increasingly contingent, flexible economy, we might explain the source of personal disintegration as a lack of critical spatial and temporal stability.[4]

Declining forms of community appear to further challenge many in their struggle to maintain individual character, self-constancy, and meaningful person-place connections.[5] Commenting on the work of the political theorist Hannah Arendt, the women's studies scholar Patricia Yaeger describes a world of shared interests, objects, and places that sets the conditions for individual and collective identity. According to Arendt, "to live together in the world means essentially that a world of things is between those who have it in common as a table is located between those who sit around it; the world, like every in-between, relates and separates at the same time."[6] Reflecting on this notion, Yeager describes a changed state of affairs as she explains how in late capitalism, the space between people appears to have lost the capacity to gather them together—to either relate or separate them—such that the world "ceases to offer the comforting illusion of dwelling in common . . . [changing] meaning-filled places into derangements of anonymous space."[7] While somewhat highbrow in their descriptions here, the ideas conveyed by these scholars are notions wholly common to the perceived worlds of lifestyle migrants in their everyday lives.

Katherine and John, a professional couple in their late thirties, told me how they left well-paying jobs and objectively successful days spent in the suburbs of Detroit to relocate to Northern Michigan, "take back their lives," and reconnect with "core values." Like other lifestyle migrants, they described feeling "dispossessed" of their suburban neighborhood and the nearby office park where they worked.

> Our key reasons [for moving] were to find work and lifestyle balance, to have greater community involvement, to raise a family. We wanted to work in a place where my willingness to work hard would be balanced by the need to

place family first. We hated feeling *dispossessed* of the city where we worked as well as the suburb we lived in and excited at the prospect of being part of a community in both work as well as personal life. In just a few weeks, we've noted the difference. We have two sons, five and two-and-a-half. [John] was working insane hours, with a long commute. Quite literally, [John] left a great salary *to take back our lives.*

Although their intent seems to express feelings of disconnection—the lack of any meaningful affective connection or attachment to place—their choice of the term "dispossession" hints at something deeper. It suggests being deprived a sense of security and, ultimately, of *home.* They went on to describe no true sense of ownership in the same way that they lacked a sense of control in their work lives. They spoke of growing feelings of being "disorientated" or "adrift" in their lives and the world.

Picking up again with Hannah Arendt's metaphor of the vanishing table—with help from Katherine and John—we see that Arendt's description can be taken to symbolize a mass-scale existential crisis or widespread dispossession. Arendt depicts this situation as "a spiritualistic séance where a number of people gathered around a table might suddenly, through some magic trick, see the table vanish from their midst, so that two persons sitting opposite each other were no longer separated but also would be entirely unrelated to each other by anything tangible."[8] This clever image is a compelling representation of interpersonal connections that in earlier generations would have been expressed in social capital building forms of civic engagement. The apparent decline in voluntary associations, which entail interactions and gatherings that act as a common table among people, is illustrated in findings of Robert Putnam and others who lament what they hold to be a tragic loss of long-standing ways of living and working together for which there may yet be no suitable alternatives.[9]

Individual Character

Having briefly explored current conditions as understood by many lifestyle migrants as well as their general sense of what is at stake, I would like to turn back to questions regarding character and specifically: What is the meaning of character when applied to self and personhood? Here I present a conceptualization of self as narrative project within which character is an essential, enduring aspect of self through time and space. Consciousness of self—in Western thought at least—is constituted and understood as a sharply demarcated, separate, and internal space. At the same time, a socially constituted moral space is a precondition of Western selfhood. As noted by Charles Taylor, in this sense we are selves only through having a place within this moral space as an evaluative framework. Within this frame, we have individual orientation to a culturally defined notion of the good. Accordingly, the self must exist among others in "webs of interlocution"—in constant dialog—within a complex social and physical geography.[10] This space of collective and consequential values is constitutive of human agency; it is where lives are lived out.

Embodied emplacement within this space is an inescapable structural requirement of human action. In short, life of the Western self entails an oriented movement through moral, social, and physical spaces.

With the ability to capture this spatial and temporal movement and contingency, narrative provides coherence, continuity, and meaningful connections between events and integration (or disintegration) of one's life through time. As noted by Taylor, "because we cannot but orient ourselves to the good, and this determines our place relative to it and hence . . . the direction of our lives, we must inescapably understand our lives in narrative form, as a 'quest.'"[11]

Narrative and self appear inseparable as narrative arises out of everyday experience even as it gives shape to that experience. It is through narrative that individuals make sense of their lives as a story unfolding in a manner that gives meaning to past events and suggests future directions.[12] Having a sense of who we are as persons requires a notion of how we have arrived at this point as well as where we are going. By giving an intelligible order to events of life, narrative creates continuity from past into future, imagined lives while acting as a critical interface between self and society. Narrative orders events in a temporal and spatial orientation particular to the individual and constructed within basic patterns shared among those in a given culture.[13] This is how individuals "lead a life," moving through moral, social, and physical space while balancing the reality of diverse elements of experience and the dynamic of a variety of possible selves with a struggle for lasting unity.[14] This process illustrates selfhood as a "work in progress," as project.

Conceptualizing self as a narrative project addresses the dialectic of change and constancy, an ongoing tension between provisional or potential selves and the need to integrate various interpretations of self into a coherent identity.[15] The philosopher Paul Ricouer explains that it is through "emplotment" that the discordant, contingent nature of individual events and experiences are rendered into a coherent, comprehensible whole of narrative account.[16] This is much more than a simple recounting. It is a combinative search for meaning. It is a quest in which separate events and experiences are unified as episodes through emplotment into a unifying story and "the unity of life considered a temporal totality."[17] Through unity of this "discordant concordance," narrative constructs character as the enduring aspect of self, a "set of lasting dispositions by which a person is recognized."[18] Together with emplotment, character allows for self-constancy in identity. It is how the same subject—a given person known to him- or herself as well as to others as an individual—may persist within a multiplicity of events and experiences in a narrated life. I turn next to "local character" in order to examine the connection between person and place in this process.

Local Character

In an expansive and broadly interdisciplinary literature on place, the term "character" is typically used in conjunction with other ideas under analysis but seldom explored in its own right. It is applied to suggest a category of familiar, often highly valued qualities and related perceptions at the local level meaningfully attached to aspects of natural and built environment in particular geographic locations. In consideration of community perception of "town character," a scholar in landscape architecture, Ray Green, points to a commonsense understanding, implicit in use of the term character as an "aggregate" of qualities that enable people to distinguish one thing, physical site, or person from another.[19] Suggesting a unique quality or even "spirit," character becomes an essential part of the idea of place and related concepts such as sense of place and genius loci as well as terms that refer to an intimate bonding of person and place such as human geographers Yi-Fu Tuan's "topophilia" or Edward Relph's "existential insideness."[20]

Discussing the concept of "place identity" in a manner that evokes the notion of character that I employ, the environmental psychologist Harold Proshansky notes that construction of self is developmentally first a matter of learning to distinguish self from other as well as from spaces in which a person lives, i.e., to recognize and maintain a unique character within a continuing narrative of self.[21] Speaking on meaningful personal connection to particular locations and identity construction and its persistence, sociologist Melinda Milligan draws on Irving Goffman's distinction between social, personal, and felt identities. Of particular importance to her discussion is "felt identity" as an individual's "subjective sense of his [*sic*] own situation and his own continuity and the character that an individual comes to obtain as a result of his various social experiences."[22]

Milligan's study of employees at a relocated coffee shop explores how individual experience is necessarily located in spaces that are at once physical realities that shape, constrain, and influence social interaction while also being sites to which social meanings and beliefs are attached. These sites rise above an undifferentiated plane of abstract space through being known and endowed with personal and cultural value until they become rich with layered sentiment.[23] Simply stated, such everyday sites of living and working are the places to which people become "attached."

The notion of *place attachment* draws together this constellation of ideas while incorporating—explicitly or implicitly—a concern with character. Place attachment has been called "an integrating concept comprising interrelated and inseparable aspects."[24] Indeed, the concept has been used by scholars in several fields, including psychology, anthropology, geography, and sociology, as a way to refer to the bonds created between people and place based on cognition, practice, and the affective dimensions of the self. Speaking in lay terms, place attachment may be defined as a person's ties to a place that result from long-term association with a particular "setting" or environment. As noted by both the geographer Robert Hay and the environmental psychologist Francis McAndrew, the literature on place attachment has developed alongside related studies of "community attachment," which have generally considered choice behavior in relocation or residential decision making.[25] With its emphasis on the significance of person-place bonds to identity, studies of attachment explore "disruptions" in this bonding as a way to better understand its varied dimensions under conditions believed to illuminate what might otherwise be an unselfconscious process or state. These dramatic discontinuities in person-place bonds are often referred to as "displacement" and are typically defined as *involuntary* breaks in attachment of person to particular place—such as those that may be precipitated in the lives by long-time residents when historically open access to tracts of cherished land is closed by new housing developments. These breaks are seen as entailing a degree of loss and identity discontinuity or "fragmentation."[26]

As noted by Proshansky, theories of self and personhood have tended to neglect the importance of physical setting to socialization and identity and have stressed constancy and stability over change.[27] With their concern for uprootedness and change, studies of relocation and displacement encourage more dynamic or systemic models of person-place bonds and identities. These studies recognize that selfhood constitutes a complex, ongoing process within an ever-changing social and physical environment. Such a model of this process of person-place bonding parallels my "self as narrative project" construct. Importantly, both address the dialectic of change and constancy as well as tension between actual and potential selves.

This dynamic is captured in work on "settlement identity" and life stages by the self-described architectural activist Roberta Feldman, as well as in research on voluntary and involuntary relocation and transformational stages in individual experience conducted by psychologists Barbara Brown and Douglas Perkins.[28] In a similar manner, Hay's article on the developmental context for sense of place notes how there are shifts in a person's life as a kind of "structure" between more stable (structure-building) and more transitional (structure-changing) periods, with the latter more frequent and prolonged in conditions of what many scholars would call postmodernity.[29] Hay suggests that an enduring self despite constant structural change and threat of "placelessness" requires intimacy, involvement, and commitment, all of which provide for greater identity continuity and "sustainability" through establishing an enduring character and encouraging place attachment as a kind of "primordial sentiment."[30] The behavior of lifestyle migrants suggests a *quest* for such intimacy and continuity through attachment to personally meaningful place.

The Search for Meaningful Connection to Place

David Hummon's work on attachment provides evidence to justify expanding the notion of displacement as used in such studies as those cited above, beyond nearly exclusive focus on involuntary disruption and loss of attachment, to include the alienation, uprootedness, or "dispossession" that characterize stories of people such as the lifestyle migrants that I have documented.[31] My work with laid-off and downshifting workers made it clear that while confidently defining oneself long-term by way of a job might have been realistic to a generation that came of age in the 1950s, when William Whyte's "Organization Man" defined devoted workers of a postwar boom, now there is no expectation of the durability of such a definition because the world of work on which it had been based is increasingly unstable and unpredictable.[32] In a departure from the ideal worker of a more standardized and regular industrial world of the last century, workers now must be multitasking, adaptable, and forever learning. This worker is the ever-adapting, multitasking "person as portfolio."[33] The cultural historian John Gillis suggests that we have entered an era in which men and women are encouraged, regardless of age, "to think of themselves in a perpetual state of becoming. We are asked to retrain, reeducate and recycle."[34]

As suggested in the above-mentioned accounts by Alan as well as Katherine and John, lifestyle migrants express a need to go to a place in which they feel they have or can make lasting, tangible attachments. As with many others who express need for connection or reconnection, Amelia has never lived in my study area. However, having been born and raised in southern Michigan, she felt emotionally tied to the perceived character of the Midwest. A middle-aged women working in software development and living in San Francisco at the time of our conversation, she sought return to self-described "psychic roots." She explains how she arranged to leave the city and work that no longer holds her:

> I spent two weeks in mid-September in Traverse City readying the antique Victorian I bought. I plan to rent it while I arrange my life so that I can eventually assume occupancy. I have developed a yearning for quiet, community, and simplicity. I have always sorely missed four seasons. I bought a wonderful book of haiku poetry extolling the beauties of seasonal essences and transitions. They get stamped onto your psyche. I am increasingly less willing to sacrifice basic human needs to pay the high price of looking out my window at the Golden Gate Bridge, then trying to make my way through a frustrating maze of traffic to simply visit the neighborhood store. You could say I wish to return to my psychic roots for the last third of my life—like a salmon swimming upstream. I can picture myself walking the gold and amber tree-lined street to the bay on a somber October day.

While flexibility in the economic sphere and what we may describe as the destruction of local places creates persistent instability and challenges the assumed fixity of ourselves and others, it has not thereby created persons who are wholly disembedded. As noted by the anthropologists Akhil Gupta and James Ferguson, instead of stopping with "the pulverization of the space of high modernity, we need to theorize how space is being reterritorialized in the contemporary world."[35] The most telling irony of these times is that as particular places possessed of distinctive characteristics that define the local become increasingly collapsed, blurred, or indeterminate, the idea or even imagining of culturally, regionally, or otherwise distinct place appears to become even more salient and sought after. One attempt at reterritorialization—even what might be thought of as a kind of "reenchantment"—are intentionally created communities in planned residential developments. Whereas neighborhoods once grew organically from the way people lived, some now attempt to synthesize them as a remedy to perceived social ills.[36] Reterritorialization here would refer to attempts to recapture, in some fashion, what are understood to be potent symbols of an idealized past. How do lifestyle migrants engage in such practices?

Preserving Local Character for Individual Character

The capacity to create and possess places recaptured from fragments both remembered—as in bits of personal experience that seem resonant with the character of particular geographic locations—and individually or collectively imagined becomes increasingly critical for both people and the places where they live and work. Lifestyle migrants often speak of the great significance of elements perceived as composing unique local character in places to which they relocate and the importance of preserving distinctiveness as marker of unity and difference against the homogenizing process of suburban "sprawl." This rapid and largely unregulated development can lead to a landscape of "Anytown, USA," a term used by some lifestyle migrants and locals alike to describe an indistinct development of chain stores along vast parking lots on congested, pedestrian-unfriendly streets. While decrying the harmful influence of mass media and consumer culture in the final volume to his famed trilogy on American history, the historian Daniel Boorstin characterized the contemporary community of the United States similarly as a commodified, largely placeless "everywhere community."[37]

Desire for belonging and concern for place preservation may be a defensive posture taken by lifestyle migrants—and others—against corrosive, market-based forces that Boorstin blamed for the destruction of place and rise of everywhere community. It is defense for the ability of individuals and families to construct meaningful accounts, sustainable narratives of self as the basis of individual character, and collective identity. It is also a defense for places to retain unique character in the face of sweeping sameness. As corporations strive to gain power, profit, and competitive advantage through increased uniformity, placelessness, and flexibility, individuals may find greater strength, stability, and personal meaning through engagement or embodied experience with and in unique places—seeking an experience of belonging and sense of place.

I found numerous examples in Northern Michigan where both newcomers and longtime residents fought to preserve local landmarks and what they understood to be basic elements of character. Take the case of "Fishtown." The future of this collection of restored fishing shanties in the coastal Lake Michigan village of Leland was placed into question when the fifth-generation Carlson fishing business no longer seemed viable. Following a comprehensive treaty agreement between the state of Michigan and five Native American tribes over fishing rights, the Carlson family threatened to shutter their business and sell the entire site. Suddenly, the possibility that this cherished waterfront could become the grounds of a big hotel or condominium complex emerged in public consciousness.

Although locals and newcomers alike treat Fishtown as a timeless monument to a rugged frontier past held in de facto if not de jure public trust—above the reach of development to change it—the controversy exposed the fragile nature of personal and collective sense of place tied to taken-for-granted physical expressions of local character. As a local newspaper article reflects, Fishtown is not only weathered shacks and aging boardwalks that serve as real or imagined relics of another time, it is the ongoing business of fishing, the life of place expressed in "nets drying and smell of whitefish and chub being cleaned and smoked. It's the sight of

Fish tug *Mary Ann*, 1958

The *Joy* and the *Janice Sue* are now owned by the Fishtown Preservation Society

For more than a century people have been drawn to Leland's working waterfront, lured by the river, fishermen, shanties, fish tugs, docks, and the opportunity to purchase fresh fish. In Leland's historic Fishtown, today's visitor can experience one of the few remaining commercial fishing complexes on the Great Lakes. There's no other place like Fishtown.

Families return to Fishtown year after year, generation after generation. Whether on a quiet winter morning or in the middle of a busy summer day, once people discover Fishtown they feel a connection. Fishtown has long been, quite simply, a treasured place. If Fishtown is important to you, think about what would be missing in your life if it no longer existed. You can help preserve this wonderful place.

Even fish tugs are like family in Fishtown. In 1958 Louis Steffens launched the newly built *Janice Sue*, which he named for his three-year old niece. Better able to endure ice and waves, steel-hulled tugs replaced hand-built wood tugs. The *Janice Sue* has since been owned by other Leland fishermen, including the Carlson family, but Leland has always been her home. The *Joy*, a trap-net tug, was launched in 1981. Like the weathered shanties and docks, the *Janice Sue* and the *Joy* are Fishtown icons and need preservation.

My father was on the water most of his life, and I spent fifty years on the water. If I had to make a choice again, I think it would be the same. I would be a commercial fisherman.
— Roy Buckler, Leland Fisherman, 1987

A busy summer day in Fishtown

Early voyage of the *Janice Sue*, 1958

Interior of brochure from the not-for-profit organization Fishtown Preservation Society.

ruddy windblown people in yellow rubber overalls and boots jumping off boats and clomping up and down the docks."[38]

Protecting certain physical aspects of place speaks directly to the question of what may be called the "cultural resources" available for constructing narrative accounts of individual and collective lives. As such, it resonates strongly with legal anthropologist Rosemary Coombe's argument regarding *signs*. Simply stated, a sign is something that can be interpreted as having meaning, which is something other than itself. As such a sign is capable of conveying information. Signs may take the form of words; images; and sensory impressions such as sound, odor, or taste; as well as of acts or objects; but such things have no intrinsic meaning and become signs only when they are invested with meaning. Drawing on Coombe's analysis, we can consider how processes of commoditization in American society driven by intense marketing and fortified by legal protections may "stifle dialogic practices—preventing [people] from using the most powerful, prevalent, and accessible forms [of signs] to express identity, community and difference."[39] How have these forces led to restrictions and constraints on signification—the use of signs to convey meaning—as well as on circulation of a wide variety of important, taken-for-granted cultural forms? If human subjectivity is fundamentally dialogic, as Charles Taylor suggests, and culture is an ongoing practice of transformative meaning making, then it is important to understand how symbolic resources available for signification may be controlled, restricted, or simply lost.

The anthropologists Rosemary Coombe and Setha Low both address actual and potential loss of such cultural resources—including elements of perceived local character—essential to individual character. They are thus concerned with possibilities or potentialities for human subjectivity. While Low's work speaks to the case of place as a personal and public resource, Coombe refers to means of expression as critical resources and "optimal cultural conditions" for dialogic practices constitutive of personhood.[40] Coombe clearly states the problem with regard to policy by stating that "if both objective social worlds and subjective desires, identities, and understandings are constructed with cultural resources, then legal attitudes toward cultural forms may have profound implications."[41] Low, in turn, warns that without some manner of place preservation "the contexts of culturally meaningful behaviors and processes of place-making disappear, cutting us off from our past, disrupting the present, and limiting the possibilities for the future."[42]

As suggested in the iconic case of Fishtown, key elements of place become not only physical landmarks in a familiar landscape but powerful local symbols that provide the substance of ideas and imaginings essential for composing self and for making the personal account, and thus the person, whole. They become the spine of autobiographical structure where lives quite literally take place. As Elizabeth Grosz suggests, "everybody is marked by the history and specificity of its existence . . . [thus] it is possible to construct a biography, a history of the body, for each individual and social body."[43]

Speaking in terms of autobiographical memory and place, the essayist Rockwell Gray asserts that "personal identity depends upon the recapture in memory of key places in which one's life has taken place."[44] Gray considers whether the phrase "take place" has significance beyond its literary usage. To say that one's life has taken place is, in fact, "a kind of pun . . . [for] we live by occupying, by *taking possession* of, a succession of places."[45] As with Coombe's focus on restriction in signification and circulation of cultural forms, meanings can also be restricted or imposed in the context of place through applying a "commodity logic." According to a fundamentally economic epistemology, what might be subjectively experienced as place, with a sense of place attachment and "possession" suggested by Gray, is conceived of as mere space in the calculus that characterizes the actions of business and government.

"Something there is that doesn't love a wall"

A legal case from my study area brings into sharp relief issues of access to and control of a resource perceived of as essential to both local and individual character. One part of this case entails a basic value that, in principle, all people should have equal opportunity to acquire or display the things that compose the prevailing notion of the good life. This is central to the peculiarly American notion of freedom in which democracy is extended from the sphere of government and political participation to the realm of consumer wants and desires. In theory at least, consumer democracy allows everyone the right of self-expression and affirmation through consumption of material goods or, perhaps, choice of residence—although people ultimately differ in capacity to fulfill desires as a consequence of such factors as socioeconomic status.

As in other places undergoing pressure to "develop," driven by tourism, inmigration, and other factors, there is mounting tension over individual and common *goods* within study area communities. On the one hand, I have found place promotion for private development in keeping with the ideal of a free and open market where people can choose within their means to fulfill individual desires. At the same time, many lifestyle migrants and longtime residents recognize the need to preserve a common good, expressed in somewhat nebulous concepts such as "open space," which may be sacrificed by largely unregulated growth.

This iconic dispute illustrates a tension between individual desire and a common good. Early during my time in the field, I learned that a Traverse City man was suing a neighbor on behalf of his neighborhood to restore a scenic view of Grand Traverse Bay long enjoyed but now blocked by a tall fence erected by the defendant, who sought to better establish personal privacy. A newspaper reporter invoked a locally meaningful, much-repeated phrase that captures how many move to the area at the expense of salary when he asked, "If a view of the Bay is half the pay . . . what's the harm when it's taken away?"[46] The ensuing court battle may be seen simply as an attempt to balance private property rights with a generalized sense of quality-of-life values and a common good. However, the case speaks to diminished access to a view basic to sense of place, an essential part of local character, individual character, and defining narratives of self and community within a neighborhood.

The plaintiff's suit describes the fence in language that carries feelings of violation heard in the accounts of lifestyle migrants. The fence is described as not less than a threat to well-being. The plaintiff's legal complaint finds it "seriously offensive, obnoxious, and darkly oppressive." They describe its construction as a "shameful and dastardly wrongful act . . . which significantly alters, in an extremely negative way, the status quo." In response to the final judgment (for the defendant), the plaintiff states that views of the bay have always been "revered" and that the fence was a "fortress-like structure" that intruded on that reverential space by creating "long, dark shadows where there used to be sunlight."[47] The aggrieved loss of a valued resource, formerly available to these neighbors, highlights the connection between local and individual character and the extent to which, for lifestyle migrants, resources of place are far from inert substances—as we will see next.

Embodied Experience, Connecting Self with Place

The desire to deliberately root selfhood in an actively cultivated sense of place, rather than in the domain of work, what we might call "career," is a basic motivation of lifestyle migrants. Now in their fifties, Joan and Peter moved from near Detroit in the mid-1990s. For a decade prior to their move, they visited and picnicked on land purchased on scenic Leelanau Peninsula with the idea of "retiring on it." Many years before that imagined day, however, Peter's chosen career in broadcasting began to unexpectedly change in response to broader changes in mass media in particular and the workplace in general. He felt unable to pursue his first "calling," as he referred to it, as a journalist. Taking time to reassess his life trajectory, Joan and Peter decided to risk taking a different path. With Peter's heretofore life-organizing career at an end, they felt freed to follow a dream of making place an essential core of everyday life, merging present self with a potential self. Cushioned by savings and equity accumulated in their longtime residence in southeast Michigan (an acknowledged aspect of relatively privileged socioeconomic status), they took a measured risk and to find or create work for themselves and relocated to their cherished "Promised Land."

Here we hear how Peter makes the physical place he loves an intimate part of self through Relph's "existential insideness."[48]

> I must tell you that there are not fewer than five days in a week where I come inside and say to my wife, "God damn, I feel loved." I live at "the Bend in the Eagle Highway." That's where I live. Eagle Highway makes a bend just like that [*gestures with his arms to point to an inner elbow*] right at its northern edge. That's the address I use. I see eagles from my porch. None actually live on my land, but I'll give them the chance. I love seeing wild turkeys. I've seen two bobcats in six months. Those are joys. I work very hard on the place I'm at to know who first farmed it and when it was bought, the successive owners. There is a stone house on the property with walls that thick [*gestures a foot in thickness*]. That kept the temperature an even sixty in summer so that it can keep milk cool.

Self and place making involve use of artifacts and place-based stories in narrative constructions that delineate particular areas of intense familiarity that organize and make surroundings meaningful. The folklorist Mary Hufford asserts that narrative strategies in accounts like Peter's provide ways for people to "surround themselves with evidence that they are at home, in a place with a usable past."[49] Place naming, specifically use of unofficial names like their self-proclaimed address at "the Bend in the Eagle Highway," provides a sense of existential insideness and feeling of belonging in encoded messages both discursive as well as in landscape features, elements basic to local character that serve as grammatical units, as signs, that may be meaningless to the "outsider" but become essential to individual character. Feelings of place attachment elevated to a sense of ownership are encouraged through limiting entrée to a particular area in the realm of signification by use of such forms. Familiarity and intimate knowledge of place can provide the basis for an implicit or explicit claim of possession, where the person "takes place" in the dual sense of process and appropriation. This claim is for stake in a basic part of self in the same way that one might claim property in one's own body—a point to which I will return to in the final chapter with my discussion of University of Michigan law professor Margaret Radin's contribution to the subject of personhood and place

Peter's words resonate with Gray's assertion that we have an "autobiographical need to re-create the past" and that "such re-creation is actually coextensive with the power of memory, *rooting* it in the [relative] stability of the spatial order" as a way of creating personal account.[50] Those who make place into home by making it a literal part of themselves experience the existential insideness described by Relph where place is "experienced without deliberate and self-conscious reflection yet is full of significances [where the person] is part of that place and it is part of him [*sic*]."[51]

As intuitively understood by lifestyle migrants, sense of self is determined in large part by what people do, and what they do is shaped by where they are in the world. Susan's case illustrates this point. In another narrative of relocation, a single woman in her late thirties who grew up in the Midwest set out in the 1990s to "find herself" in a career with a Silicon Valley software firm. When the world of work in the high-tech boom lost its meaningfulness and began to erode Susan's faith in career for providing an enduring basis to selfhood, she reconsidered her earlier commitment to climbing the corporate ladder. She spoke lovingly of the local character of place when describing how she chose to leave behind a high-paying job for a life deliberately embedded in the landscape of my study area. Here she clarifies her meaning of place: "It's the water and the dunes, the open space, the seasons. You feel part of the outdoors up here. You feel like your life is not your home, the footprint of your house, your work. You realize that it's bigger than that. It's a lot bigger than that. Your life kind of expands. It expands even into that old boat stored back in the woods."

Susan's description expresses how her *self* became a literal part of place, how she has taken ownership of it as a part of personhood. She explains how—through connection to place—your life can be "bigger" than home and work. This is the "something more" referred to and passionately sought by lifestyle migrants. As noted by local writer Kathleen Stocking, people sometimes seek out places to feel that they belong to something bigger. Stocking left New York City when she needed "birds and trees and the observable minutiae of seasons so I could feel my life as a stream of little movements . . . huge hills and big lakes and that sense of panorama and distance."[52] Both Susan and Stocking describe how what we might think of as a person's psychic space can be enlarged. They suggest where personhood and place are entwined in embodied experience such that physical *things* such as that "old boat stored back in the woods," as a feature of local character, become an acknowledged element of individual character in the composition of selfhood. They act as a kind of sign for the self. Further, both women are talking, in part, about experiencing a kind of self-integration in various elements of their lives quite distinct from the existential predicament suggested in Alan's account of "struggling along" in a career that came to violate his core values.

Susan notes that feeling connected with place before might have happened during intense moments of letting go during a vacation experience, but that amounted only to a single "compartment" in an otherwise fragmented life. Integration involves letting all the parts come together. Knowing that her sense of self is so much a part of this place, she fears the changes that economic growth and development might bring. It is again the fear of an encroaching Anytown, USA, or everywhere community. In her description of this fear, she recognizes that other people's need for place might have less to do with the connectedness that is important for her and more to do with simply having "space."

> But from time to time, I feel some anxiety. The anxiety I feel is that more and more people are going to come up here and it's going to become more *civilized*. I can't stand new construction. When I see subdivisions being built and that kind of stuff, [it] causes a lot of anxiety because I feel that I have a need for more space, personal space, than these people do. I must. Those people are happy living in New York City. Everybody has their own personal space. You want to be close enough to be part of a community, but I'm always feeling crowded, which is why I live up in a little town on Leelanau Peninsula.

Susan describes what it means to be a part of place by living here and making it her own through the rituals of everyday life: "We've got friends that are farmers and go up and help pick cherries and stuff like that. It's a part of life. I've just had some incredible experiences that I would never have had on vacation because I live here. I'm a *part* of it. That's part of my life. I don't need to take a vacation to do that. It's like camp all year round. We've got a fire pit in my backyard. This is probably why I'll never leave. It's the way everybody should live . . . [*laughs*] in my opinion. That's how I feel." Susan again talks about how she does not want a place of temporary refuge, such as one might escape to in order to find peace and tranquility only to return to a life that is somehow wanting. She wants to "surround" herself with such a place. Like the local author whose eloquent prose began this chapter, Susan needed land and country around her so that she could feel that she belonged to something bigger than herself. She realizes that her understanding of place is more profound than that of someone just passing through. Lifestyle migrants recognize the importance of place for identity. They have put place ahead of work in their equations for the good life. In their compelling narratives of relocation, they show us how embodied experience gives them meaningful connections to place, the physical landscape, and the intangible spirit of history. It is about something bigger, greater than themselves and their lives of finding relative stability for a sense of self.

PART IV

Moving On

Ovwerleaf: Entrance sign for campground where Susan spent
several months living after quitting her job, leaving California,
and seeking to start over in the study area. Photo by Brian Hoey

CHAPTER 10

The Option of Elsewhere

In America the theme of moving on " . . . appears on every cultural horizon. We write it and paint it. We sing and recite it. We see it in the wild geese over our fall pastures; we hear it in the early morning rumblings of the eighteen-wheelers. We smell it along our coasts, in the mud of the great Mississippi, over the wild prairie grasses of the Missouri breaks. We feel it in our bones and sense it in our roots. It is as generic to the concept of America as freedom itself."

—Frank Bryan, "Rural Renaissance: Is America on the Move Again?"

The idea of relocating to promote a change in one's life is by no means unique to the present day. Neither is the desire to define oneself as an individual with the freedom to choose. Relocating has always offered opportunities for many kinds of change. What I call the option of elsewhere is a basic cultural theme and cherished right of American life—even a defining characteristic of the nation's democracy. It is a foundation of the American notion of personal freedom. According to the sociologist James Jasper, Americans have generally tried to define their collective identity by a lack of place attachment: "We see ourselves as people who are ready to move anywhere to take advantage of new opportunities. For us the road itself is a place, in fact our favorite place. . . . Roadsides, boomtowns, and riverboats are all place where Americans feel at home, constructing a sense of identity built around movement rather than place."[1]

There is a basic tendency to see moving as starting over and as a possible solution to present problems. This restlessness and faith in the capacity to make a fresh start are an essential part of a cultural heritage that may have historical roots in America's immigrant tradition. The stories of immigrants have served as compelling, idealized examples that teach us that our world can be remade through individual effort and determination. An immigrant history appears to normalize the act of relocation and provide the basis for trust in the possibility that a deliberate and radical disruption in one's life is normal and even admirable.

The American belief in individual freedom and taking responsibility for one's own fate is closely allied with an abiding faith in the market. This is one powerful reason why many Americans have little problem with placing blame on the poor themselves as a group for their state of poverty. Rather than looking to structural inequities or lasting social problems—to those faithful to a belief in the justice of apparently impersonal market outcomes—the poor appear deliberately stuck and entrenched in the misery of their own misfortune. It seems that they are in a state of poverty because of the weight of their own choices or even their personal traits. Following this logic, economic failure or financial ruin becomes an individual moral failing.

In her study in the early 1990s of autoworkers in the Midwest called *The End of the Line: Lost Jobs, New Lives in Postindustrial America*, the anthropologist Katherine Dudley found that the prevailing view—adopted by the workers themselves—was that they were responsible for their own misfortunes and perhaps even "deserving" the downsizing and restructuring that constantly threatened them and led to thousands of layoffs.[2] We tend to see the economic market "as the simple aggregation of large numbers of individuals making informed, autonomous decisions, unconstrained by government policies or structural forces. As a result they are responsible for what happens to them."[3]

As in my own family's immigrant stories, and as in Horatio Alger's rags-to-(relative)-riches tales, most Americans tend to focus on the individual as the master of his or her own destiny. Who more than the lowly immigrant ancestor has taken the necessary leap of faith to take control of his or her own life and force dramatic change through the act of relocation? The greatest success stories in America as a free-market society are the so-called self-made men of industry and those "lone eagles" who now characterize economic success in a gradually more postindustrial economy. It is stories such as theirs that have defined an American character.

While as a form of literature, autobiography is not unique to American shores, as a literary form, it embodies characteristics that are peculiarly American, including a "valorization of individualism and its focus on the success story. . . . [Thus, it] has always been eminently suited to the dominant American temperament."[4] As American autobiographies go, Benjamin Franklin's is perhaps most iconic. It established as a central piece of our mythos that personal transformation is possible through migration and that the country itself was—as both an idea and a place—a world of possibilities and new beginnings fully realizable in the lives of ordinary people without regard to status or class association.

Freedom to Search for "Something More"

Nearly all lifestyle migrants in this project provided an autobiographical narrative of relocation. During the course of explaining—even defending—decisions to relocate that often meant leaving jobs or potentially rewarding careers and uprooting family, they describe periods of looking for "something more" in their lives. Generally these feelings arose from personal dissatisfaction in work life, but career discontent was not a necessary condition to impel people to embark on a quest for something more. Sometimes these periods of seeking simply grew out of a sense of possibilities connected with other places. Lifestyle migrants often spoke of how they were *generally* happy with what they were doing and *basically* satisfied with where they were living but still felt that they needed to explore other "sides" of themselves. They believed that new places would allow them to do this.

A young couple planning on children, Ben and Kelly explain how they did not run from anything unpleasant. They were drawn to imaging other lives and potential selves. They recognized and enjoy a flexibility that allows them to pick up and move simply because this is what they want. In their experience, the flexibility that I have associated with an emerging postindustrial economy is not threatening. At the time we met, they had only just arrived in the study area. Kelly was in high demand as a nurse in the local hospital that served a wide geographic area undergoing a surge in population. Having saved up for the move, Ben was content to spend time looking for a satisfying job. I first met them in the cafeteria at an outpatient clinic while Kelly was taking a break from her duties. As they sipped coffee in the Spartan lounge, Ben spoke about where they were at when they decided to relocate. It was a place of comfort, a shared sense of flexibility and a faith in their capacity to make the right decision.

> BEN: So we were not displeased with Charleston [West Virginia] at all. We had no pressure to go anywhere. We both had jobs that we liked and felt fulfilled. We had a great group of friends. We had a good church community. We were kind of equal distance to our two families. We didn't have to go anywhere. So that took all the pressure off.
>
> KELLY: Yeah, we were both working.
>
> BEN: Right. So it was just like, "We're fine." We didn't have to do anything. This allowed us to make the decision. Whatever decision we made had to be a very good one—not just the first train to come along. We were going to wait until something felt like it was right for what we wanted and that we felt good about because we were leaving a good situation. Why would you leave something good to go to something that was questionable?

Ben and Kelly relate a story of an unfolding relationship as well as an early commitment to living in a place that supports a particular lifestyle. Their early lifestyle commitment guides subsequent decisions and becomes not only a foundation to their relationship but also, as suggested earlier, a kind of moral orientation. When I spoke to them during this early period in their relocation, they were looking to find a house that they would be happy to call "home" and maybe even to start a family—both of which they had by the time I returned to the area in the summer of 2010. In the meantime, they rented downtown and got a better sense of the "lay of the land." Sufficient savings of several months' rent and living expenses helped cushion the transition, and they felt secure for now with Ben not working. As I listened to them, focus on place first was essential. It was a sense of flexibility that allowed them to be open to finding the ideal place. I am not surprised that they, a young couple at the relative beginning of their working lives, embrace flexibility as a core theme for their story. It is essential not only to the character of the contemporary economy but also more broadly to a society composed of what many scholars have suggested are increasingly loosened bonds akin to the qualities of "flow" described by Lewis Mumford as he sought to understand cultural and social shifts in American society that would lead to defining patterns of residential migration and community life for the twentieth century. In the following passage,

Ben speaks in terms that echo the sense of possibilities Mike (the Pie Guy) had graduating with a degree in engineering and contemplating whether to join the ranks of Oldsmobile in Lansing or opt for something and somewhere else entirely. Ben explains:

> Coming out of college, I sat down and said: where do I want to live? I don't have any strings attached. I can go anywhere in the world I want and do anything that I want. I took a fairly cautious look at a couple of different cities that I thought I would like to live in. If I'm going to work maybe ten hours a day, what's important is that I still have two-thirds of the day. So if I don't like my job then I darn well better like where I live, or my whole life is going to suck. I can control that piece. When Kelly and I started to talk about our life we said, "We're not company people." I'm not trying to build a career with DuPont or whoever, and neither is Kelly. So this was part of our relationship, and we made a *promise* to ourselves, which grew into a plan over time.

The promise they make to each other is not to any particular life at that point but to a *way* of life. They have made the oft-heard lifestyle commitment and a pledge to remain true to themselves. It is as much about what they do not want to be—about setting the limits of what is acceptable—as about what they wish to be. Their account resonates with a sense of being relatively unencumbered, flexible, and essentially free.

BEN: So everything has sort of—I can't say has fallen into place because for something to fall into place you sort of have to have a *mold*. We didn't. But I think flexibility and staying true to ourselves and our relationship came first. Most of the people we've talked to are somewhat envious of us having taken the opportunity to *create* our existence that way. I'm not needed on the family farm, you know? I'm not needed to be the next generation of wheat farmer. I'm not needed to be the next generation of shopkeeper. My dad didn't die in a mining accident. I'm not the sole breadwinner for my mother. Neither is Kelly. So, why not? Perhaps it's selfish, but that's okay, we're allowed. And if we're not, we're doing it anyways.

KELLY: That's right [*laughs*].

BEN: That *flexibility*. We've come at it with this whole relationship—it's not just finding a place to live. It is flexibility. That is the piece of our life that gave us the opportunity to make this kind of a broad decision that "We can just pick up and go someplace." It still exists in our lives. So, if we get to two years [living in the study area] and Kelly's frozen to death, I don't know a soul, and we're miserable, we can pack up our stuff and move to Albuquerque—if we want to. We are totally devoid of pressure. I don't mean that we don't have relationship pressures or financial pressures, but we don't have anything that forced us here or is trying to keep us here. We are not bound by anything other than our own desire. That's a very comfortable and fortunate place to be.

Returning to the engineer turned pie maker who started his own small business in Traverse City in his early forties after leaving a corporate life in California, we can hear Mike's own sense of flexibility. In this conversation, Mike described laying out a contingency plan that he and Denise came up with as soon as he was granted a loan from a local bank to start their pie shop. With foresight and planning, they were prepared to go into a dramatic lifestyle change and to shift gears again—even if it meant going back to a corporate life.

> So now somebody is really going to loan me money! So then we went back through all the charts that we had made again. It's like, "Do we really want to do this?" We're getting to the point of no return where I would *actually* leave my job—making eighty-plus thousand with full benefits and stock options—to do this. At some point either you have the *vision* or . . . *blindness* to just do it, or you recoil and say, "Well, I'd better not do that." I just thought, well, I know people at Lockheed-Martin. So, if it falls through, I have a bailout. Our out would be leaving [the study area], which would be rough on the family, but we were ready to do that.

Place First, Work Second

Much like Ben and Kelly, Carl and Liz were generally satisfied in their working lives. However, similar to John and Katherine's experience, they felt completely *dispossessed* of Cincinnati, Ohio, as a place. They described their sense that it was possible to become "mired" in a rut of work that kept you stuck in a physical place. And place was too important. As with other lifestyle migrants, they made a commitment. This is expressed as a promise to get "unstuck." Carl and Liz moved to the area just over a year before I spoke to them. A couple in their midthirties, they did not have children and did not see the move as one to start a family. Carl was working in a local private school as a music teacher, and Liz was giving music lessons out of their home. When I first spoke to them, we gathered in their thoughtfully decorated home tucked into a grove of plantation pines sown to curb soil erosion in the windswept glacial plains above Traverse City over a generation ago. Speaking of their former life and place in Cincinnati, Carl began:

> Our life was fully booked up with work and we were happy professionally, but we still really did not *fit* in that place. We decided that life's too short and our time on earth is . . . [*laughs*] limited. If we're going to make a move—if we're going to do something—the longer we sit here, the harder it was going to be to leave. We did a lot of research the year prior [to their move] because we had made a *commitment*. I remember driving home from one of our many escapes up here and right there in the car . . .
>
> LIZ: We shook on it.
> CARL: We shook on it! We said we're going to move. We're getting out. That's when we began to get serious.

When asked what it was about their former place of residence that was so unsatisfying—despite being otherwise professionally happy—they speak of identifying an inner need and acting to fulfill that need by finding a place where they felt most "at home." As I heard in other interviews, they identified this need as one based on a "spiritual" connection to place—to the land.

> CARL: I don't think we could put our finger on what we were unhappy about before.
> LIZ: Was it the economic situation or where we were living? I think if you had to put in a nutshell what made us decide to move here, it was a spiritual decision based on where we feel most connected and at peace. Where do we feel best internally? It was always *up here.*
> CARL: It certainly wasn't economic—for financial security.
> LIZ: I would say it's primarily the *land.*

Patrick echoes the sentiment that it is important to at least be in a physical place that is personally meaningful and rewarding, regardless of one's work. Like Ben, Patrick is a social worker. As we heard earlier, when I began my research he was in his early fifties and had moved here with his young family in the late 1970s—caught in a rising tide of white flight from Detroit. Patrick relates his own story of working in the Detroit area, where he often felt unsafe both on and off the job. While his fear might not have weighed as heavily in his deliberations about the course of his life if he were still a single guy, in the story he told of this time he had just become a father. As I sit back in a comfortable chair in his downtown office, scanning the shelves of clinical books behind him, Patrick squints his eyes while recalling the period of decision making that came with the birth of his daughter—now more than twenty years ago: "That was a real significant change in my life. In my work setting, I had a couple of experiences where I was physically threatened. So, it was if I'm going to do social work and be broke, I might as well do it where it's going to be pleasant and safety for my family will be less an issue."

Patrick and I talked for several minutes about how he felt confronted by a genuine terror of gangs in the Detroit area and by an increase in drive-by shootings in the 1970s: "It was those forces driving things. Up here was an area of vacation that we had come to a couple of times. We didn't know anybody. I guess, like us, people are coming to a place with no connections and staying and *making it work* because they're *committed* to the place itself." Here Patrick speaks of commitment in terms of being emotionally devoted to place itself and the promise that it holds for another life—this one free of fear. This promise ultimately draws people like Patrick and his family to a place where they have no connections but pledge to "make it work."

Sitting in the deeply wooded backyard of his recently purchased home in a small neighborhood among the scattered developments of modest homes in the plains west of Traverse City—not far from Carl and Liz—I listened to a local artist while two wood thrushes called to each other in the background. Martin is in his forties and lives alone. Before moving to the area he had been coming up for several years seeking inspiration in his work. Like other lifestyle migrants, Martin recognizes the importance of finding a place that is personally satisfying—regardless of what else one does. He recalls how he felt living Downstate: "I was finally realizing that I wasn't really happy there. I wasn't being so successful that it would make up for not being where—in my heart of hearts—I wanted to be. I figured that if my life was going to be moderately unsuccessful, it might as well be in a place that I loved rather than a place I didn't."

As I have already demonstrated, physical place—as well as the idea of place—is immensely important to lifestyle migrants. One reason for this importance is what appears to be a genuine effort to seek what human geographers and other scholars have called the *therapeutic landscape*—a healing experience through personal connection to place. As defined by the geographer Wilbert Gesler, who first coined the term in the early 1990s, the concept should broadly focus our attention on "physical and built environments, social conditions, and human perceptions [that] combine to produce an atmosphere which is conducive to healing."[5] It is within this broad conceptualization that I have found meaningful application in my own work through discussing the importance of place—understood as both physical and ideological in nature—for individual and collective health. Therapeutic landscape has become an important theoretical contribution to health geography, whose emergence as a specialized field parallels an earlier turn by cultural anthropologists generally away from a limiting perspective of place as merely the physical space or bare material context within which cultural practices take place. Rejecting the notion that place is a largely neutral setting—a container within which social and cultural life unfolds—ethnographies within the anthropology of health, for example, have for some time presented a dynamic, relational view of physical and mental health. This view holds that well-being involves complex interactions between people and their social, cultural, and material environments.

In recounting their narratives of relocation, lifestyle migrants routinely search for compelling ways to express the importance of place for personal well-being and identity. I was captivated on that springtime afternoon by the particular way that Martin, with his artist's passion, described his powerful sense of place. He began by evoking his earliest feelings about being "called" to the arts and about his personal struggle to face what he believed that calling would mean for his life. As it turns out, early misgivings were warranted as that pursuit would challenge him deeply. It would also bind him inextricably with this place where the landscape became a fundamental part of his self.

> A sense of place was very important to me as a kid. I know that to be true. Early on I . . . [*sighs*] recall feeling that I had a calling—in the religious sense—to be an artist. Even as a child, I didn't feel qualified enough to meet the needs of this calling. So, I felt a conflict and did my best to avoid it. My idea of artists was that most were poor, had unstable relationships, and went through a lot of grief, angst, and misery. Though I didn't feel at home in suburbia, I felt like I wanted to be comfortable in life the way that suburbanites are comfortable. I avoided the calling as best I could by living that life. Finally, though, I had to fulfill my calling because I got a little crazy—life

began to come apart for me. I understood intuitively that I had to paint. So, I got to work doing this thing that I didn't feel capable of doing. In finally responding to that, I knew that I had to respond to what was really in my heart. And landscape was it for me—it always has been. This place became very inspiring—it's a place that I'm in love with. It's hard to point out exactly what it is because there are so many different fascinating and wonderful environments that I can feel a thrill from looking at, but around here it's something about the light and the atmosphere. It's just the shape of things—the textures and colors.

As used by anthropologists, such a notion of landscape as evoked in Martin's account is understood as a culturally mediated production, a symbolic transformation of our personal environments writ large. Such an understanding takes into account humans, the anthropogenic environment, and the manner in which this milieu is conceptualized, symbolized, fashioned, and experienced in different places and times. Similarly, the landscape concept is used in health geography as a metaphor for a complex layering of personal and cultural understandings, history, social structure, and the built environment that converges in particular places.[6]

Weighing a Heavy Decision

Lifestyle migrants who undergo prolonged periods of searching and those who experience a more sudden personal change that precipitates relocation seem to share a process of weighing where both attempt to make sense of often conflicting desires and different life choices. For those undergoing extended searching, weighing may be a highly formalized process involving widely ranging research into many aspects of the decision. It may involve detailed lists of pros and cons—as in the legal pads I kept hearing about—that are reviewed periodically by would-be lifestyle migrants as information is gained and as feelings evolve and have different bearing on the meaning of that information for any potential decision about relocation. Decision making can be a lengthy, ongoing process where the lists are revisited as a kind of "reality check."

Kathy, an area native, and her husband, Dave, who is from the Detroit area, had lived in Traverse City for several years as a married couple at the time of my fieldwork. Dave's work frequently takes him on the road. The need for Dave to do much of his work elsewhere compels them to reevaluate their decision every so often—wondering if it might be better for them to live closer to where he needs to travel for work. They approach this reevaluation methodically.

> KATHY: We have these discussions, you know, with the legal pad in front of us and "*Down*state" on one side and "*Up* Here" on the other and list things out like income, housing, and people—because all our relatives are down there too. We have no relatives here.
>
> DAVE: [*laughs*] That may be a good reason to stay here.

For Mike and Denise this process of weighing takes on a similar methodical, calculated form. Mike describes the way he and Denise worked their way through the decision to relocate and to completely change their lifestyles from one centered on his career with a large corporation to one dedicated to building their own small business.

> We went through a series of evaluations where we just listed pros and cons and places and assigned numbers. The company would have moved me to Denver or Albuquerque, but my mom and grandma had moved out to live in the [San Diego] area by me. I didn't feel like I could move to some other foreign place and drag them along so we realized that—if we're going to move—we were going to move back to Michigan. I'm the only child. There's no other family for them to be around. That was one of the very weighty factors for here versus when we looked at Portland, Denver, or Salt Lake City. We tried to rank them by the factors that are in *Places Rated* like education, recreation, jobs, health care, and those kinds of things. Then you add in the emotional factor and try to come up with an answer. We went through that many times.

Ben and Kelly also embarked on a long, fairly systematic process of eliminating potential places. This process grew out of their early commitment to each other to forego potentially more materially rewarding and socially recognized career moves in order to emphasize the lifestyle choice they made to live somewhere with high quality of life that fit their vision of the ideal place. It is not only a process of research, learning, and compromise among many options but also a negotiation between one another as they weigh.

> BEN: We sort of had worlds [their different lives and backgrounds] colliding. So, we said let's entertain the notion that we could live someplace else. I remember one evening in particular where we sat down and started listing out criteria about places—things that we like. Some of these were absolutely opposed to each other. For example, we said that we want to live in a small town, but we want ethnic diversity, good schools, and a nice library. We want four seasons and to be able to do stuff in the winter, but we also want to be on water. We want to be able travel, but we don't want too many people coming to visit. We want an airport. Basically, we want all the services but none of the hassle. We wanted to have a community that we felt would be a good place to have our own family.
> KELLY: We looked at schools, the housing market, and the financial market. We took those things—knowing that there was no utopia out there—and said, "Okay, where do these kind of places exist or where do we think they might exist?" We took the US map out [*laughs*]. . . .
> BEN: The idea was that we were going to identify a dozen or so communities, to do some research, and visit one per month for a long weekend. We started this long before we were married. We would usually leave on a Thursday evening

and get to where we wanted to be on Friday while businesses were still open. We'd go around and get a feel for the place, have dinner, and then plop down and have a beer someplace to talk to the people there—kind of chat them up a bit. Before we left we'd get the Sunday paper and read that on the way home and talk about houses being in this price range, what the want ads looked like, and the editorial section to see what this community was about—were they flaming liberals, staunch conservatives, or what?

A lawyer now with his own local practice, Bill describes another careful process of getting to know a place. He is in his midforties and has children approaching high school age. For Bill the process is akin to building a court case. In this case, it is about having to justify the move from a highly successful and relatively secure position as a full partner in a California law firm to heading out on his own in a small community of Northern Michigan. Is this a defensible position?

On the day we first spoke at his legal practice in a lovely old brick building in a quaint bay town spread out along the sparkling water of Grand Traverse Bay that had helped draw him here, I spied several large binders on the tabletop near us plainly bursting with paper. They looked like family albums or scrapbooks where each one was, seemingly, assembled with great care and reflection. At some point during the conversation, he hefts one with consideration and slowly hands it to me. Its substantial weight catches me off guard, and I nearly drop it to the floor. He winces momentarily—clearly protective. He explains that for years before his move in the late 1980s—just in advance of the Internet age—he subscribed to local papers from the area. He wanted to read about and develop a feel for the place. The newspapers would be sent cross-country in big bundles with more than a week's worth of news tied up inside. Pouring over these stacks, Bill collected stories that reflected what he understood as the *character* of the place. He was trying to get to know it. Ben and Kelly too sought to know the ethos of a place through their weekend-long visits to prospective hometowns. In addition to the local papers shipped to him thousands of miles away, he spent hours in libraries researching—and requesting through interlibrary loan—dozens of academic articles on urban to rural migration. As I flipped through the binders, I recognized many of the same scholarly titles that I have used in my own research. Like a lot of lifestyle migrants, Bill was putting his professional training to good use in his relocation plans. In his case, Bill was using his legal training to research an argument for moving to the study area.

He explained this thoroughness as a strong desire to know where he stood in a big picture of national trends. In this way he was somewhat unique. Most lifestyle migrants had only general curiosity about whether or not they might be part of a larger movement. For Bill, however, he needed to know that he was not alone—or even maybe a little bit crazy—for thinking the way he did. Was there *precedent* for his decision?

> I had to make sure that at least at some level I could make sense of it economically. So I started gathering material about Northern Michigan. I

subscribed to both the *Traverse City Record Eagle* and the *Leelanau Enterprise* when I was out in California. I did some other research on migration patterns, trying to understand why I would want to move and to see how I fit into the grand scheme of things. I remember in particular [an author] by the name of Jack Lessinger [promoter of the notion of "penturbia" to whom I referred in Chapter 6] who had written about the subject. I read a book of his and then started reading the academic literature on migration.

In his story, this lengthy and thorough research was entirely consistent with building a case—not only for himself, so that he could have some kind of rationale, but also so he could sell the idea to his wife, who wasn't initially inclined to make any kind of move from their sunny California home.

So in May of '86, I announced that in May of '89 we'd be moving to Northern Michigan. She sort of laughed it off. At that point we were living in California quite comfortably and enjoying ourselves. About a year later I said, I just want to remind her that in two years we would be moving to Northern Michigan. I continued my research, continued my practice, and another year came along and I said, "This is fair warning, in another year we're moving to Northern Michigan." I think that's when she began to take me seriously. We made a trip up here. We had family and friends in Michigan. It was probably March of '89 that I announced to the firm that I was moving. We wound up here in May of '89. I think if you don't approach a move like that with a little bit of discipline, you can't do it.

Reaching the Breaking Point: Narratives of Conversion

We have heard stories of migrants with relatively long, deliberative processes of weighing alternatives and reaching meaningful and consequential decisions. Despite the significance that events in this process may carry for them, lifestyle migrants like Bill tend to see them somewhat differently from those for whom there has been a clearly defined turning point in the course of their life that is often described as a more pronounced break leading to a kind of personal *conversion*.

Although conversion is typically understood as taking place more or less exclusively in a religious context, more recently it may be seen in popular descriptions of intense moments of individual crisis as well as more prolonged periods of personal growth as people move from one way of understanding themselves and the world to another. For example, the term is now routinely applied to the experience of individuals joining secular movements. In the case of feminist activism, women may describe or be described as having undergone a kind of conversion where they feel that they have come to realize the truth about who or what they are. This usage may also hold for "coming out" when applied to the experience of gays and lesbians who come to personally acknowledge and openly embrace a particular identity— perhaps for the first time—as their true selves.

Lewis Rambo, a professor at the San Francisco Theological Seminary, describes conversion not as an inner event or singular moment in a person's life, but rather as a complex, multidimensional process. While Rambo provides a heuristic, stage model intended primarily for considerations of religious conversion, I am taken by how nearly all the stages that Rambo describes have clear parallels to the experiences of lifestyle migrants with whom I have worked. As the first of seven parts of the model, *context* is less a distinct stage than the overall milieu within which change takes place that can variously facilitate or restrict individual thought and action. Familiar to the stories of many lifestyle migrants, the *crisis* stage entails a kind of break or rupture in the status quo, taken-for-granted world involving what Rambo terms a "trigger" through the interaction of both external and internal forces—factors that contribute to action and change.

For those destined for an experience at least akin to conversion, this crisis is followed by a *quest* wherein the individual seeks new sources of meaning. In this stage we see a good deal of individual variation in response to crisis in terms of its intensity, duration, and scope. The next two stages in Rambo's scheme, *encounter* and *interaction*, more directly fit religious conversion as they involve contact with advocates of an alternative ideology. It is possible, however, to think of these stages as a generalized joining of those on the quest with different ways of understanding the good. Basically, I can find parallel here with the variety of ways that lifestyle migrants come to challenge—in some way—the status quo. In a *commitment* stage, lifestyle migrants can be seen to make their decision and lay the groundwork for reorienting their lives while adopting a new lifestyle—as we saw clearly described in the story of Carl and Liz, who made a promise to each other. In the final stage of *consequences*, there is not only a culmination of effects of the experience but also ongoing assessment of the new orientation where individuals evaluate whether or not it is viable. This stage is consistent with what I have described as weighing, which—as we have heard above—continues as an ongoing personal negotiation in the lives of lifestyle migrants well after their relocation.[7]

For those who experience something approaching the *epiphanic*—a moment of profound realization that may emerge out of the "crisis" stage in Rambo's scheme—it may appear by their own account to be incongruous with the rest of their lives. Unlike those from whom we have heard from so far in this chapter, there was no formal or conscious decision making prior to that moment. In relating their relocation narrative, these lifestyle migrants mark certain parts of these stories that in hindsight appear essential to setting them on the road to a turning point or break with the past. Susan's case is a good example of this particular narrative understanding. She was in her midthirties at the time of our first conversation in a conference room at her place of work near downtown Traverse City. She was in a relationship with a local man from a farm family with deep generational roots in neighboring Leelanau County. They were planning to have a family. Susan grew up in metropolitan Ohio and relocated to California in her midtwenties to ride the rising wave of the Silicon Valley tech boom.

The shift in Susan's sense of self and the nature of the world seemed sudden and practically inexplicable in the moment that it took place. Today, however, she recognizes it in the context of changes not only going on in the business world around her but also inside of her. In retrospect, she sees her crisis as part of a longer process. It was the changing economic reality of high stakes software development that was increasingly dependent on bottom lines and shareholder satisfaction and her own loss of faith in the meaningfulness of the work to which she had earlier committed herself.

> I had gone as high as I could go and didn't want to go any further—I was not willing to play the games. It was very isolating because the whole company was being torn apart. The president was being ousted and the vice president of sales—my boss—was being kicked out. I was all alone with these new guys telling me that I'd better get out of their way because this is what they are going to do with the company. It was unbelievable! I lived in this beautiful house up in the mountains. I thought my life was there and everything was going good. But within a two- or three-day period, it was like: "I'm going home." For the first time in my life, I realized that I just couldn't keep going in this direction.

She explains the break with the understanding that time and emotional distance has given her:

> I walked away from five thousand stock options. They all thought that I was going to a competitor: "Oh, you must have another job." There was all this gossip going on. I was, no, I'm *leaving*. "Well, what are you going to *do*?" I didn't know. I didn't work for five months. I went out there [California] with all this energy and ambition, and I hit a point where I couldn't go on that way—money isn't everything. When I left, I didn't know what I wanted to do. I was thirty-some years old! What I did know was that I needed some kind of distance from the computers and the craziness [*sighs*] and everything, you know? It was kind of like an epiphany [*laughs*].

In this way, we can see how lifestyle migrants who undergo more abrupt change leading to decisions to relocate can go through a process that can be likened to conversion. In what may at least seem like a single moment, they describe going from one point of view, way of believing, or moral orientation in the world to another. Their descriptions of this experience are like that of an epiphany—Susan even uses that term. I do not mean to suggest that these more sudden turns are always in the form of an unexpected perception of the essential meaning or purpose of their lives, but there appears a distinct moment where a critical realization takes place—as in a *crisis* stage. This realization is the turning point and the beginning of a transition—or *quest*—which, as an individual process, can unfold with relative rapidity or be much more prolonged in nature. In more protracted cases, lifestyle migrants may come to understand that they are finally fulfilling what seems like a promise made to themselves at some point in the past. In this way, a lifestyle *commitment* appears to serve them just as well as those who show themselves as being far more methodical and deliberative in their decision to relocate and whose stories do not entail the quality of crisis that we see in the tales of migrants like Susan.

Not surprisingly, there are differences in the amount of time people need to react to personal watersheds. As we have seen, some will almost immediately take action to bring about change in their lives while others bide their time by taking small, incremental steps in a manner parallel to the methodical weighing we have seen in other cases. Regardless of how they choose to respond to the crises, they remember in great detail the physical conditions—as well as the features of the time itself—during these pivotal experiences. Some seem to have them as a kind of slow accretion of events causing a final cascade when the volume of experience reaches an apparent threshold or reacts to some kind of catalyst and they realize the need for change. Others may also have this more gradual accumulation, realized later only in hindsight, but are pushed over a threshold by some kind of singular event.

I first met Alan—from whom we've already heard—when my wife and I were looking for a place to live while I conducted research. During a planning visit, I called about renting an apartment. A local real estate agent walked me through the building. Answering her questions in polite conversation, I described my reason for moving to the area. As I spoke, a man emerged from behind the kitchen counter, where he had been quietly making repairs. In paint-splattered coveralls, he gripped a putty knife with an expectant stare that unnerved me. I involuntarily took a step toward the door. Why would this scruffy handyman show such interest in my research? As it turned out, he and the agent were husband and wife. In what would become a familiar story line, they described how they had left well-paying jobs in southeastern Michigan a few years earlier. Alan and Beth were two more lifestyle migrants who had moved to the Grand Traverse region. It was in this move that Alan became a self-proclaimed "corporate refugee."

In a subsequent conversation, Alan described having felt stuck in his life. After a number of years of self-doubt about the direction his life appeared to be heading, he was ready for something to challenge his still entrenched position. There was an existing connection to Up North and this weighed-in on his decision making. Although there is a long process of accumulated experience and choices, it came down to a single moment that he could recall with great clarity. In this moment, everything shifted, and the weight of meaningful possibilities tipped an inner scale that pushed him to embrace change and make his own lifestyle commitment. His crisis reached a moment of clarity that lead to the experience he relates below.

> Some people experience a vacation and say, "Boy, I'd love to live in Hawaii." Some people have their vacation, and they think, "Oh, that'd be great to live here wouldn't it?" Well, I was coming up [to Traverse City] on weekends. I felt, gee, this is *different* up here. There's something that I can't quite put my fingers on. I was not able to identify it, but I can look back and reflect and figure it out. I remember driving down [a tree-lined road outside of town] one day and . . . I was making a decision. Beth and I were having problems. She was going to move Up North—I wasn't so sure. So I was driving and I started looking around—looking at the trees changing colors in September. Why would I leave all this for what I got down there? Maybe I should leave all that for what's up *here*. I remember that day as clear as a bell. I was driving down the road looking out the window and I realize that I'm fucked up.

I need to keep all of *this*. I apparently have to give up something to keep all this. So you finally say, I'm forty-five, am I gonna make it to sixty-five? Am I gonna make it to fifty-five? Am I gonna die from an ulcer or a heart attack?

Watershed moments like Alan's drive down a tree-lined road in autumn may act as catalysts that compel people to make decisions about the course of their lives. They may make lifestyle commitments and relocation decisions based on these promises. For Alan, the event was an ultimatum delivered by his wife. These events can include such seemingly positive experiences as the birth of a child or a promotion at work as well as those more widely considered negative experiences such as a death in the family or being laid off from work.

A psychologist and writer with whom I briefly worked on a popular press article early in the project, Victoria Secunda found that after the death of parents, adult children—including those already in middle age—went through an important shift in their identity. In research for her book *Losing Your Parents, Finding Your Self: The Defining Turning Point of Adult Life*, Secunda found that regardless of the quality of their relationship with parents, 70 percent of those interviewed felt liberated after their parents' death and driven toward finding greater self-reliance. She also found that the experience of losing one's parents left many emotionally unmoored. Indeed, it meant the ultimate loss of a childhood home and the experience led a significant number to completely reappraise careers in a search for meaning that redirected and oftentimes rejuvenated them—even while causing some angst and confusion. After the death of parents, more than half the people in Secunda's study changed careers—sometimes relocating geographically in the process—perhaps freed from a fear of disapproval or direct obligations of care.[8] Mike made the point of sharing with me that he had made his dramatic break from a corporate career to making pies shortly after the death of his father—something that he considers significant in hindsight.

Another lifestyle migrant relates her story of a traumatic shift to simplify her life in the aftermath of a personal tragedy. Barbara describes her prior work: "I used to sell electronic components, mostly military, but had several commercial accounts. A very demanding job! But then I had an accident. I was run over by a pickup truck and couldn't work. I told my husband that now was the time to move if he wanted to. We bought property, sight unseen, sold or gave away most of our belongings, and relocated." Within months they were living in a remote cabin, completely "off the grid." As a child, she had moved first from Detroit to Los Angles, California, in the wake of the race riots of the early 1970s. Now as an adult, her decision to move to rural Michigan coincided with the very year racial violence struck that city hard and left people stunned and reeling with shock. Not surprisingly, she said simply, "I will never return to either city or any other metropolitan area again." What appears to occur in these watershed situations is that these individuals reach a point where they feel that they are out of normal time and given pause to reflect on the meaning and direction of their lives. It becomes an opportunity for assessment not unlike what we know as the culturally constructed midlife crisis.

A self-conscious and articulate informant with whom I spoke early in the project, Jim perhaps sensed my uncertainty about where I was going with the research. He offered a bit of reassurance by explaining to me how his own story of reevaluation and relocation was quite typical of what he heard among others who had moved to the area. A middle-aged man with grown children and former executive of a successful software company in southeastern Michigan, he moved to the area in the early 1990s and eventually ran his own national consulting business from his modest home in rural Antrim County. During one of our conversations, he relates the drama of his own crisis.

Jim describes a brutal layoff from the company that he helped build. The experience helped him to realize his need to have greater control over his family's life rather than depending on the company to always be there. This was a theme common to many lifestyle migrants, regardless of whether or not they experienced a layoff. Like others, Jim used preexisting connections to this place as a way of "falling back," as he put it, in order to recover—or as we clearly saw in Martin's story—to heal. We hear about this particular strategy from both Alan and Jim, who each owned cottages in the area that became places of personal refuge. Jim used a family cottage this way until he got back on his feet after his layoff. Ultimately, these cottages may be expanded—as in Jim's case—to become full-time residences and sometimes the sites of home businesses as well. As I will discuss in Chapter 12, entrepreneurialism among lifestyle migrants is high. "We are typical in many ways. We owned a place Up North. When there was a life change we decided to forego the city life and move *up*. You're going to hear that from a lot of people—that same story. Something like "Well, we had a cottage up there for a lot of years, and then when the plant burned down . . ." or "The kids graduated . . ." or whatever—some kind of life experience after which they decided to move Up North. That's what happened with us." Consistent with the theme of conversion, Jim experienced a critical disruption and fundamental breach that lead him to seek meaning and embark on a personal quest.

> My life ended as I had known it to be—my *career* life. Fortunately, I was able to draw on a deep reserve and solid foundation. I knew that I wasn't going to be in corporate America any more. It was so brutal. We were in this meeting, and there are only three of us: My boss, the president, and me. My boss says to me, "Ah, Jim—you're done with the company." I say, "What do you mean done with the company?" "You don't work here anymore. As of tonight you don't have any life insurance, you don't have any health insurance, you don't have any pay, you don't have anything." It was just three months ago that the president stood up and told the sales staff how these people we're working with [are] the best of the best, blah, blah, blah. It was like milk and honey coming out of this guy's mouth—that's why it was such a surprise.

Jim recalls the very moment when he knew there was no going back. He could only move forward to a life as yet undefined but as self-reliant as he could make it: "I knew the moment—it was like an epiphany—where I knew that my life was going to be different. I was never going to let that happen again. I was never going to put myself in the position where someone could hurt me that badly, that fast."

In a voice that seemed to echo this crisis of faith and breach of social contract, Peter described how it was necessary first to find distance from his everyday life before he could make the radical change that he knew he must take in order to keep his life "on track." This involved taking what was at first considered a temporary break from the routines of work in order to refresh and revive the mind and spirit. His break came in the form of a paid sabbatical in which he was able to fundamentally question where he was going with his professional career. This opportunity allowed him to make the decision to reorient and relocate.

> I used that time for study, reflection, and reading, but I think I knew when I left that I wasn't going back. When I left the TV station in Detroit, I knew I would never go back. It was a sad decision because I had made a commitment to news that was different than the commitment most people make to their job. I was disappointed, disillusioned, unhappy, and upset that I had to give up what I considered to be a life's calling, but I couldn't find a way to continue. I could not find a way to operate in television journalism—it has just changed as a profession. I had to find something else.

When Peter found that he had reached the end of his career, when he found that he couldn't find a way to continue that life any more, he focused on starting over. He knew above all else that he wanted to live Up North. At least that made sense to him, and he would do what he could to "make it work." As with other lifestyle migrants, it was like fulfilling a lifestyle commitment. In Peter's case, this promise was made through the act of purchasing land in rural Leelanau County years earlier. Perhaps he had thought that land would be used to build his retirement home. As it turned out, however, it became a place of early refuge—what might be called preretirement—where he could launch a new career as a small business owner.

> Even when I was in Detroit and celebrating the city I still sought this *outdoor* feeling, this Up North sense of things. I'm not sure what it is—buying fresh asparagus or fishing for trout. My work had given me that same sense of calling. Once that work became impossible to do then the chance to do something else in the *place* where I had always sought to be was present. I had bought this land and come up here for a long time, so my wife and I just decided that we were going to do this and find a way to make a living after we got here, which is what a hell of a lot of people do when they come up here.

Like many lifestyle migrants, Peter is very self-aware of the meaning and significance of the decisions he has made that have led him from one life to another—leaving behind one career for another, one place for another—in order to find a more personally satisfying place both physically and metaphorically. Relocating in order to pursue a new lifestyle is a fulfillment. Sometimes it may not be until many years later in life that this promise is kept. It may not come until the waning days of working life, and in this regard it is not all that different from what we might expect from traditional retirement.

My conversations with Alan often returned to the theme of retirement in which he speculated what it might mean for someone who left a seemingly life-defining career well before typical retirement age and who continued to work after relocation. Alan left his job as a gray suit clad corporate executive making over $100,000 a year. What was the man without the suit? So significant was his corporate ensemble that he jokes about "indoctrination into the suit culture" of the large company that he worked for. He recalls, "One day I showed up wearing a brown suit and I was just kind of taken off to the side and told, 'We don't wear brown suits— it is blue or gray. Don't you ever go to headquarters in anything but a blue or gray suit. And that's dark blue or gray, Alan. Do you understand?'" Today you do not see Alan in a suit of any color. He is content to own and manage rental properties as well as be the coverall-clad maintenance man I had met during my search for an apartment. In the cool weather, when we began our regular conversations, he appeared in uninterrupted flannel. When I would see him about town, he would be rambling around in a beat-up red pickup truck that he joked allowed him to be "undercover." By this he meant he could blend into the local baseball cap and Carhartt wearing, pickup truck driving crowd. Nobody would ever suspect him of his former suited and Towncar-driving life. As you may recall, I certainly had no such suspicion upon our first meeting when he emerged from behind the kitchen counter.

Though he was very busy tending to the needs of his buildings and tenants, when we spoke of where he was at that time, Alan normally referred to himself as retired. What does this mean? Like other self-proclaimed corporate refugees, he used the term in contexts where he wanted to emphasize that he has given up some *version* of himself or left behind a life or a lifestyle that he wanted to change. In other conversations, he spoke of a future retirement and thus acknowledged that he had yet to reach the end his working life. When we figure how many hours a week he put into his work since the move, it is equivalent to a full-time position.

By our calculations, Alan put in much more time doing things related to his maintenance work than he generally accounts. In particular, he spends a lot of time doing what he likes to call "running around talking to people" and filling other more informal responsibilities related to his role as property manager. He does not feel any need to account for this time as *work*. This unconcern is common among many of the lifestyle migrant small business owners with whom I spoke. "Running around" feels more like engaging in everyday social interaction, especially when one of the things which most characterizes life in the Traverse City area for migrants like Alan is that locals know each other and deliberately take time to stop and chat. There is a palpable sense of community from this kind of contact. Making time for that is important to him as it definitively helps to express and support his lifestyle choice: "That's one of my *commitments* to my lifestyle. Beth and I laugh because growing up my daughter watched me wearing suits and driving a company car, and my [much younger] son is now growing up watching me driving an old pickup truck and plowing snow, wearing Carhartts. Man, those kids are going to have stories to share. 'No, dad was this . . . !' and 'No dad was this . . . !'"

Thus, in Alan's usage, the term "retired" does not mean that he no longer works. He is making a statement about having left behind a part of his life that was defined by a particular kind of work and by the lifestyle to which that work contributed. He left a career, quite literally gave up this path, and, therefore, we would say he retired, but he had by no means stopped working. He had simply chosen to define himself in opposition to that past. But like the ambiguity his youngest and oldest children might one day have about what kind of person dad actually was while they were growing up—was Dad a suit or a Carhartt man—Alan was not always sure himself when it came down to typical categories: "To this day I don't know how to define myself. Beth has finally acquiesced to my preferred definition [or] my preferred word, *retired*. I prefer to say that [*laughs*]. I guess I'm not. I'm not retired but I find it easier to define myself that way."[9]

Freedom and Flexibility

Any additional measure of real or imagined freedom that people may have gained in today's "flexible" economy—like that celebrated by Ben and Kelly—appears to come with some cost. All too often this freedom is experienced not as joyous release but rather as absence of meaningful sense of community, increasing alienation, and feelings that lifestyle migrants like John and Katherine described as dispossession. Without clear guidance, people may feel anxiety or even fear. How do we make decisions about how to spend our time? It may be easier for people to act as if there were no options and as if they did not have a choice.

The freedom experienced by many in American society today is not what they might have wanted out of the social and economic changes in which they have—perhaps unwittingly—participated. According to the social psychologist Walter Anderson, we are all now "'forced to be free' in a way that Rousseau could not have imagined when he coined that famous phrase. We have to make choices from a range of different stories—stories about what the universe is like, about who the good guys and the bad guys are, about who we are—and also have to make choices about how to make choices. The only thing we lack is the option of not having to make choices, although many of us try hard, and with some success, to conceal that from ourselves."[10] Similarly, Barry Schwartz, another academic psychologist, has written on what he calls the "tyranny of freedom." In his view, the proliferation of choices in American life can be experienced as a burden. Although we value freedom as autonomy, when there are so many and potentially conflicting options out there, "you have no one to blame but yourself if you choose badly . . . the combination of the escalation of expectations and this self-blame are both the result of a multiplying of options."[11]

For lifestyle migrants, the desire for self-improvement and fulfillment through seeking greater control and balance in integrated lives entails a vision of the good that requires letting go in order to realize the potential self and using this vision as a means of guidance on a road toward greater personal fulfillment. Lifestyle migrants appear to prioritize place over work. Although work may remain a central part of their lives, particularly for the small business owners like Mike or Peter, decisions about work are guided by lifestyle choices from the realm of leisure as opposed to that of production. This more leisure-oriented realm is highly individualized. A perhaps uniquely American sense of freedom is consistent with this. Today freedom seems oft conceived of as the ability to construct one's own life without being forced to follow fixed standards. For many, the balancing act is ever more between a simultaneous desire for engagement with and retreat from the world, which may keep them in motion, relocating as they chase after an image of other possibilities and explore the option of elsewhere.

CHAPTER 11

Potential Self

> The conditions of time in the new capitalism have created a conflict between character and experience, [and] the experience of disjointed time is threatening the ability of people to form their characters into sustained narratives. . . . The dilemma of how to organize a life narrative is partly clarified by probing how, in today's capitalism, people cope with the future.
>
> —Richard Sennett, *The Corrosion of Character*

Although relocation offers opportunities for new beginnings, we have also seen how dramatic changes in one's life can be a source of insecurity, uncertainty, and even fear. Regardless of the underlying reasons or circumstances, even in the best of all possible worlds relocations can be stressful on relationships and challenge personal identity. For lifestyle migrants, life in other places may offer an alternative to individuals and families seeking to break from a given model of success. The potential self serves as a means for many to negotiate the harsh reality of everyday balancing between work and family obligations and economic challenges. Lifestyle migrants speak of sacrifices in their allocation of time to family, community, and self made possible by holding on to the promise of an imagined self. Lifestyle migrants are both willing and able to act on a lifestyle commitment rather than adapt to existing conditions through the imaginary of potential selves.

Here Alan describes his own fears of leaving the corporate world for a life on his own. Despite the challenges of that world, it had become a ready form of identity, provided in part through a great deal of routine. What would it mean to let go of that? "When I moved up here, we moved into the river cabin. It was only nine hundred square feet. We came from two thousand square feet, so it was a squish. We lived in there for about a year. I think what kept us there was my hesitancy to make any more moves until such time that I knew that we can *make it work*." I wanted to make sure I understood what Alan meant by the fear he said that he felt during that transitional period. I asked him to clarify.

> Financial fear. Just to make sure I could cover our costs. I was planning on staying in Northern Michigan, but I wasn't sure about taking that financial plunge. During that time did I start thinking about looking at another job? Yeah. Going back to the [corporate] world I was in. A *regression* back to where I was at. I never shared that with Beth, but I was thinking that this is

not my comfort zone. No W-2 income. You know, it was not my comfort zone. There was a two-year *transition*. I came here deliberately, but it doesn't mean that you're comfortable when you get here—you have fear.

As with other lifestyle migrants, Alan can look back on and reflect on this period of *transition* from one world to another. He sees this time in a different light and, in retrospect, understands what he was feeling.

Now I understand it. I was scared to death when I first did this. There's a lot of security to a W-2 income, having *a job*, but I remember very distinctly why I didn't like it. [There] was a lot of *insecurity*. You were battling for your job every day. It was politics, and I'm not a politician. When you come up here, self-employed and worried that you're going to have enough money— what helped me was my accounting and financial background. I laid out a budget and figured out what we needed and could afford. Now I've got it understood. I've got a steady income where I have total control—I am the one that's taking the risk and I'm the one that's expecting the rewards. It took me a couple years to understand it. I was scared to death. I had to go through a couple of annual cycles, which is my business training—you had to go through an annual cycle and see what the ups and downs are and where are the expenses. Then, okay, this is alright. I can do this.

Alan emphasizes the need to get comfortable with changes. There is a transitional period of adjusting to a new reality and personal identity that must be forged in that new place. A comfort zone needs to be created. Mike was also setting out on his own after allowing a job in corporate America to long define who he was. Both men express how the discomfort of being "on their own" was eventually replaced by an important sense of greater control and ultimately greater self-worth. Mike expresses his doubts, insecurities, and quest for control in this way. "It's one of those things where I think I'm the only one in my family to go to college. So there was at the time, 'God, am I really going to make it? Can I do it? Am I going to make it in the business world with all these big companies?' It's not like I didn't have any confidence, but there was doubt. You've made it and supported a family in the corporate world, but can you make it on your own—flat out on your own? You can't hide behind the corporate identity. Even though I was a manager and had a certain amount of autonomy, you're still a part of a large corporation."

Then, tellingly, Mike takes his two hands and thrusts them into the space between us—making a motion as if he were grabbing a large bowl: "I wanted to get into something simpler that I can get my hands around." Then his hands slowly come apart with his palms turned downward as if he was going to rest them on a table in a gesture that appears as if he is searching for Hannah Arendt's metaphorical table: "I want to get something where I can control my own destiny instead of just sort of floating with this company."

We can see how experiences such as those described in Alan's and Mike's stories reflect beliefs and behaviors of many lifestyle migrants that are not—as they may superficially appear—simply about coping and adapting to a new environment. Rather, they are primarily about a need to use destination places as a means to reconcile different visions or versions of self and family that are purposefully set apart by an act of relocation and a particular notion of the good underlying the lifestyle commitment pursued. For many migrants, something like Alan's little cabin on the river helped to construct the necessary space to do this essential identity work.

Many lifestyle migrants commented on their uncertainties and fear about whether they could "make it work." Both Alan and Mike relate their experiences of adjusting to life outside the corporate world and the exultation of freedom combined with fear and doubt that comes from wondering if they could make it on their own. For those lifestyle migrants whose stories are closer to that of George and Allison, the *risk* of relocation and pursuing a lifestyle dream is even more present. The couple is in their midforties and newly married. Prior to their relocation, they lived and worked in suburban Detroit. George recently had gone to school for computer programming. After checking help-wanted ads for a few months in Traverse City, he took the first available job in his new field—despite the fact that there might be more opportunities and higher salaries within his field of programming in other geographic areas.

Although it was with a small company, George was confident that there was a real chance to explore his creativity. It turned out that because of their size they required people to wear many hats. Unfortunately, they determined that George was not a good fit because they did not consider him capable of taking on additional managerial responsibilities. In the end, there was nowhere for him to go within the ranks of the small software company. Despite this, George and Allison both seem pleased with the fact that they still called Traverse City home. When we met to talk about their story, George had just been laid off.

> GEORGE: I saw an ad for a programmer in the Traverse City area in a family-oriented company. I'm a programmer. I got an interview, and Allison and I sat down and talked about it. Even before I pursued the second level, which is okay, you're accepted for an interview, do you really want to go? The recruiter kept saying "Are you sure you want to go up *there*, because it's a big change." And we talked about the fact that coming to Traverse City would be a cut in pay. Do we really want to take a cut in pay? I guess they had a number of other candidates, and it basically came down to sitting down at the table and them saying "Hey, you're going to go from $60,000 to $40,000," and the other guys said, "I really can't do that." So the company was kind of a little gun shy at that particular point. So every candidate they got, it was "Don't forget to ask them this," and "Don't forget to ask them that."
>
> ALLISON: And make sure your *spouse* is actually into moving. Cause a lot were not really all that willing to get up and move. They would have a glowing career down *there*, and they'd have to give it up.

Allison, however, had no glowing career Downstate. In fact, not only was she generally unhappy, she had no reason to feel at all secure about her job. Nevertheless, leaving her job and putting all the eggs in one basket—his basket—was not an easy or comfortable move. It was a risk even if her prospects were less than clear should they have stayed put.

> ALLISON: I was working in Livonia [a suburb of Detroit]. I was an adjustments coordinator for a third-party workman's comp insurance. I had left it before we moved up here because [*sigh*] I was not happy with it. The company was going through too many changes—they were going under. They didn't know if you had a job or not. I was getting tired of it. I wasn't moving in the company and the people I was working with were just complaining all the time. So I decided for my sanity that I just had to quit.
>
> GEORGE: We had lived together for four or five months when she did this. We were making some pretty good money between her income and my income. And then she quit and that hurt, but we survived.

George was also highly motivated to get out of the work situation he was in before moving to Traverse City. He describes his unhappiness before their move as well as his sense of opportunity in a new beginning. Relocation to a new job and a new place, however, turned out to be a tremendous risk with real consequences. He had been working in an upscale suburb of Detroit, but while he liked the work, the situation was unpleasant.

> The vice president of the company was my boss—who is now the president of the company. It was a very small company, and there were personality problems. He would badger his employees . . . call you "stupid" in meetings and say "What are you crazy?" I don't need this *shit*. The new company I came up to [in Traverse City] encouraged new ideas. But unfortunately the fit wasn't there. They told me this about two weeks ago. So I was laid off after almost seven months. They gave me a severance package, which they usually don't do—they felt kind of guilty, plus they gave me three grand to move back [Downstate] if I want to.

I wanted to know how much time George and Allison planned to give themselves in order to get back on their feet here in the Traverse City area. Was there a point at which if they were not finding work in his field that they would take whatever they could get? In the meantime, how were they managing to get by?

> We paid off all the bills that we owed with the severance—June's paid off [and] July we have to come up with. The money that they gave us to "go back home" we've used to buy a car and a computer. So, we're living off our savings. We've got about four grand right now. Allison's got a job. What she makes right now is enough to get food and keep gas in the car. Mine will have to take care of the rent and car payments. The weirdest thing about life is that it just *is*. Life happens. You think you're in control, and then you realize that you're not. My maturity level at forty-five years old is different. If this had happened to me ten years ago, I'd have been devastated.

Despite the cushion of a negotiated severance given out of apparent guilt on the part of his employer so that they could go back Downstate, they instead chose to use that money to regroup and focus on staying in the area. He invested in a computer and some software central to his field in an attempt to remarket himself. Another chunk went to buying Allison a car so that she could commute. Funds were quickly drying up. Allison found herself struggling with limited options for work. Eventually she was forced to join the ranks of working-class laborers. It is enough for now simply to get food and keep gas in the car. Allison relates her story of reentering the workforce at a different level than what she was used to: "[At first] I had stayed home and then we decided that we needed more money coming in. So, I was the Easter Bunny at the mall for a day until I got claustrophobic and couldn't wear the bunny head anymore. Basically, I was in it for five hours, got out, got in the car, rolled all the windows down, came home, and cried: "I can't do this anymore, don't make me" [laughter]. Then I signed up for temp service jobs. But they weren't coming through, and we needed the money, so now I work at McDonalds!"

Allison and George came up here to follow a dream, but when he was laid off they found themselves caught without the income necessary to sustain the dream. They had not given up, but they know it will be a struggle and that they may not be able to remain. I have talked with other people who have moved here and who feel that they cannot live the dream of being Up North—even though they live here. Inspired to relocate to the area for a variety of noneconomic reasons, but with less education than most lifestyle migrants, many younger singles end up working in the area's large service industry and feeling somewhat left out of the Great Northern Dream. In many conversations, I heard them speak of long strings of service jobs while struggling to find a place to live that they can afford and where they do not have to live with roommates. Many of them find that they are always holding out for the summer tourist season, making do through the winter and waiting for the boom when work is plentiful and labor is often short. The challenge is for finding year-round work and a way out of what one person called "playing job of the month."

In talking about this way of life, it is perhaps not surprising that people see a gap between where they feel they are and the social status enjoyed by the people that they frequently serve who have also come here for the good life. They complain that there is "nothing in the middle" between these two positions and that you "either work in McDonald's or you 'have a career,'" as one somewhat bitter young woman told me. This fits with the understanding—held by many living in the area—that you must either be from a well-connected local family or be well educated in order to find a way to the "inside," where good work is available. Stuck in the job hopping of seasonal service-based work, one woman in her late twenties who had come up here to take pleasure in life Up North told me, "It's about learning how to play the game, otherwise you either *are* 'them' or you work *for* 'them.'"

Not all these marginalized migrants are twenty-somethings looking to start a life in a fun, outdoorsy place. There are also plenty of college-educated members of the middle class who have worked for years in reasonably well paying professional jobs only to find themselves in situations where they must join the working poor if they wish to stay in the area. We saw that Allison found herself in such a position after the "basket" that held all their eggs unexpectedly broke. This was also the case with Linda. A single professional woman in her early thirties, Linda followed her dream of living Up North by seeking a transfer within the financial company she worked for. They had some local branch offices in the Traverse City area. Unfortunately, hitching a wagon to the company to take her on her dream turned out to be a risky move. Her job was cut when the company was forced—by the bottom line and shareholder demands—to restructure. Unless she would consider moving out of area, she was unable to find another position. When we first spoke behind the stunning new Traverse Area District Library overlooking Boardman Lake at the heart of Traverse City, she was only visiting the area. At the time, Linda had already been forced to return Downstate. She had moved back in with her parents and was living in a kind of limbo—not knowing if it was possible to keep the dream and return to the area that she had grown to love beyond all her expectations. She returned periodically to "stay connected," as she put it, and to look for job opportunities. I continued to speak with her during these occasional visits. I wanted to know how committed she was to coming back to Traverse City and whether she had set some kind of goal about when that needed to happen, or not.

> I know that I'll have to [set a goal]. I really thought that I'd have something by now. It's been very difficult for me. I know that to stay here I'm going to have to take a cut in salary, and I understand that. I'm trying to get prepared, but I also don't know how to make my bills on seven or eight bucks an hour. I have to find a room to rent, and what do I do with all my stuff? Then I have to put that in storage and pay for that. I paid $625 for my apartment in Traverse City, and I have seen some for less, but even if I go lower, I'll have some kind of car payment because cheaper rentals are far out of town and require at least a fifteen-minute drive. I did get offered a job, but it was eight bucks an hour. I'm adding up all the numbers, and I really want to stay, but how do I do that? I won't be able to pay my bills. I'll live off my savings, but my savings are only going to go so far. Being in a position like this is like you don't really belong anywhere, you know?

In one of our conversations about his choice to give up a life's calling in journalism for a life Up North as a small business owner, Peter commented on how he feels there must be many people chasing dreams up here who cannot seem to make it work. While most lifestyle migrants stress the need to feel connected with place even before they speak about the necessity of work, Peter feels that you must enjoy what you are doing not merely where you are. Is it enough just to be here? When faced with the possibility of just "getting by" on whatever work was available, Peter recognized that place may not be enough to make a life meaningful—even if it had inspired a lifestyle dream. "What's most important is what you're doing, not where you're doing it. And while where you're doing it may be wonderful and ought to be wonderful and it's an important part of the picture, if you're in the most beautiful place in the world and you're doing something that you loathe then you shouldn't be there—or you shouldn't be doing that [laughs]. I can think of a couple of people now that just seemed to wander from job to job who really want to be here but can't find a way to be comfortable."

In these discussions of struggling to make it work despite the difficult adjustments that many lifestyle migrants must go through on personal and economic levels, the conversations often turn to consideration of what it means to be happy or successful. Participants in my project related their own—often evolving—ideas of what happiness or success meant to them. Not infrequently, they separated out different ways of looking at success—from both personal and professional angles. For those who have left their careers and now are only "just working" and doing whatever it takes to stay, the only notion that matters is one of personal importance. In Alan's case, he left a well-defined, high-rung position on the ladder of corporate America for his own cobbled together business of managing and maintaining rental properties. Success by Alan's standards became a completely personal definition that reflected a decision to relocate for lifestyle. "How much of life and where you live do you just accept and say 'I'm going to be happy.' Happiness is what you make of it. The notion of success in the corporate world is how much money you make and what position you hold or how many people report to you—climb up that corporate ladder. But what is personal success outside of your work? Is there personal success outside of your work? When you only look forward to the weekend—when you can drive down that tree-covered road—is that success? I think you have to reassess what is success. Success is being able to live your life the way you want to live it."

In what is perhaps the most inclusive, articulate statement by any lifestyle migrant that I have heard on the idea of success, Susan relates the common tension between potentially competing, individual notions of success. As we heard previously, Susan's life took a turn when she had a crisis experience in a Silicon Valley software start-up that shifted her understanding of the world of corporate work. After she had left that company, pulled herself together, and moved up to Traverse City, she had achieved personal success by virtue of making it work. She had been able to pursue her dream of living Up North in fulfillment of her own lifestyle commitment. She achieved a life composed of a strong personal engagement with community and place.

On the other hand, however, like Alan in the beginning of his new life without the suit, Susan still had demons within. She fought ghosts of a career past that continued to assert themselves—causing her to question her very identity. If she is not struggling to climb the ladder of professional success then who is she? Echoing Peter's doubt, there is the question of whether personal attachment to place can be enough. Susan shares Alan's early fears that go to the very heart of identity, but she also shares his understanding that there is potential strength in *letting go*. She describes a major component of nearly every story of lifestyle migration. Her words express the challenges of fitting in when the full scope of what life Up North means becomes real and when pursuing the dream becomes a full-time job of making it work: "*Professionally* I'm struggling. I'm thinking I'm way below my potential and what I've *done*. I've done a lot of things already—some incredible things. But *personally*, I'd say that I am successful. I've been struggling for many years to get into this space where I've *let go* of a lot of things—that was what I wanted. So, I'd say personally it is success."

Much like Alan, Susan also felt she needed to separate success into distinct parts, one professional and the other personal to correspond with what seemed separate domains—one work and one family or, perhaps, self. I wanted to hear more about this from Susan. Did she feel that she *needed* to make this split?

Well [*laughs*] I have to. I'd be feeling like a total failure these last couple of years if I didn't. I would have gone somewhere else if I felt that I was failing. It's *ongoing* too. You have this idea that this is what I want to do, this is what I'm prepared to do and what I'm willing to do, but it's a daily thing. You're constantly saying, "I can't do this anymore." Not just financially. Who am I if I'm not sales director or whatever? The question "Who am I?" was constant. It was like you'd sway back and forth, back and forth, so even if you'd think "Oh yeah, I want to give up my career," you don't realize how *entwined* it really is with your whole identity. The reality is that every single day when you wake up it's not as easy as it sounds. It is *everything*—the crowd you hang out with and the friends you have, the family, the people that you date. To fit it into this who you think you are is just a constant thing. It gets easier only when you *let stuff go*. That's how I feel right now. When I say personally successful, I feel like I'm just letting it go, you know? It's been three years of Do I? Don't I? Can I? Can't I. Can I really? Because if you let it go, who *are* you?

We have heard about a fear of letting go of an identity that has given some measure of shelter—even as it might have nearly suffocated. This was evident in both Alan's and Mike's stories. In Susan's case, she had come to rely on external valuations of worth and allowed her professional roles and successes to define her not only to others but also to herself. What would it mean to pursue the good life where this meant that profession would become secondary—simply a means to be here in this place? How would she redefine herself or be redefined by others?

The dream I had was living up here in a little cabin [*laughs*] where I was outside all the time with kids and a dog. Implied in that vision was the fact that I was going to be surrounded by people that understood, accepted, and valued me. I didn't realize until I got up here that I had always allowed people to value me based on my professional successes, because that's where I was comfortable. When I came here with all these farmers and construction workers, I just felt I didn't know who I was—they didn't know who I was. It was so frustrating. It was like "Don't you know who I am? Don't you know what I've done? Don't you know what my skills are?" It was feeling like an outsider. These are tight knit communities of extended family around here. They're huge—ten kids—and they've been here forever. I was an outsider.

Susan describes the sometimes difficult transitional period of personal growth that lifestyle migration can provoke. Susan is realistic in that she acknowledges that her image of the potential self may require adjustments. Adjusting your expectations is okay. The struggle leads to understanding and the ability for her to let go of the past and to other ways of valuing and determining her self-worth and measuring success. "It was very difficult to figure out who I was because I hung on to this professional relationship. I walked away from that—gave it up. So, I had to find some other way to fit in. I didn't know that I was coming up to deal face to face with who I am. I thought I was going to come on up and find a little niche and be successful and everybody would see. I'd have my little dream world." As so many lifestyle migrants have related in their relocation stories, starting over requires both physical and emotional distance and the changed circumstances that open up new possibilities for individual discovery. Finding a place of refuge is about recognizing this fact and knowing that the place itself should provide some kind of support. At the very least, it should inspire.

For most Americans, the meaning of life has become a continuing effort to be one's own person and to—quite literally—find oneself. This has perhaps long been the quintessential American task. The freedom characteristic of today's flexible society is largely without guidance from traditional sources for making choices. Although the business sector may flourish on the freedom and flexibility of an apparent new world order, for individuals and families it offers little direction for making the choices that will determine how we live our lives. In the context of trying to make a family, what amounts to a breakdown in the old consensus requires that everything be rethought literally from the base level, the individual, on up. Robert Bellah explains that the tendency of Americans to view their primary task in life as a long struggle to find themselves as individuals "in autonomous self-reliance, separating oneself not only from one's parents but also from those larger communities and traditions that constitute one's past, leads to the notion that it is in oneself, perhaps in relation to a few intimate others, that fulfillment is to be found. . . . In this perspective, even occupation, which has been so central to the identity of Americans in the past, becomes instrumental—not a good in itself, but only a means to the attainment of a rich and satisfying private life."[1]

Many Americans appear to recognize the importance of finding structure in order to ground their account of self in some meaningful framework. For lifestyle migrants, this involves a kind of therapeutic quest for community.[2] The very act of relocating for community and the awareness of the relative uniqueness of challenging status quo notions of right action for how to prioritize life decisions that places work first and place second provide lifestyle migrants with a kind of framework for understanding their lives. An insurance professional in his early forties with a young family, Matt frames his life in terms of the decision to relocate and the lifestyle choice his family makes.

> Our family has been coming to the area for many years. Like many people we know who vacation here, we have all schemed and dreamed about how to live in the area. But in most cases no one has had either the job opportunity or will to really sacrifice what I call the "urban lifestyle myth" and make the

move. I was a professional in the insurance industry for sixteen years in various capacities. After selling my business in 1999, my wife and I decided to make the migration Up North. We had no job plans, and I was giving up on the career that I knew for sixteen years to live here. We went through all the discussions, pros and cons for kids, careers, and etcetera and took the *leap of faith* to move and live in this place. Why? We were attached to the natural beauty and wanted to live the lifestyle and pace of a small community.

Like other lifestyle migrants whose stories I have shared, Matt and his wife went through years of dreaming, weighing, and waiting. Finally, they decided it was worth a degree of risk to give up a career for their lifestyle commitment. It was taken as an act of faith in order to have the Up North way of life in a small Northern Michigan community and to act on their existing sense of attachment to the place from earlier family vacations.

We have been here now for three years. As most things in life there are positives and negatives. It is still often very interesting that we actually walked away from our old lifestyles and to live in this particular place. The comments we get from friends and old business associates are sometimes very interesting. Most seem to be envious of where and how we live but can't or won't make the jump themselves. Some can't believe that I walked away from the traditional business world and career path at age forty—sometimes I can't either. Unlike most of my friends, whose career or job dictates where they can or will live, I am just the opposite. We decided *where* we wanted to live and worked our jobs and incomes backwards into it. That seems like quite an unusual approach to many people. I still get offers and tinges of motivation to go back to what I grew up with and lived and sacrificed [for] for so long, but the force to stay is strong. When those instincts come to the forefront, the sense to *repress* them steps right up to smother them back. As a family we decided to make less money to have more lifestyle. I know my children better than I ever thought I would. The desire to live in this place is real, strong, and sometimes, unexplainable in tangible terms.

Like other lifestyle migrants, Matt and his wife continue to focus on the importance of the lifestyle choice, the therapeutic potential of community and place that weighs more heavily than even some kind of "instinct" to return to a past life of sacrifice devoted to a more traditional model of putting work first. In Matt's account, *instinct* is another word for the past career ghosts that haunted others like Alan and Susan. In the final sentence of this excerpt from our conversation, we see how Matt invokes a powerful, intangible, even mystical quality of place, a kind of enchantment that holds his family here, repressing any desire to return to another world and another life. In this way his own story echoes the travel story of Cyrus Howard related in the brochure described in the Introduction. This enchantment, a commitment to place, becomes a restraining force that keeps him following a path more consistent with his current notion of the good.

Emotional Downsizing

Having time is essential for self and family. It is vital for recreative activity. Martin, the local artist who came here to find spiritual nourishment and healing, reflects on this with the intuitive insight and sensitivity artist's sensibility affords:

> It's really important. It's partly that artist aspect of me that needs unscheduled time. I call it hang-out time. There's something re-creative or creative, whichever way you look at, that comes out of the unstructured that can't come out of structure. I don't know why that is, but it's the creative part of one's own life. I don't think that that's just true for artists. It's some sort of intuitive, creative process that makes psychological as well as physical health—the more I can get the better. I'd love to have even more time alone. Not alone as in isolated sense, but alone from the demands of work.

For many moving to the area, relocation involves re-creative time through the very act of making a home. Some inherit family cottages in dire need of repair in order to make them suitable as year-round residences. Others will make a project out of an old farmhouse purchased at auction. Perhaps unconsciously they recognize that in that foundation and weathered frame there is an opportunity—as one couple found—to restore or even redeem something in themselves. This redemption may be had through the dedicated personal revival of a dilapidated old homestead.[3]

While Americans have always been motivated to move by a desire to do better economically, there is also a tradition of choosing relocation as a way of getting in touch with what might be called the higher things in life that include one's most inner self. And so it has to do with not only material gain but is also about fulfilling potentials. For many people, however, the promise of a potential self may be all that is possible given the real constraints on time that are characteristic of today's families.

As we have heard in the stories of lifestyle migrants, many feel a profound sense of having lost control of their lives. This is most acutely experienced in the loss of time for self and family. As people experience the "time bind," they may choose to delegate increasing amounts of responsibility for those things that they would have once done themselves. This delegating can be described as a kind of domestic "outsourcing" wherever parts of the family production process are shunted to outside contractors. Others are paid to carry out the acts that would have once been among the defining aspects of good parenting. Meanwhile, parents hold on to hope that the situation could be different, more consistent with inner desires and even enduring cultural conventions and expectations, if only time and circumstances would allow it. Beyond this, families are less responsible for the production of entertainment or recreation. Today leisure activities are produced ready packaged for consumption by families and individuals as part of the supposed "simplicity market" of time-saving goods. As a trend, this furthers the shift in meaning making toward the sphere of consumption and away from production while leaving people less skilled in the important emotional work of being a family.

As corporations continue to physically downsize by cutting costs through lay-offs and scaling back to improve efficiency, many workers employ a personal-scale *emotional* downsizing in a roughly parallel process.[4] We see this route of emotional downsizing displayed in the stories of lifestyle migrants who talk about how before their decisions to change their way of life they had wished their family could do more activities together, but who tended not to given time pressures. They refer to how they wished that they could hike or play board games together. These are things that would require them to be "unplugged," as I heard increasingly during the latter period of my research. However, pressures of everyday life and work too often meant that people felt they needed to lower their expectations about what was possible. In this way, the actual and the ideal grew more and more distant so that things like watching a movie together becomes "enough"—it comes to "pass" as an acceptable substitute for idealized family engagements. Over time, emotional downsizing might be followed by emotional "outsourcing," where children are left in the supervision of hired caregivers who engage them in the kinds of activities parents wished to do with the kids, but felt they could not given other pressures.

In this unfortunate process of attempting to deal with time pressures as well as the additional strain that the looming threat of layoffs imparts to working life, people may deny not only their own emotional needs but also those of family members. This environment of overwork and anxiety requires all to engage in making do with less time and with less of the attention, relaxation, understanding, and support that greater time can afford. The course of emotional asceticism is taken as one defense against having to acknowledge the human costs of the loss of time at home. Time is personal capital. The degree that people have this for themselves is the extent to which they have the capacity to invest personal energy in their families, in communities, and back into themselves.

Here an important distinction must be made between the kind of minimizing involved in the act of downsizing emotionally and the desire for simplifying one's life. Minimizing or downsizing in this sense should be seen as adapting on a personal level to potentially destructive conditions. It involves choosing to be "less" in a personal sense in order to potentially gain more financially even when this gain is acknowledged as a sacrifice. It is coping with the status quo, not challenging it. Simplifying, however, involves scaling back or restraining economic commitments while emphasizing what people might refer to collectively as the simple things in life, core values. There is a profound shift to finding other measures of success. It involves a back-to-basics mentality where questions of enrichment come to the fore and people begin looking more closely at questions of personal growth, family, and community.

With a shortage of time in the present with which to do the vital emotional work of family, emotionally downsizing workers can only imagine that they would fully meet emotional needs if only they had the time. In this way, an imagined future provides a place for a potential self with the time and skill to do what is known to be right and who dwells in fantasized harmony. In a way, this kind of possible future gratification is consistent with the old model of working and putting off until retirement. In the imagined future of the potential self, the kinds of important productive activities that a family must do in order to function in a way consistent with cultural conventions for the good family is gradually replaced by mere promise. This potential self is not unlike the families that we "live *by*"—the imagined family of possibilities and promise—as opposed to that family that we "live *with*" and actually find ourselves in.[5]

In their darkest hours, when all hope seemed to consist of distant imaginings of potential selves or possible families, lifestyle migrants who sacrificed prior lives to work allowed themselves to envision other times and other places. The option of elsewhere held the promise of transformation, re-creation in another time and place. It appears that for lifestyle migrants there is an understanding that small places like those in the Grand Traverse region effectively concentrate experience and thereby the collective memories of family members. This concentration of experience and memory may then serve as important physic "glue" that helps hold a family together through the bond of common experience and understanding. People live, work, and play in small areas, and without intention more can be shared. Lives seem less fragmented, more integrated.

Emotional asceticism characteristic of lives fled is expressed in many stories of lifestyle migration. Despite appearing to offer a defense against the personal costs of loss of time at home, it merely entails adapting to these conditions. Downsizing emotionally does not require one to challenge conditions. Lifestyle migrants may be distinguished from others who struggle in that they chose not to emotionally downsize. While emotional downsizers might imagine a potential self, lifestyle migrants attempt to realize this self through changes brought by a lifestyle decision to relocate and begin again. Lifestyle migrants have the ability, wherewithal, and the will to "let go" and to realize potential selves.

It's Different Up Here

Leisure may be defined simply. *Webster's* identifies it as "freedom provided by the cessation of activities; especially time free from work or duties." As a more complete expression of leisure, we know from discussion above and studies like those of historian Cindy Aron that vacation experiences can become exercises in self-definition.[6] By allowing individuals to break even temporarily from everyday routines and experience a departure from the normal, where one enters a space of other possibilities, these occasions allow people to explore new or different dimensions of themselves and to conceive of other prospects for their lives.

In a manner similar to research concerning work and family boundaries and construction of individual and family identity, scholars of lifestyle migration describe relocation behavior as typically entailing an ongoing project in order to emphasize that it is much more than a single act. This is consistent with assertions by the sociologist Anthony Giddens that self-identity has become an increasingly reflexive project—something on which the contemporary person must continually reflect and work.[7] This concern is central to recent tourism studies with which those of lifestyle migration share close kinship. In part, this closeness comes from the fact that many destination areas for lifestyle migrants, like those of the Grand Traverse region, are historical or emerging tourist hot spots that actively engage, as communities, in construction and marketing of place as a consumable lifestyle, whether to short- or long-term consumers. Importantly, scholars such as Michael Hall and Allan Williams address a close connection between tourism and migration in their discussion of "tourism-informed mobility," where prospective migrants are exposed to particular places that they come to idealize and imagine as future home.[8]

For many lifestyle migrants, the connection between prior experience as tourist and their eventual decision to relocate in order to pursue an idealized vision leads to ongoing construction of self-identity after their move in terms analogous to those experienced and expressed by vacationers.[9] As we have already seen, however, lifestyle migrants like Susan are quick to distinguish themselves from tourists, whom they characteristically come to see negatively as an unattached and potentially destructive force that may damage the very qualities of place that attracted them.[10] Second homes—typically used for family vacations—can play an expanded, transitional role as migrants segue from occasional short-term visitor to full-time resident.

As I discussed earlier, Up North is taken as more than relative geographic location. Up North is seen as a state of being. Not surprisingly, out of the total number of 128 people interviewed for this project, eighty-two vacationed here either as children or adults. As in Jack's case below, many came to family cottages, where they could take on what I call a *cottage persona*. As in Jim's case, many of these second homes were converted into primary residences when migrants chose to leave careers or otherwise start over. Many of these houses had already been in the family for more than a generation, while others were purchased years earlier in anticipation of retirement but previously used only on an occasional basis for temporary escape.

A professional in legal services in his midforties, Jack explains that for his family, coming up to their second home is an opportunity to be different and break from the everyday of struggling to balance work and family in his practice Downstate. While at the time of our conversations he was still working in the Detroit area, they planned to relocate and were at that point spending long stretches in the summer and weekends throughout the year at their second home near Traverse City. Jack is sensitive to the difference between these two worlds because he was at that time straddling them. Sitting in the newly finished log cabin, perched at the head of a long sloping meadow commanding stunning views of a river valley below, we talked about what it meant to be Up North as opposed to back Downstate. Checking first to see that his cell phone would not disturb us, he described experiencing a kind of "split personality."

> I'm completely different when I'm here. I don't lift a finger when I'm Downstate. I don't cut my own grass. I don't shovel my own snow. I probably don't have a hammer in my house, but here I'm constantly outside. It's funny though that those things that I hate to do Downstate, I'll do here—like I don't read Downstate for enjoyment. It's just completely *different* here. I don't understand it. We don't take naps Downstate. My wife and I will take naps *up here*. The kids are different up here. The kids do needlepoint. The kids don't do needlepoint Downstate. I don't know what it is. If it's being by

yourself where you can open your windows and sit around in your under-
wear and look at the bay and do needlepoint. There's no question it's a
totally different life. I don't know whether it's this environment or what. It's
the people and the open space.

In a different conversation, I was speaking to a middle-aged couple with grown
children who have just relocated to the area. We discussed what this relocation
meant for them on the spacious porch of their small chalet-style home, overlooking
an open field where deer are ambling about—grazing in apparent content. Frank
and Cindy came and went out of the house engaging in our conversation in a tag
team fashion as they tended alternately to iced tea, a ringing phone, and a needy
cat. Down at the edge of the field and beyond the road, the cerulean-blue Torch
Lake—widely noted for this distinct color—stretched out before us. From time to
time during our chat, our eyes drifted and lingered on the lake's sparkling waters
in the evening sun. I have been told, with some authority, that it is considered
one of the most beautiful lakes in the world. Looking at it in this moment, I was
inclined to support the assertion. As we sip our tea, they talked about the kinds
of things that living here has both required and allowed them to do. As Jack suggested, it is not just about different kinds of activities, however, it is also about an
entirely different sense of self.

> FRANK: Before I moved up here, I never lifted a saw in my life. Now, I'm building
> fences and all that stuff. Most of those fences down there [*he gestures to the field
> of deer below us*] are all built with a handsaw. Finally I got wise and bought a
> chainsaw.
> CINDY: I think he's got a lot of talents that just never surfaced because he was
> *too busy*. So, now it's *different*—it's just totally different. It's become all about
> discovering gifts that you didn't even know that you had and the desire to
> work on and develop them. It's been a much richer life—not financially, but in
> experiences and togetherness.

For Frank and Cindy in particular, but not unlike the kinds of experiences that
I have heard from other lifestyle migrants, their relocation allowed them to create a
physical and emotional space where social interactions can take place that did not
seem possible where they lived before, where they had become stuck in routines
that effectively precluded even their consideration. It is as if they not only started
over in terms of making a new life for themselves as a couple but also cleared the
way for rediscovering and refiguring old connections with extended family. Interestingly, their home is now a kind of vacation destination for relatives. In this
space—that serves as a refuge—old wounds are being slowly healed:

> FRANK: I've got two brothers that I didn't talk to for twenty years. I'd see them
> now and then but I didn't talk to them. But now one brother comes up five
> times a year for weekends. We're really close now. [My other] brother and I
> didn't talk since we moved up. He has hard feelings about something, but then
> they came up two weeks ago and we all sat down and talked about things from

when we were kids. It's like it's a better *atmosphere* to do that here. I think if we were living Downstate, I probably never would have talked to my brothers. Now we'll sit down at the table with the kids here and there, and we'll get into some pretty deep stuff—stuff I don't know if we'd talk about when we were down *there* [*he gestures by pointing in a southerly direction*]. But our environment down there wasn't the kind of place that you'd invite people over to stay. Here we say "Come on over, we've got rooms." It's like a bed-and-breakfast.

CINDY: There's healing. It's created a space. It's that dynamic of moving *up here* when you don't know anybody else, you can either become a hermit or you can reach out and meet people and even reach *back* to your family.

Cindy and Frank's story emphasizes how their relocation decision allows them not only to redefine their own lives and relationships and to discover previously unexplored aspects of personal potential, but also how it creates a physical and emotional space for reconnecting with relatives. Although they may have been closer in terms of miles before their relocation from Downstate, the rush of everyday life provided ample excuse to explain away the absence of one another in each other's lives. By choosing to break from the routines of the past driven by busyness, Cindy and Frank unwittingly opened up the possibility of new beginnings in the whole family.

Without knowing the profound importance of the possibilities created by this space, one might characterize the interactions there as a family simply spending "quality time" together. But quality time is bankrupt for the emotionally downsized and offers far too little in the way of nourishment for those starved for real, meaningful human interaction. Alan relates how he has given up attempting to manage time and personal and family needs and abandoned his prior belief in the artificial proposition we know as quality time. He talks about how he now feels that his life is a more integrated whole rather than a fragmented collection of parts loosely held together by his effort to patch things together through temporary fixes—of which quality time was one. Speaking of what were different categories in his life before, such as his role as "husband," "father," and "friend," Alan says now:

I can actually put time against them. They are all important in my life. [*stammers*] They were important before in my life, but now they're important so that this can wait. I can go be Dad for a while, whereas before you'd have to put in your calendar to be Dad or to be Mom. It's a lot different. Quality time—what does that mean? What it means is that you get this allotment of time to go spend with your kid for this period, and it has to be quality because you have this little window of time. So it had better be intense. That's a real bullshit term. Somebody came up with this term in corporate and made it more palatable so that they can get more out of us!

The very idea of quality time is a powerful symbol in the struggle against growing time pressure in private life. As unrealistic and ultimately self-defeating as quality time is, for many families it holds the oft-unattainable promise that such necessarily programmed periods of intense togetherness can smooth out the roughness in relationships caused by ever-thinning degree of real, meaningful contact and sharing. The perception that time is something like money, to be spent or saved, is fundamental to American ways of thinking about and relating to time. Time becomes something else when individuals or families begin to imagine alternative lifestyles where they imagine having greater control over time. While stressed-out workers might rely on quality time as a way of carving out at least temporary shelter for relationships, lifestyle migrants go beyond seeking refuge in time. By placing primacy on place, lifestyle migrants such as Cindy and Frank restructure their own lives in order to make a more complete refuge in both time *and* place.

As we have seen in the accounts of physical and emotional passages to new lives, the relocation narratives of lifestyle migrants relate their experience as a kind of liminality—a basic part of their process of negotiation between material and moral domains. A term to describe a state of betwixt and between, liminality comes from the Latin *limen* for "boundary" or "threshold." As used by cultural anthropologists, it has generally referred to rites of initiation or "passage" that involve certain basic elements that include a transformative period where status and identity are stripped from the individual. Influenced broadly by the foundational work of sociologist Emile Durkheim, the anthropologist Victor Turner focused his research on social processes and systems in periods of change. Specifically, he spoke of "social dramas" to emphasize the performance of ritual as well as the opportunity for change by breaking from established norms and of liminality as a kind of "interstructural stage."[11] Much like the stages that Lewis Rambo outlines for religious conversion, Turner held that social dramas have several observable phases ranging from breach, crisis, and redressive action, to a period of reintegration.

In Turner's understanding, the first of these is signaled by an "overt breach or deliberate non-fulfillment of some crucial norm."[12] Precipitated by this breach—as we have seen in the accounts of corporate refugees—the crisis stage that follows forms the critical, liminal period in which a threshold is crossed between more or less stable phases. As we have heard, lifestyle migrants who leave the self-consuming stress that they experienced in corporate careers frequently recall a distinct, often epiphanic moment—or sequence of such moments experienced over a longer period—that results from a breach where the meaning and purpose they had previously found in their work evaporates or the faith or trust they held in an employer was somehow "violated." This violation extended at times to core personal values as well. In light of these challenges, personal narratives are shaped by crisis as those who construct them attempt to make sense of new understandings while weighing options and exploring alternatives. In the following stage, they attempt to redefine themselves through forms of redressive action such as that taken in the act of relocation itself. Their relocation requires that they literally move from one life and social world to another where—in a final phase—they must find ways for personally meaningful reintegration into that new place.

CHAPTER 12

Making Transitions

Transition, 1a: passage from one state, stage, subject, or place to another: CHANGE b: a movement, development, or evolution from one form, stage, or style to another 2a: a musical modulation b: a musical passage leading from one section of a piece to another 3: an abrupt change in energy state or level.

Perhaps the most distinctive aspect of twentieth-century American society was the division of an otherwise potentially far more unified life into a variety of functional sectors splitting up home and workplace, work and leisure, white and blue collar, public and private spaces. At the same time, ideas of family, home, community, and place remained closely related and intertwined in individual thoughts. As we have seen, lifestyle migrants seek the greater balance and control they believe is more consistent with their inner selves through integrating what are increasingly fragmented, compartmentalized parts of a whole life. In the absence of guidance from traditional sources about how to achieve an integrated life, families are thrown back on their own opportunities and resourcefulness. As I have shown, place may play an important role in the attempt to integrate these domains.

The meaning of home is one category undergoing reinterpretation. Not so long ago, the home served as a private and largely feminine domain to be sheltered against a public, exclusively male domain and place of business. Although most take this for granted as the "traditional" home, this meaning of home emerged out of the effects of the Industrial Revolution at the second half of the nineteenth century. For many today, home does not function well as a haven or refuge from the outside world—if indeed it ever has. The American public are perpetually reminded by television commercials and print advertisements that being "with it" is about being "connected," "linked," "hooked-up," or "networked." Home is becoming less and less a place of return and more and more a point of departure. At the same time, the consumer economy responds by attempting to make everywhere a home away from home. People may be advised to get out of the house so that they can find refuge somewhere else—away from all the distractions there.

A transition in the meaning of home was also exhibited in the "domestication" of the workplace, including the relaxation of corporate policies on dress and the use of office space. There have also been growing numbers of people who turn their work into home by moving production into the home space and who now work out of their houses. This is something made ever more possible by technological change, changes in corporate policies, and broader cultural changes in how home, work, and the relationship between these domains is conceived.[1]

Despite the onslaught—or perhaps in response to it—there appears to be a rise in home-centeredness in American culture. A walk through virtually any department store today is educational. In aisle after aisle one finds the promise of instant "homeyness" in products that often aim for "retro" design styles that blend elements from the past as if to throw us back aesthetically to a time presumed to be somehow more wholesome. Retail and service industries aspire to provide things that help to "make a home" fast, easy, and cheap. Kmart's deal with Martha Stewart's multibillion-dollar industry at the end of the twentieth century was indicative of this need for "homemaking" now made accessible to not only a price-conscious middle class, but also an aspiring working class.

Paula is a single woman in her forties who moved to Traverse City to start her own business as a personal chef. During a conversation with Paula in her first new house in a neighborhood of Traverse City, I asked her what she felt "home" was. She began to think about it as where she grew up. Her words also express a sense of disconnect, of being unmoored, as the only place she had known as home—her childhood residence—was sold. Now she has the chance to try to make a home here in this house: "For a long time, the house that I grew up in was home. My parents sold it three years ago. That was the only house that I ever knew. I guess it can be a place where it's just that you *feel right*. Sometimes it feels like you've been there before. It's just comfortable. Like when I was looking to buy a house here— it's completely intangible."

For Carl, home is something experientially defined. In a manner not uncommon for lifestyle migrants, Carl describes an intangible connection to this place through his family's summer cottage. As previously noted, eighty out of 128 project participants vacationed in the area at least once—many while growing up. Nearly a quarter of that number had some kind of family cottage or second house. The cottage became home for Carl while the house Downstate was merely a place of residence. To use a tired but appropriate cliché: home is where the heart is. Carl's heart was unquestionably Up North. In the manner that Thomas Bender suggests that we define community, home is best defined by a quality of experience.[2] Here it is a feeling of belonging to something greater such as we heard from Susan in her reference to the "old boat stored back in the woods" and an enlarged psychic space. Here Carl explains:

> I was one of those that spent summers and weekends in the area growing up. Having been in the Detroit area, my family was lucky enough to have a summer home. But this was always home, whereas going back to the house near Detroit—it was always the place where you worked, went to school, and resided until you had an opportunity to get away. So, this was always *home*. I'm not sure why that was. I grew up outside Detroit, and that was the *residence* of my family. This region was where I felt at home. Liz and I wanted to return home. I think that is why we chose to move here. It wasn't because of jobs because we did not have jobs. We figured that jobs would follow. We were prepared to create our own employment, and it has worked

out. I think home is a place where you are closer to the land and feel more of a connection to other people and other living things. It is a place where you can count stars—it's amazing to me that people actually live in places where they rarely or ever see stars. This was a place where you could see stars, so it had a magical quality. Maybe it is sort of primal, in that sense of returning to something basic and deeply connected to something that has been going on for centuries. I never felt that kind of connection in the city.

In the 1990s, with the primary home being overrun, many in the middle class worked harder and longer to provide money to pay for second homes or vacation houses that might serve as a refuge where everything else is intentionally left behind. These places do not share the dual daily burdens of being both house and home. I know Downstate families who choose to spend important family holidays in their second houses—making temporary migrations to these places. In this way, they accentuate the distinct, ritual nature of the events set apart not only temporally but also *spatially* from everyday lives.

Locally, these homes are decorated in the cottage style now characteristic of Up North and virtually codified in lifestyle magazines such as the local spin-off publication from *Traverse Magazine* known as *Northern Home*, a self-proclaimed guide "For the Way You Live Up North." They are filled with stories of family memory—becoming heavy with the artifacts of past vacations, days of beachcombing, childhood dreams, and the symbolically charged flotsam of the celebrated good life of days spent, as one local author has put it, "in the North Lane."[3] I have heard many people explain that the more traditional cottages still contain no television or have standing rules regarding their limited use—presumably to focus attention away from the outer and other world.

As we have seen with Carl's remembrances of happy summers in childhood and Jack's reflections on a distinctive *cottage persona* that so differed from his sense of self Downstate, people develop a greater sense of attachment to these second homes than to their primary residences. These removed places—as refuge or asylum from the everyday—can serve as vital personal repositories for evidence of familial and friendship bonds where *remembering* is now a central cultural practice and the essential ritual of a healthy family life. According to the cultural historian John Gillis, "memory has tended to migrate to summer or weekend houses."[4] Not surprisingly, much of the housing development in the Traverse City area is second home construction. As I have previously noted, these second homes may become primary residences in retirement or in lifestyle migration both deliberatively chosen and—as in cases like Jim's brutal layoff—due to sudden shifts of direction that can come without much warning.

While addressing the emotional as much as more widely discussed legal issues surrounding inheritance and use of second homes in her book *Passing It On*, Judith Balfe describes how what the sociologist Peter Berger terms "mediating structures" play an essential role—though taken for granted—in people's everyday lives. These structures, in the form of a variety of small-scale, voluntary associations—as well as the second home itself in Balfe's argument—serve to mediate or "stand between" individuals and families and the macro-order institutions of society such as political and corporate entities that operate at a vast scale. Following Berger's analysis, Balfe finds that despite the unparalleled power of the macro-order "mega-structures" of contemporary global society, they are experienced by most persons as so unreal that they "cannot generate the stable values that [they] need to live by—whether they work to sustain those mega-structures or work to oppose their effects."[5] Further, Balfe states that "without stable values, people can scarcely trust and build upon their own experience, having enough consistent faith in the future that they believe in the efficacy of their own actions in ensuring 'for themselves and their posterity.'"[6]

In Chapter 9, we explored place as a central element of lifestyle migration. In Chapter 11, I began to explore time as perhaps of equal significance. Much of the questions about lifestyle, quality of life, and livability deal with how we spend our time and, in particular, how time supportive of meaningful, nurturing relationships with the family may be lost. We frequently hear discussions about how as our time and attention is increasingly divided, we lose quality in the way we spend our time. Paula moved here after a series of lifestyle moves. She spoke to me about home and further about her sense of "pace."

> My lifestyle was going out every night. Most of us hung out and rode horses, and to pay for this habit we all had second jobs at night. We spent too much time working and cramming fun in with too much partying, drinking, and smoking. I decided to move and start over. It became a completely different life—a different pace. I went crazy the first month after moving Up North. I stood in line at the bank and would tap my foot and snap my fingers and say "Come on come on, I've got somewhere to go!" And everybody is chatting, and you couldn't do anything fast. I was used to something different. I didn't even realize it until I went somewhere else. I was forced to slow down—after all, this was going to be where I lived.

Temporal and spatial relationships between home and work have been changing in response to broader social and economic changes in the United States. The ongoing negotiations of individuals and families between conflicting personal, familial, communal, and workplace obligations and their meanings present a challenge for lifestyle decisions. In one of my conversations with Mike, he expressed how important it was to be able to share his work life with his family. The separation that had existed before his lifestyle migration was forced on him from the outside as part of living in a world of corporate work. He genuinely wanted to *integrate* work and family life, but prior to relocating and recreating his life, he was unable to fulfill this desire.

For Mike and lifestyle migrants as a whole, the good life should be integrated—both spatially and temporally. It felt right that he should be able to share the lessons of work with his children and to have them partake of a greater share of his own life. Using skills from his management positions in corporations as well as his engineering background, he constructed a life and business plan that would allow for that lifestyle. In a small-town places, the more focused geography and tighter layout of the community could encourage greater mixing through the scale and sheer proximity of everything—work, home, school, and recreation: "I wanted something where we could *integrate* the whole family with everything just a few minutes from home and no freeways to worry about. This seemed to be a good combination of that and the cost of living is much less than out there in California."

While not every lifestyle migrant starts his or her own small business, Mike's path has a strong appeal for those seeking a greater sense of control over the circumstances of their work and family life. As suggested by the work of economist David Snepenger and others, entrepreneurial tendencies are strong among lifestyle migrants given their strong desire to claim control over the domain of work while financing commitments to improve quality of life.[7] Interestingly, several of Mike's former coworkers from the defense contractor in San Diego—who either opted to voluntarily downshift like Mike or were involuntarily downsized—ended up starting their own small businesses. Mike heard of one guy who landed in the New Orleans area, took the concept of a breakfast restaurant, and hired a locally popular restaurant out in San Diego to help train him. Now he has a series of restaurants in the Florida Panhandle and Mississippi. Another guy went to central California and opened up a chain of fish taco stands and has a very successful business based on a concept borrowed from the San Diego area—from where they all moved after leaving the large defense contractor for whom they all work. While not everyone went on to own their own businesses, Mike suggested that the others ended up in small companies, applying their skills to often quite different projects. For example, one individual ended up working with a golf company to develop a better putter using his aerospace experience.

After the dependency created by corporate life—like some of his past colleagues—Mike was looking for greater self-reliance and the ability to determine his own self-worth through this control. Pursuing an integrated life is an attempt to bring the family that we live *with*, the family of our everyday, and the family we life *by*, the imagined family, closer together and possibly to merge them. Although lifestyle migrants stress the need for integration, it should be recognized that this desire is pursued in the context of an overall commitment to a lifestyle defined by notions of simplicity, balance, and overall "quality of life." The sociologist Christina Nippert-Eng has found that when work and home become inadvertently integrated without the careful consideration given this process by lifestyle migrants, people will expend great amounts of energy making and remaking boundaries in an attempt to maintain control. Her study suggests the potential risks of the integration of what many people actively endeavor to keep separate spheres of work and family life.[8] For Mike, greater integration meant bringing a sense of greater control to a life that was already fraught with insecurity.

> I think in a big company—like where I was before—sometimes you can question your own self-worth. Every day that you go in, you may do some phenomenal white paper on a new program that will bring in business, but there are days of just pushing papers across a desk. You don't see the results of what you're doing. So, the question is what *value* did I provide today? You can see that *here*. Every day you can see what value added. It's on a simpler

level. From a self-worth or self-confidence level of providing value to my family and building a base or a foundation that will endure, each day I can feel that I am making a step in that direction. We bring the kids in—so I'm benefiting their lives by having them work here. My son is eleven, and he can help customers. He can run the cash register. He makes pie dough with me on Sundays. My daughter is sixteen, and she can do any job here. She understands the value of good work and responsibility. Those are things that affect the whole family. My wife is not full-time anymore, but she is in here to work on holidays as needed. It's a real family group. We all feel better about where we're going.

Owning his own business means the possibility of fully integrating and balancing his work and family life. He sees their relocation as clear pursuit of this lifestyle and the concrete, methodical steps needed to eventually realize the potential self that has guided his family through the transition. In Mike's case, he planned for a number of years and had the skills and resources to make it work. Most importantly, this is not a short-term solution to contemporary work-family problems like relying on artificially constructed quality time. It is a wholesale rearrangement with positive long-term consequences for self and family.

It enables us to spend more time with the kids. It's not just two weeks of vacation. You can take more time off and go places with them during the slow periods. It affects the family and it affects the psyche. We made the right move. There's more control of your destiny. [*Speaking of his work before now*] What would happen if I lost my job and how will I provide for my family? Up until my mother passed away in August, she was my bookkeeper. My mom had failing health over last few years. She wasn't financially independent to retire, so we provided her work. So, I got to see my mom—in addition to my kids—involved in the business. It was all integrated into the lifestyle. The business became part of the lifestyle versus somewhere to go for eight hours a day to make a living. It became part of connecting with the family and connecting with people and the local folks—that is very satisfying.

Integrating, balancing, and connecting. This is the stuff of lifestyle dreams and the offspring of its promises. Owning his own business afforded Mike the possibility of doing these things for himself and his family. It is also about integrity and truthfulness. It is easy to see in the same way as understood by lifestyle migrants like Mike as being true to one's self and to others.

You can connect with real people. In my old job you had your customers whether they are a national laboratory in New Mexico or the Department of Energy back in DC. But here I have people coming in every day to us from the neighborhood and we *connect*. We can contribute to the schools. We can give back. In San Diego, the company used to do this on a larger scale, and here we can do this as a business and contribute to charitable educational projects. That feels really good. It's not the name of a business behind a glass window where people wonder what goes on in there. People know what goes on in here. People *know* us. We know the people, and it is a small community where that can happen, and it's the type of business where that can happen.

For Liz and Carl, the question of integration and balance was more than a dream—it had become necessary to personal health and well-being. It became a matter of identifying fundamentally important things and finding a lifestyle that integrated work, family, and community in a place believed to support a lifestyle commitment. During one of our conversations, Liz spoke to this.

> I think it probably was a health issue. I had been diagnosed with a form of manic depression and had spent several years trying to get all of that straightened out. Once I was healthy enough to make some decisions, I realized that my career path just wasn't working. How I lived was a lot more important to me as well as being able to live in a place where I could take care of myself better. I don't think it was like I was diagnosed one day and the next day we said "Okay, we're moving to Traverse City." But the experience of going through that changed the way I look at things. [Now] I go for a walk every day in the woods. That's just one pretty simple thing that has a huge impact. My life has slowed down a huge amount. Sometimes days will go by where I don't leave the house except to take the dogs out because I *work here*. I don't think that we realized that we were in the rat race *before*. We had felt really stuck.

In an manner akin to Alan's discussion of how you just "end up" living a life and might find that life at odds with a sense of oneself, Liz spoke about their former lives before moving to the study area. I remember that Carl said to me at one point, "I'd be really depressed if I died in Cincinnati" before he elaborated further:

> I think we both just *ended up* there. We had both gone there for school and then stayed, and so it wasn't a choice that we really made, and then we got involved in a life there. You know how things happen. You find jobs or create an occupation for yourself. It wasn't a place either of us chose to be in other than for school. I think getting out of that, taking the plunge so to speak, and taking the risk of moving just freed up a lot of energy. It just changed a lot of things besides just our occupation.

As we have discussed previously, Liz and Carl describe their journey to this new place and the life they have created here as a journey while being careful not to have it characterized as some kind of *escape*. We could describe their relocation as being about leaving behind certain things—such as fear—but it was more clearly about value affirmations in this place as a kind of refuge for personal growth and healing. Carl explains that integration and balance takes on spiritual dimensions far beyond personal finances and economic considerations.

It wasn't an escape to come up here. It certainly wasn't easy. On a really fundamental level it was driven by a more spiritual . . . *quest*. It was not so much trying to escape but actually trying to *integrate* more balance into our lives. It is a big word. It probably means looking at what are our core values. What is it that you can take with you that is really meaningful? Certainly family is at the top of the list but [also] community and a sense of place where you can live a life that is in *balance*. I think that is a very hard thing to do. So, I look at spirituality in that way of trying to integrate all those facets of life and to put them in balance. It's actually having the time to spend with family and friends, to think, to read, and to enjoy the out-of-doors. Those are things that money cannot buy. It is said that the best things in life are free, and the other part of that is that is that the best things in life you cannot buy for any amount of money. You know people are thinking that I can buy time or I can go away on vacation and buy a little piece. I think we came to the realization that we could not buy what we have up here for any amount of money. Moving here was the only way to really integrate our lives the way we wanted and to have this lifestyle.

They assure me that moving here was the only way to really integrate their lives in the way they wanted to and to find the lifestyle that was consistent with the core values they identified as a necessary part of a spiritual quest or journey that has led them to this place, seeking a holistic sense of self. Carl describes:

In Cincinnati we didn't have family so there wasn't that pull to remain there. But we had friends, and we had a network of colleagues and acquaintances that we considered a community, and we had really fantastic employment opportunities and choices. We both had businesses that were very successful. All the ingredients were there to keep us there but yet there was something about the lack of connectedness to the land. For me, it had a lot to do with community and living in a place that I could *believe in*. I found myself saying that again and again that I wanted to live in a place that I can believe in. For me that means a sense of belonging where you don't feel that you are an outsider and a misfit in the larger society.

Together these testimonies indicate the increasing importance of "home" for self-identity in the face of broad changes. Lifestyle migration is one response to the perceived assault on the home. As we have heard in the accounts above, it is an attempt by some to gain greater control of *both* place and time through relocation.

Making It over the "River of Doubt"

Lifestyle migration is a story about transitions. It is necessarily about movement. People leave certain places for others. They also pass from one stage to another in their lives defined, at least in part, by lifestyle choices. Their lives have a certain rhythm. Certain passages are punctuated by key turning points that can lead to periods of potentially tumultuous change and eventual calm. Personal development and growth is part of the narrative of these lives. We have heard stories of embracing and fearing flexibility, narratives of conversion, of seeking to identify core values, of letting go, of committing to lifestyle dreams and striving to follow a life path that is believed to be true to self. All these stories can be framed in an overriding concern for identifying the good and orienting oneself to this intensely personal but ultimately often shared notion of what makes a life fulfilling.

While these are conscious choices to change, transition is not always easy. For lifestyle migrants of average means, it is often a real challenge economically and personally—so many changes in so little time. The story of lifestyle migration is about transitions as people move from one stage of their lives to another from what might have seemed a life-long career to preretirement or to raising a family. The key is *deliberateness*. The changes, and any struggles to adjust, are immediately recognized as being one's own responsibility. How are the uncharted waters to be navigated to what is at least an imagined safe haven or harboring refuge of stability?

We have already heard something of Alan's story of leaving a corporate executive position to move Up North and how his narrative expresses a personal struggle of transitioning from one identity to another, making personal adjustments, and finally arriving at a place of greater comfort and self-confidence. It was about giving up the framework that had defined his identity, his former commitments and identifications, and about the disorientation that this entailed. For some time at least, it was not entirely clear to Alan what *the good* was. His relationship to the good was in a state of flux as he transitioned from one life to another, caught for a time somewhere halfway, suspended in a potentially perilous liminality. As we have seen in his account, there is movement from breaking with the past by physical relocation and a kind of moral reorientation. For Alan it took at least a year until he felt comfortable with the move and with his new self apart from a world that always provided, if nothing else, a readily available definition of self and the good. Now he is reoriented.

> The first year was a struggle. I used to wear out a horn in a car. Now I think the horn in my truck is not working for lack of use. For the first year or two that I was up here, I kept saying, what is this place? They don't work. I growled and growled. It's different. People do work up here. People work hard. But people don't have that same intensity. I was stressed like crazy for the first year or so. I was like a fish out of water. I tried hard to run my own company and smile at the employees every day, but I was just too intense. They had a hard time relating to me. But I had to have the company to be comfortable when I first came up here. Now, I don't need all that stuff. It was just that initial *break*. I just had to have faith that I could make it work without all that stuff.

While there are undoubtedly those who struggled and then left the area after a time, for participants in this project reaffirming the decision amounted to renewed vows of the original commitment to core values reflected in the lifestyle choice. As I have discussed, our cultural traditions as a society define the meaning of achievement and the purpose of human life in ways that have left the individual in a kind of liberating but potentially frightening isolation. Flexibility is the catchword and the order of the day. The ultimate goals of a good life are matters of personal choice. Being in a liminal period of transition, temporarily unmoored from a borrowed but still orienting vision and a not yet fully realized expression of one's own potential self, exposes us to the reality of our own self-doubt about the meaning and direction of our lives.

Mike sums up his understanding of this fear and uncertainty for taking the plunge into the unknown—that potentially dreadful period of transition—from the familiar path one is on to the other side, where the unfamiliar gradually clears and the new land becomes more comfortably familiar. He describes a sense of disorientation much like that we heard from Susan earlier that is concerned with identity as well as having a very spatial dimension. He recognizes that he is no longer placed on an organizational chart that locates him within a broad hierarchy of social relations and roles. In this passage, Mike illustrates the essential link between identity and a kind of *orientation*. Knowing who you are is to be oriented in moral space where questions arise about what is good or bad and about distinguishing between what makes a life worth living and what is only a distraction. "For a while [after leaving a corporate job] you don't have any sense of yourself—of where you are. For some people that's too great a void. That's why some people don't take that extra step. They can't handle it: 'I'm not on an "O" [organizational] chart. I'm not getting my annual review and my set of objectives for the year.' I don't have any of that. I take this step and I could be a complete failure or I could be okay. It's up to me to decide. Maybe [some people] don't want to decide. It's too stressful." Pausing for a moment to recall feelings that emerged around his own decision to enter "the void," Mike gestures in the air between us in an effort to give me a sense of his orientation in this space. Sitting before me he holds one hand out to his left clenched in a fist while he gazes into his right hand, held close to his face, palm up. He continues, saying "I think it takes a while from knowing where you fit *there* [*shaking his left hand*] to knowing where you fit *here* [*offering out his right hand*]." Waving both hands before him in the space between these two points, he finishes: "There's a period of not knowing." With obviously spatial dimensions as related in his account, Mike has clearly identified and illustrated the liminal that lies between what may be very differently defined identities, different lifestyles, and different locations.

Mike and Denise explain the transitional struggle as an adjustment the entire family needed to make. Children were uprooted. An established pattern of relating to one another is suddenly and completely altered. Maybe spending so much time with each other is not such a great idea after all.

> DENISE: I remember moving the children and the emotions that went along with that and having to deal with their pain. They went through a lot of pain for this move. We missed our friends and everything when we moved. We had to start over.
> MIKE: And the whole dynamic of us working together. We hadn't done that before.
> DENISE: Oh yeah. That's a whole other point.

MIKE: You don't know what's around the corner for the business. You both have the best interest of the business, but there's nobody who's laid out the map: here's what you do. So you're making decisions every day and not always do you agree on them.

DENISE: Lots of time we would agree on an issue but we would disagree on the urgency. I like to have things fixed right away, and Mike would say it would come in time, and that would send me! I was, no, I want done now, right now! I knew it was going to be a real challenge for us to work together, which it ended up being.

MIKE: It was a learning thing, but we've sorted it all out.

Although Denise felt the crisis of identity more acutely than Mike, he nevertheless went through the period of uncertainty and self-doubt in his own way. He explains that ultimately it did not really matter who he was during his transition as long as he knew that he was no longer what he was leaving behind and he had set his sight on a vision of potential self consistent with the lifestyle commitment that he and Denise had made to each other. As suggested by Charles Taylor, knowing who you are entails being able to find yourself oriented in moral space where questions arise about what is good or bad. It is also about distinguishing those elements that make a life worth living. Again showing the importance of a kind of spatial orientation, Mike explains how he got beyond the liminal to a more comfortable, self-assured place:

> You're just marching every day ahead as if you're walking along the edge of a tall building. All you see is where you want to go; you kind of don't notice that it's far down. Then again, it is like I've jumped into a pool, and I've got to swim to the other side. No matter what, you've got to swim. I think personality-wise, feeling like I'm a provider you've just got to do it. So the identity part—for the first year or so—it didn't matter who I was. I knew I wasn't *that* anymore. Now, it was just do whatever it takes to get this off the ground. Then, okay, this is going to work. That feels good now. I can see how it's going, and I can feel good about it. But the jury was out for a long time. Am I fool? Am I a success? Somewhere in the middle? What am I? You don't know.

In this conversation, Mike elaborated on the process of crossing the river to reach the other side. Again, we see the fundamental uncertainty about status and self. Am I a fool or a success? Perhaps caught between the two? We get a clear picture of the importance of being oriented. We see how this orientation is not only within a moral space of questions about good and bad, what is worth doing and not, but also how it is bound up with our actual physical *bearings* in the world and with how we locate ourselves in a moral, social, and material landscape. To speak of *orientation* is thus more than mere metaphor. Temporarily lacking a stable framework or horizon through which things take on stable significance and with which we can weigh possibilities and actualities as either good or bad,

meaningful or superfluous, left many lifestyle migrants such as Mike, at least temporarily, unsure of how to move. Ultimately, Mike could fall back on the knowledge that he had planned well and thoroughly thought through the process of
building his business. He is an engineer by training and was a manager most of
his former career, so he knows how to put together a plan that can work. While
not every lifestyle migrant planned and strategized with the intensity and degree
of deliberateness that characterizes Mike and Denise's story, the common thread
through all these stories is a need for what most referred to as *faith*. Fundamentally, it is about having faith in the decision and in the ability to make it work.
Mike explains that it is about faith in their commitment and the capacity to stay
the course.

> It's one of those things where if you're standing on a board going across the
> river and you looked down you might say, "Oh shit." But if you don't then
> you just walk across. You're looking at the bank and you don't look down.
> I really didn't look down. It's a lot of unknowns when you start a business
> from scratch. Part of that faith was seeing the Joshua Pie Company [where
> he and Denise vacationed regularly in California] succeed for twelve years
> before I even started my business. I knew that I could make it work. There
> was a model. I never really got to the point that, "Oh my God, this isn't
> going to work." I never got to that point. Maybe, this is a lot of work. Not
> like being at a desk with a secretary. So we never really completely doubted
> what we're doing. We are fired with the feeling of starting something suc-
> cessful. There's huge, huge gratification, and so I was focusing on that versus
> "what if." I think that is having faith.

What is faith? Our popular understanding would surely emphasize it as having a set of beliefs and as trust, but faith should also include an understanding of
fidelity to one's promises and convictions—it involves *commitment*. It also calls to
mind a sincerity of intent, and so it involves authenticity. And faith comes in many
forms. Mike and Denise are perhaps iconic—each in their own right. Mike represents a methodical approach. His faith comes from confidence in the plan and
his intent. Denise, however, represents what we might recognize as "true" faith—a
sense of faith consistent with our everyday understanding of acts of faith taken as
trust. Lifestyle migrants run the full range between the approaches represented
here by Mike and Denise. For Denise, faith is wholly about *letting go*, trusting, and
relying on inner guidance largely separate from an emphasis on analytical process.
Like most lifestyle migrants, regardless of the path they ultimately choose to realize their visions, Denise looks for guidance through "opening up to it" and by letting go and identifying what is understood as the true self inside. This inner self, it
is hoped, will be more stable and secure when compared to the outward self caught
in the conflicting demands of the world. Although Mike's final approach may be
different, we already know from listening to his story that he plumbed the inner
spaces of self to find what mattered before taking action and that he remains true
to his conviction. Like Carl and Liz so eloquently stated earlier, it is a question of

identifying "core values" and making a commitment to live a life that is faithful to them and that expresses a fidelity to those convictions and a sincerity of intent.

> MIKE: It's been a watershed kind of thing—a watershed event. It's been one to the other. Doing what we did was huge. It was a huge difference in self-worth or satisfaction of what you're doing on a daily basis. As far as looking at the future and what possibilities there are, it's a huge difference from there to here.
>
> DENISE: I think it teaches you that in a leap of faith, a true leap of faith, where you're really faithful, it usually works out. You calculate the risk, but then you go, okay, we're very committed to making this step and not looking back.

I wanted to make sure what she meant when she said faith. Having heard different dimensions, I wanted to see if I could focus in on anything in particular. Was faith here meant as faith in themselves, each other, or possibly some kind of coming together of supernatural forces?

> DENISE: For me, it is all of the above. For him, not so much. For me, my faith is boundless.
>
> MIKE: You need a longer tape [*referring to the fact that I was recording that early conversation on a cassette tape*] if you want to hear about Denise's faith—it's much broader than mine.
>
> DENISE: We approach life a lot differently. I'm incredibly philosophical and not terribly intellectual. It has to do with opening up to guidance; there's guidance out there that's just astounding. Most people don't allow themselves to *open up* to it. They close it off and then think they have to do everything themselves. You need to get in touch with something deep inside you.

Regardless of faith, Mike explains that in their particular case they did not simply leap. Using his methodical approach, Mike built a *bridge* between two lives and explored contingencies as a way of trying to mitigate both the risk of breaking out and the impact of personal liminality. "Worst-case scenario, I'll go get another job. Say I have to leave and start over for Lockheed or something. I had contacts and enough of a track record to find an opportunity. It wouldn't have been a real happy time to do that, but we're going to be fine. We were not going to starve on a street corner somewhere. We built a bridge. We closed a loan on the new business in March, and I resigned in May." Although not every lifestyle migrant is so systematic—some simply leap—what Denise describes is a process that is very much a part of many narratives of relocation and transition. In any new work after migrating, there is always the risk of consciously or unconsciously ratcheting up the dedication of time and energy to a point that one loses sight of the original commitment to reprioritize and allow greater time for self and family. It is a question of *restraint*.

Scott, a divorced former workaholic from Downstate, left a very well-paying job as a personnel director at a large company. He relates his story from the catalyst to change through his continuing effort at personal restraint so that he does not return to the life he left.

My then-wife indicated that I wasn't family oriented enough and [was] paying lip service to a "family-comes-first" ethic. She was correct. After the move, I assumed that I would find work quickly—albeit at a lower rate. After seven months of part-time at a book store and as a day laborer, I found an office job that paid $13,000 a year [in the mid-1990s]. I went from eighteen-hour days as a personnel director and no hobbies to seven and three quarter hours and more hobbies than I have time to do. Since then, I've found myself in the unfortunate position of having been promoted up the corporate ladder from a trainee [in my department] to the [second position], and I'm up to twelve hours a day. However, I've refused four opportunities outside of Traverse City, including one that would have paid $150,000 per year—roughly four times what I was earning at the time. It's not easy—they really want to promote you and it gets *weird* if you turn them down.

Recall Alan's story of needing to step back from plunging into becoming head of a small company after he relocated—something that he felt was necessary in order to remain in his "comfort zone" at least at first. This lasted only until he realized this decision was simply because he was uncomfortable having left—or possibly retired from—the career that had defined him for so long. Once he *let go* and let himself find new meanings for his life, he found work that allowed him to remain true to his original commitment to live a life more focused on well-being, quality of life, personal growth, and family.

Like others that we have heard from, Mike found himself slowly building back up to some former level of intensity. It had a lot to do with finding a greater sense of security. He knew that was something he did not have before when he was in the corporate world. Now he could only make this for himself. But what exactly should it look and feel like? And so the risk was to end up deep in self-consuming work again. He explains that he built a bridge because "I wanted to definitely make sure that everything was in place first." Yet the drive to continue building continued even once everything was in place. Denise discusses the process and the restraint that is ultimately essential in order to maintain the original commitment to balance:

Then what? I'll tell you what happened, he did it again! Then you went, "Maybe we need to do more to shore it up." You build a bridge and it's holding stuff but maybe you ought to shore it up a little bit and make sure that it's going to hold what you think it's going to hold. That's what it felt like to me. Just the thought drained me that he was going to open up another shop. I couldn't handle it. Emotionally, I couldn't. For me it felt like he was shoring up in an effort to feel that security. In actuality maybe it needed to be shored up, but I think that you're backing off on how many extra posts you're going to put under the bridge, which I think is good.

As we have seen in Mike's story, the idea of building a bridge has great significance. Bridge building suggests making links. It speaks of bringing together and ultimately merging sides. Here Mike is bridging two worlds or two lives as he aims to fully enter a new life, in a new place. But he is also building a bridge between the family of everyday life, caught in the push and pull of conflicting obligations, desires, and definitions, and the family of imagination, the potential family of promise. It is an effort to merge and provide integration between the families we live *with* and the family we live *by*. This is an effort that can lead to a less divided, more holistic sense of self where aspirations and the everyday continue to edge closer together, as opposed to the abbreviated, compartmentalized alternative of the emotionally downsized self.

Letting Go and Being True

As noted previously, many lifestyle migrants appear to reach what might be called a turning point that, regardless of their age, could be likened to the crisis of identity and challenge to self that we have come to associate with the self-doubt and second guessing of midlife. Speaking of the more common midlife transition, Gail Sheehy, author of *Passages: Predictable Crises of Adult Life*, invokes the sense of flexibility that is part of the double-edged sword emerging out of a postindustrial economy and society of loosened bonds. This is the flexibility that simultaneous liberates us as individuals but threatens us as persons. Here Sheehy only celebrates the sense of freedom and describes a journey of self-discovery. As in the author Ruth Luban's image of the corporate refugee, cast out or self-exiled from one world, finding a way through unknown territories toward eventual asylum in a "New Land," Sheehy writes a travel story of "moving away" where you are in control.[9] This control, paradoxically, is achieved by letting go of all but your inner sense of what is right and identifying your "true self," with the ultimate goal of the good life as an intensely personal experience. As we have seen, this paradox is intuitively understood by lifestyle migrants, whether in midlife or not.

> Let go. Let it happen to you. Let it happen to your partner. Let the feelings. Let the changes. You can't take everything with you when you leave on your midlife journey. You are moving away. Away from institutional claims and other people's agenda. Away from external valuations and accreditations, in search of an inner validation. You are moving out of roles and into the self. If I could give everyone a gift for the send-off on this journey, it would be a tent. A tent for tentativeness. The gift of portable roots. To reach the clearing beyond, we must stay with the weightless journey through uncertainty. Whatever counterfeit safety we hold from over-investments in people and institutions must be given up. The inner custodian must be unseated from the controls. No foreign power can direct your journey from now own. It is for each of us to find a course that is valid by our own reckoning.[10]

As I suggested earlier, there is a distinct similarity between relocation narratives of lifestyle migrants and the literary genre of travelogues. Here in the United States, these travel stories are typically spun around a quest for finding or rediscovering the essential nature or character of America through a journey that weaves its way through small towns and close-knit communities along back roads. In the process of this outward roaming, there is an inward journey of personal growth, a discovering or rediscovering of one's own essential nature or character.

Susan knows she has embarked on such a journey. Her passage is about letting go completely of the external valuations and accreditations, in search of her own inner validation and guided by her own inner compass on a course set by her own reckoning. Her lifestyle vision and commitment to her inner self led her to seek the good life here. As in other cases, Susan went through a reorientation to the good in a process of shedding or letting go layers of social expectations or definitions of an outward self in order to expose a more authentic self as a source of moral guidance. For lifestyle migrants, the good life is found by getting in touch with this source. Living a life that is consistent with or faithful to the direction of this inner source is having a life worth living, a life more full of purpose and meaning.

> One of the few memories I have of being little is that feeling of the world is just totally possible and I'm going to be great in it. Then you lose that along the way. I remember just being unhappy as a child and always feeling outcast that I spent the next twenty years trying to become things. Whether it's successful in your career or having a title or a salary or a label, it was always I am this or I am that or I did this or this is who I am sort of thing. I look at part of my struggle career-wise as I was collecting titles and jobs and thinking that would make me somebody. I think when I talk about *letting go*, it's like that didn't make me anything. I landed in Leelanau County, and nobody cares about any of that stuff I've done before or the places I've been or the friends I've had. I thought those kinds of things made me interesting, but they didn't. I mean, nobody cared. So how much money I made before didn't matter. The job experience, the degrees I have don't matter. It's like, wow, then what *does* matter? That's what I've been trying to find out because none of that stuff matters. Something drove me to put myself in a position where I'd be forced to do that.

PART V

Conclusions

Overleaf: Construction on an exclusive residential development on a ridge top overlooking Lake Michigan that was traditionally open to locals but is now off-limits. Photo by Brian Hoey

CHAPTER 13

Migrants and Locals

Here come the artists with their intense faces,
with their need for money and quiet spaces.
They leave New York, they leave L.A.
Here they are—who knows how long they'll stay

[chorus:] It's a Boomtown
got another Boomtown
and it'll boom just as long as boom has room.

Here come the tourists with their blank stares,
with their fanny packs—they are penny millionaires
Something interesting happened here long time ago.
Now where people used to live their lives the restless come and go.

Nice to meet you, nice to see you in a sheepskin coat made in Korea.
Welcome to the new age, the new century.
Welcome to a town with no real reason to be.

The rich build sensitive houses and pass their staff around.
For the rest of us, it's trailers on the outskirts of town.
We carry them their coffee, wash their shiny cars,
hear all about how lucky we are to be living in a . . .

The guy from California moves in and relaxes.
The natives have to move—they cannot pay the taxes.
Santa Fe has had it. Sedona has, too.
Maybe you'll be lucky—maybe your town will be the new . . .
— Singer/songwriter Greg Brown, "Boomtown"

So far I have focused on the effect of economic, social, and cultural changes on working families and decisions that people have made to cope with these challenges. Specifically, I have concentrated on the decision to relocate as a way of redefining life priorities and attempting to rebalance work and family obligations. But what is the consequent impact of in-migration driven demographic change on places and, in particular, the longtime residents who live in these places? At the same time that there is the influx of middle-class families in destination communities, there are large numbers of rural working-class people moving out from areas traditionally based economically on agriculture or resource extraction, in a continuation of long-standing trends, in order to find more diverse and better paying work opportunities in metropolitan areas. Because of the very selective nature of migration, even in locations where there is an approximate balance of in- and out-migrations such that there is no net change in population, we can expect significant changes to take place in the demographic profile of such an area.

In areas of the country where lifestyle migration is taking place, in-migrants can be quite different than longtime residents in terms of their socioeconomic status as well as other factors such as political leanings and ethnicity, and as discussed earlier in the context of community studies such as one from Lyn MacGregor, their "ethics of agency" or "logics of commitment." In the case of the Grand Traverse area, ethnic difference was not a factor, with well over 95 percent of the population of residents and in-migrants described as "white" in official figures. Thus, ethnic difference does not play a role in the local dynamic between these groups. Rather, this relationship is framed largely on perceived class differences and, in particular, closely held assumptions about what income differences meant for what people would believe and how they would behave—despite how these expectations were frequently at odds with what both project participants and I observed.

One of the most common issues in rural or micropolitan areas with high in-migration of the relatively affluent is a dramatic increase in property value that leads to increasing financial pressure on longtime residents with much lower income. The new elasticity of place made possible by the globalization of resources and an economy that promotes flexibility presents new challenges for how places, and people, acquire meaning. On the one hand, this elasticity can contribute to local revitalization, new modes of resisting change, and the assertion of local identity. At the same time, as I suggested is true with changes in the nature of work, it threatens to erode the stability and continuity that are constitutive of lasting and meaningful identity and connections. It is a double-edged sword. One way that the character of place and thus the means of expression and resources for creating self-image can be manipulated is through a process of rural gentrification.[1] Property value increases can lead to a "rural ghettoization," where locals are effectively pushed out of areas in demand into less desirable places and housing that are likened, in this view, to urban ghettos.[2]

Also locally important is the demand for access to scenic lakefront as well as former hunting and fishing areas in heavily forested areas and river valleys. In many rural locales rich in such natural amenities, there is high demand for picturesque views such as in waterfront and hilly, forested areas. This demand leads to increased privatization of land as property formerly held by a single owner may become a hodgepodge of individual owners. As recent arrivals buy up tracts of land to build dream homes, traditional access through familial or social connections to longtime local property owners is challenged. In turn, the attraction to in-migrants of physical place may serve to later limit the opportunities for them to enter into the common space of local community they had sought by inspiring them to erect physical and social barriers between themselves and longtime residents.

In what has become a familiar story, after growing up in the area, Dan moved away to the city to look for more promising opportunities for work. After a short time, however, he realized that there were things about life in Northern Michigan that he regretted leaving. These were not related to economics. There was a sense of place and belonging that haunted his days in what seemed like a kind of personal exile in foreign lands over a thousand miles away. Moving back several years later, he found that the place where he grew up had undergone changes that have made his home much more like everywhere else. It seemed much more like Anytown, USA—the local shorthand for strip malls and chain stores. Despite these changes, Dan feels that it is still a better place to be. Here he describes the most troublesome changes and what these mean to him. In his account, we see that he laments not only a loss of access but also a *way of life* that characterized a different time that is, perhaps, disappearing across a wide range of rural places in the United States.

> I still enjoy it here. I have no wish now to go elsewhere to live, but sprawl is very apparent. I'm very habitat sensitive. I used to be able to go two miles south of town and there was nothing there. And you'd go down in the river valley and nothing was ever posted. It was very *open*. There wasn't a problem with trespassing—we'd just go. In high school we used to have guns in the back of our cars because we'd get done with school and we go hunting. But now there are so many places that are becoming subdivisions, you know? There goes the habitat. Or they've been posted so you don't have access anymore, and it's usually because somebody from out of the area has moved in and then they've bought it. "Okay, now I have *my slice* of Northern Michigan. Now you fuck off." And there go the orange "No Trespassing" signs up all over. It never was an issue—we always knew if somebody owned it. Through a group of people: "Oh, my dad knows this guy—it's no problem." So, we'd go hunting and it was no problem. Now it's the opposite of that. Now instead of going two miles out of town, I have to go twenty.

These kinds of tensions are often based on what seems like a "clash" of value systems that in some parts of the country is described as a simple case of the locals versus the newcomers. Where I once lived in northern New England, the term often used for these newcomers was "flatlander"—a term that reveals a geographical component where upland dwelling folk felt threatened by outsiders. As a society, Americans tend to understand these tensions and misunderstandings as a *culture clash*. Possibly the first use of this term to describe the situation where rural areas experience high rates of urbanite in-migration was by Michigan State University sociologists Michael Price and Daniel Clay, whose research in the early 1980s concerned "structural disturbances" in rural Michigan through the phenomenon of turnaround migration noticed only a few years earlier.[3] Today, the construct of culture clash seems de rigor for any popular discussion of urban to rural migration.

Longtime local residents in rural areas may value more open uses of land, whereas recent migrants moving from crowded metropolitan areas may value having their own "space" apart from others and can afford to pay for this. Certainly this is Dan's understanding: "I've got my slice." Not surprisingly, some lifestyle migrants expressed a desire for seclusion and privacy even as they spoke of the value of community. We have seen how they routinely emphasized the desire to find a kind of refuge. We can expect to find that locals, as well as lower-income migrants, are more dependent on embedded social and communal networks. These networks contribute to their quality of life. More affluent in-migrants, however, can more easily ignore this stock of locally embedded social capital as they will be able to substitute their imported financial capital by paying for certain goods and services as opposed to relying on existing social or communal networks for support.[4]

Patterns of interaction carried by migrants from urban or suburban places, where one would expect to find greater separation of work, residence, socializing, leisure, and education, might make it seem normal to individualize everyday practices. This could include choosing to do things as individuals and valuing privacy above participating in traditional communal activities such as country dance or fraternal organizations that overlap with the interests of local families over a number of generations. For the corporate or urban "refugee," it might be more important to seek privacy and isolation than to engage in the kinds of social activities that create and maintain reciprocal relationships among residents. Idealized visions of potential selves, particularly as attached to a vision of the Rural, are not infrequently unrealistic and challenged by complexities of community life where different groups may be pitted one against the other over how local resources are defined and used.

In fact, the influx of lifestyle migrants may precipitate conflicts as individualized claims on these resources, including previously undeveloped land, made in the context of creating affective, place-based identities together with an accompanying romanticized discourse may stand in sharp contrast to traditional, utilitarian, and communal notions of place. This kind of conflict is, not surprisingly, played out along lines of insider and outsider and along associated socioeconomic class lines. Unless action is taken by newcomers to build reciprocal relationships by actively contributing to social bonds of community and what may be required to build new relationships, what the political scientist Robert Putnam defines as the "features of social organization such as networks, norms, and social trust that facilitate coordination and cooperation for mutual benefit."[5] Sounding like many of the midlife downshifters to the area, Jack explains:

> I love the fact that there is community here, and the people are wonderful, and I enjoy meeting more people all the time. But I don't think I would have moved here to move into a neighborhood. That wouldn't have been why. Privacy is a luxury. It really is. I'm fortunate that I can afford that. I wouldn't move up here to meet new people. Now if I had a young family I would. I don't think I would move in a new subdivision in Traverse City. I would probably be more than happy to live in a new subdivision when I first got married. I don't have really young children at home anymore. I'm looking for something different up here. It's not that I don't want community—I mean, I love meeting people—it's just that I'm looking to *get away* a little bit.

It is important to recognize that lifestyle migrants in this area represent a wide range of interest in engagement in community life. Some would rather stay out of active participation and enjoy local place by letting what they understand as community be something of a backdrop to their private lives. They appreciate community as an aesthetic quality. As Jack so clearly illustrates, being without young children at home may suggest less need to engage with others through children in neighborhoods or schools. Just as geographic and social mobility variously necessitate and allow for changes in the ways that people relate to others and view common interest and difference in conceptions of community, so too does movement through the life course. Others like Katie, who relocated recently with her husband as a dual-career household, view community as inseparable from physical place and shaped by geographic and demographic scale: "The other meanings of lifestyle adjustments to me are more of a small-town feeling, a feeling of community, like a cohesive community, not based on religion, race, or ethnicity. But a community *based more on geography*. We live close together and these are the people that work together and go to church together and go to school together and we are a community. That was part of what we were really excited about." Katie identifies a basic analytic understanding of community—in the most traditional sense—as being common interest shared through geographic location. Many sociological and anthropological studies do show that geography often does serve as an essential element in defining identity and, particularly, in the act of defining "other" in opposition to self through physical distance—we are "here" and they are "there" kinds of thinking. In short, attachment to place may be a means of symbolically constructing boundaries that delineate "insider" from "outsider." Importantly, physical proximity does not necessarily lead to common interest, though it can certainly be the beginnings of associations that lead to shared identity. In short, one does not typically become a "local," or gain entrée to extant community in a particular place, by simply taking up residence in that location.

Although in his study of urban to rural migration in Montana, Patrick Jobes does find that in-migrants have a "hunger for community," it does not appear that they are prepared to work consistently to construct it. In Jobes's study, exurbanites largely wanted "community to almost magically, though sensibly in their minds, converge around them."[6] This seems consistent with lifestyle migrants in my own study—such as illustrated in Katie's comments. Most migrants in my study, however, are at least interested in partaking in community life, if not through the Elks club or spending time at the local feed and grain store, then through being "good neighbors" who know the people around them and are available to provide help when needed.

Although the claim of importance given to community in lifestyle migrants' lives is promising, the focus continues to be on self-interest, where right action is found in following a personal idea of the good understood as what feels right. It is something that promises to increase individual well-being and quality of life and to provide the basis for greater narrative unity through grounding in a particular place. Despite the potential for a revitalization of community and for more meaningful, purposeful lives through engagement with community and place, if community means nothing more than a gathering of similarly minded people for purely individual interests, whether planned or not, community is reduced to nothing more than lifestyle enclave.

Robert Putnam became widely known for proclaiming what he considered the profound extent of decay in America's civil society. Putnam would no doubt expect to see declining civic engagement in rural communities with high in-migration from urban areas. Armed with an array of statistical data that appears to indicate serious erosion in America's social capital, Putnam outlines several explanations for the decline in what had been an American inclination toward participation in civil society. It was a propensity for civil life that so impressed Tocqueville in the early part of the nineteenth century. Because of the importance of civil society to the consolidation of democracy, Putnam places special emphasis on the issue of declining political participation. His primary aim is to demonstrate more broadly that the decline in civic engagement of all kinds—including religious affiliation and membership in such organizations as labor unions, PTAs, and civic, women's, and fraternal groups—is part of a related phenomenon that needs to be identified and addressed.

Despite the fact that more Americans than ever before are of middle age and hold advanced degrees—both of which have traditionally fostered greater associational involvement—Putnam finds that aggregate membership in associations appears to be either stagnant or declining. Today most Americans appear far less involved in their communities than they were a generation or more ago—an assessment that is echoed in popular culture. Among the reasons for the decline, Putnam's findings suggest that increased physical mobility has reduced the social rootedness of the average American and that changes in scale, including those in the US economy, have led to increased shopping from home (online and catalog) and with it the replacement of community-based businesses by distant multinational firms. In addition, he identifies a technological transformation of leisure that is radically "privatizing" or "individualizing" leisure time so as to reduce opportunities for building social capital through participation in group activities. Further, he claims that Americans are becoming less "neighborly," that is, that people are socializing less with their neighbors and are on the whole less trusting of others.[7]

Following Putnam's reasoning, can we expect something different in the case of lifestyle migration where there is a shift from a largely rural, working-class population, many of whom have long-standing family and social ties in the area, to a largely transplanted more urban-cultured middle class? Can we expect lifestyle migrants to have the desire to maintain and expand existing social networks and thus truly participate in local community rather than treating an ever-diminishing community as a picturesque set for the performance of private lives? My own expectation prior to beginning the project was that for many of these migrants, establishing meaningful social ties and roles in community life would be taken as fundamentally important to quality of life. I felt that one of the motivations for relocation was the desire for a human scale relationship with place of residence that included not only the physical but the social world as well.

Nearly all the participants in my project stated that "community," however defined, was important to them in their decision to relocate. Although less than half of 128 formal participants were actively involved in what we might characterize as community building by way of regular attendance in town meetings, volunteering in local organizations, or other such activities of deliberate interaction with others in their places of residence beyond necessary encounters such as through work, it was important for the majority of participants to feel that they were engaged in some way with community. This was true even if this amounted simply to walking through the downtown shops, spending time in public spaces, and being recognized by others as a resident. Not surprisingly, for participants with young children—unlike middle-aged migrants like Jack—active involvement in community building was highest even if this was limited to school-based events. Almost all participants, regardless of age, expressed an interest in getting more involved in community planning and decision making in order to protect the quality of life that they came here to enjoy—although barely one quarter of participants had attended planning meetings or felt "up-to-date" with important local issues facing the community over land use and development initiatives.

Although I spoke individually with both longtime residents and in-migrants, generally there were few opportunities to see the two sides face off candidly over the issue of in-migration-induced physical growth and social change in the area. While town meetings would sometimes heat up, it was not always easy to identify the parties involved, and the emotion was typically directed at town officials or at the tourists who were generally referred to as "fudgies," in a manner that tied them to their penchant for the sugary treat commonly sold in shops around the area. During the early months of my project, I stumbled upon one of the many discussion groups or "web boards" that were popping up all over the Internet as a way for people to exchange ideas and often to wrangle, anonymously, over ideas and current events. One local manifestation of this phenomenon was an online forum set up on the homepage of the local paper, the *Traverse City Record-Eagle*. "TC Talks," as it was known, became a very active online population of both current and former locals together with established newcomers as well as would-be in-migrants. The discussion thread that I reproduce here took place in the first half of 2000. It was initially started with a query by the user "Jeff" from Chicago, who wanted to have more information from residents about the prospects of relocating to the area. This was a fairly common sort of query. The request for feedback quickly became an exchange over the meaning of in-migration to the local area.[8] The discussion took place under the heading "Author Topic: Transplants to Northern MI":

JEFF: I love northern Michigan very much and am considering moving there. I am interested in feedback from anyone that has moved there recently as to how they like it and are doing.

MISSY: It is beautiful country, but I feel like I live in a "mini-Downstate" without the Downstate problems . . . so far away. Same people with the same attitudes are just transplanted to northern Michigan. It is like everyone is rushing to northern Michigan to live in a bubble, protected from the real world.

TODD: This is a great place to live and there are plenty of outdoor activities in summer and winter. The pay isn't the greatest and both people do have to be working to make it. But life is a lot more relaxed up here and for the most part people are friendly. Although there are a lot more people from Downstate moving up here it is still a great place to live.

SHAMUS: Northern Michigan is many things to many people. I grew up here, and moved away, only to return. I returned for the land I love that is in my bones and the bones of 5 generations. It is my home. It saddens me to watch it fill up with people who do not have this kind of connection. This area is being colonized. Ford Explorers are taking over. They are shaking their fists, and driving too fast to the mall through streets that look just like the ones they left back in suburban nowhere. They buy their luxury condos on the golf course and snarl at us locals as we serve their whims in restaurants and resorts. Why don't I leave? Because on my days off I can drive out to the woods. If I go to a secret spot I can get away from the fudgies and I'm back in the land my grandfather knew. No offense, but please don't come here.

BETTY: I'm sorry that you feel that way, however, I am entitled to live anywhere that I choose. And my choice is the Traverse City area. I am looking for a peaceful area where I can live out my life. I'm not looking to raise "heck" or speed around. I'm looking for "peace and tranquility" and many people have pointed me in this direction. Granted, I am not from your area and do not have family there. But that doesn't mean that my children can't move near me and raise their children and start a new family tradition. May God grant you peace and tranquility because you will need it . . . because no matter how you feel, I am still going to move to the Traverse City area.

FRANK: Don't pay any attention to the whiners. If you want to live here, then you just come right on up and make yourself at home. There is plenty of room for you and your family. Some people just have a hard time seeing things change or they see all change as negative.

BETTY: Thanks for the kind response, Frank. Most of the people on the board have been very nice but there is always someone with a negative attitude. I'm over 21 and a nurse and will go where my heart leads me . . . to peace and tranquility in nature. I love the outdoors.

JEFF: As to Shamus's comments about wanting to preserve what you have—I couldn't agree more. I have always been a "small town" person mentally—even though I now live in Chicago. My dad lives in a small Indiana town where some can trace land holdings back to the 1840's. The sense of community is what makes it all the worthwhile. I have a very deep respect for that and of course the land, its people and its history. The type of people Shamus is referring to however are becoming way too common all over. If you want to keep them out the answer is to keep what Shamus calls the "colonists" out first. Without the "colonists" they won't come. What are the colonists? The McDonald's, the Wal-Mart, the developers, the materialists, etc. Stop them and you will substantially stop what follows. I was in Aspen in the late 70s and I saw what they did. Even though locals fought the McDonald's hard and fast, the "colonists" still came. Eventually the locals lost. However, losing one battle doesn't mean a "war" is over. Northern Michigan is a new time and place. Lessons can be learned, victories won. If Shamus wants to preserve Northern Michigan, I think the answer is to stop development that attracts the wrong people and encourage preservation activities that attract those that are like-minded.

CHERYL: It seems to me the people who are transplants are very actively involved in the preservation of neighborhoods and parkland. It certainly would not make sense to move to Traverse City and work toward making it like the area they left.

JANE: I was a transplant and I think if both "Natives" and "Transplants" compromise, it would make for a more harmonious relationship. The natives complain that the transplants ruin the landscape, but if there were sufficient zoning codes this wouldn't be allowed to happen. I feel so fortunate at being able to raise my family in such a wholesome, healthy place with nature at your fingertips. Yes, it was frustrating when we first moved to have to go to Grand Rapids for major shopping sprees, but we were well aware of that when making our decision to move there.

TRENTON: I think you make a good point. I grew up in Traverse City and remember the days before the malls when the only night the stores were open was Friday. My family like many others would go to Dills for the Friday night fish fry then go shopping on Front Street. Front Street was like a mall with [Montgomery] Wards on one end JC Penny on the other. Friday night shopping was a social event, as you knew most everyone and it afforded you the opportunity to discuss local politics, schools, and sports. I moved from TC to Seattle only to find much the same thing going on there as in TC only on a larger scale. The Californians have discovered Washington and are moving there in mass. They soon forget why they moved there and have now built a new LA in Washington. During my visits to TC I have found much of the same mentality. The colonization of TC with Detroiters is an abomination. They have begun to build a little Detroit. The development of the malls has created a Front Street of tourist trap type stores. The mystique of TC is gone forever.

CHERYL: I moved here 13 years ago, but I could live here 40 years and still be considered a Downstater by people who were born in TC. In the thirteen years I have been here, I have been active and interested in efforts to manage the growth of Traverse City, which are spearheaded by people not born in TC. They recognize growth is a good thing, but not growth for growth's sake, not to the level of TC becoming very much like the communities from which they moved. While at the same time City and County Commissioners cry about the "Downstaters" (a euphemism for anyone moving from any part of the country) ruining TC, they consistently vote for more roads, more building, parking structures, the elimination of green space, etc. and do nothing about traffic and affordable housing. And they are most generous to developers (no matter where they are from).

The beauty of this thread is that it is an exchange between people representing virtually the complete range of voices that I have heard regarding in-migration and its potential impact. "Missy" feels that "Downstate" attitudes are transplanted "Up North" making the area a kind of colony. She also feels that the escape is an illusion. "Shamus" joins her in this understanding and recognizes that place is imagined. Place becomes different things to different people. For a multigenerational local, it is something quite different than to a refuge-seeking urbanite whose very consumption of the idea of place is seen as a kind of colonization. "Trenton" later joins in with a lamentation over the loss of a fragile "mystique" of community and place, lost to what seems like inevitable change through growth. "Betty," a would-be migrant, asserts her right to the pursuit of happiness wherever she may find it and lays out her plan to define herself and make a life in this place through a pledge to not cause any trouble. "Jeff," the thread's author, asserts his intent to respect local community while fingering the real colonists as the corporations who, presumably, are reacting to demographic data that suggests that setting up shop in the area makes increasing economic sense as local buying power continues to rise. Both "Cheryl" and "Jane" recognize that the blame for growth must be at least partly borne by the local authorities and, to some extent, voters that approve policies that affect patterns of growth and development. "Cheryl" also points out that newcomers may actually be more active preservationists than locals in keeping with what might be called a "gangplank" sense of their potential for activism. The gangplank or "last-settler" syndrome, as one might assume, suggests in-migrants are keen to be the last one in to an area. They are happy to be there and do not want anyone else to make the same choice to move to the area. By seeking privacy, solitude, and separation through distance, the supposition of the gangplank and last-settler perspectives is that in-migrants would want to prevent more people like themselves from relocating. After all, it is in-migration that may contribute to spoiling the very qualities of place that attracted them by generating economic growth that can lead to the sprawl and crowdedness that characterized areas fled.

Echoing sentiments evident in the discussion board, former resident and author Jack Ozegovic wrote a book to chronicle what he feels is a vanishing way of life—the presumed outcome of a culture clash between locals and newcomers. Ozegovic's book was inspired by his twenty years living in the area and describes the people and places that were part of what he characterizes as a rural "sub-culture" distinctive of the region: "This book is my description of the good life . . . without being too sentimental. However, a certain sorrow emerges as I recall the dismembering of the serenity and freedom that once existed there along with the steady obliteration of an irreplaceable scenic landscape."[9]

Much like the accounts of cultural anthropologists working among the Native Americans in the early part of the twentieth century, *Northern Spirits Distilled* was written with a kind of *salvage* mentality "in order to record certain aspects of this regional lifestyle. The people and stories and the unique landscape are both rapidly vanishing. This was one of the reasons that motivated me to leave the area."[10] Like these accounts, Ozegovic sees a way of live vanishing through inexorable change. He blames in-migration for the loss of a way of life in Northern Michigan as well as for his choice to leave the area in order to become a newcomer himself someplace else. The passage below captures a wide range of views on the possible impact of urban-rural migration:

> When these migrations occur they can result in upsetting the cultural balance of a given area. The newcomers, while claiming to search for a more

tranquil life, can actually transport with them the aggressive and arrogant actions they claim to be retreating from. They help create clogged streets, often adding to the preponderance of more aggressive driving habits. With the advantage of great wealth, they can also inflate local real estate values, creating pricey homes which the native resident cannot afford. I observed in our township a wealthy newcomer demanding protection from the rural volunteer fire department. He wanted services, but it was beneath his dignity to turn around and volunteer himself. New arrivals often did not share the values of being an old fashioned neighbor. Being a good neighbor was highly cherished in rural communities at one time but is now vanishing, as many newcomers prefer to remain anonymous. These migrants, wherever they go, just by their numbers, destroy the very thing they claim to be searching for.[11]

Like those in the discussion thread, the lifestyle migrant Jim referred to people—like the newcomer in Ozegovic's story—as "colonizers." He felt that they "just take from the area without making any real investment in the quality of life. They don't want to know anybody. They bitch about services and what's lacking. They distinguish themselves by what they wear and what they buy. They are so self-important. They think of everyone who lives here as though they are in some kind of backwater, provincial." Jim believed that there were two other categories of in-migrant. He characterized members of the first category as those "who had undergone some kind of change in their lives." As you may recall, Jim was involved in a brutal, personal layoff from a software company that turned his life completely upside down. He says, "These people want to become a part of the new community through living and working there. They get more self-fulfillment out of being involved in community here than from their careers." He considered himself a member of this first category. The other group he called "gray." This was because they seemed "neither here nor there"—although it could just as well be considered a reference to hair color. As retirees, this group was largely content to "settle down" such that rather than getting into local issues or organizations, they were content to lay low.

Mark Smith, local schoolteacher and writer, has produced a number of articles that focus on how local place is imagined by outsiders and how these visions are then, perhaps unwittingly, adopted by locals themselves. Smith considers the meaning of in-migration driven by the desire for place and for lifestyles defined by leisure and status. He begins by envisioning a Visa ad featuring the small town of Leland, in Leelanau County:

"Up in Michigan's great north woods there's a town where all the locals wear moccasins and drive big boats to work. You can sit above the harbor and eat ice cream all day, while the sun sets lazily between two majestic islands in the great blue distance and the fishing boats bring in the chub [a small fish]. There's a little place on the harbor called The Cave where all the locals eat smoked chub and drink cherry wine 'til the cows come home. But remember, you won't be able to pay for your chub with American Express. So be sure and bring your Visa card, and have the time of your life. 'Cause that's

definitely the way to go." Whatever! Hey, do you ever wonder when they'll
get around to featuring Leland in a Visa ad? Actually, Leland already is a Visa
ad. It's just that it hasn't actually been written up yet. Throngs of improbably
dressed visitors see us as the perfect getaway place, and many of them manage to actually move here, bringing with them their own special mindset.[12]

His worry concerns the loss of real, meaningful community in favor of an imagined form wholly disconnected from real circumstances where a place like Leland
becomes a state of mind.

As I discussed in this chapter, rising property values and changes in land ownership and use can lead to profound dislocations of long-term residents who have
relied on traditional access to certain areas and who are often displaced by housing
and other costs that they can no longer afford. This can lead to rural ghettoization
as a companion process to gentrification. Research conducted around the country
on the values and orientations of newcomers versus longtime residents suggests
significant variation in results depending on the particular demographics and history of a given area. However, the idea that there is necessarily a clash in values
and beliefs between the two groups is generally not supported. One area where
differences do appear is in the meaning and function of community. If community
serves only as an aesthetic or wholly imagined thing for in-migrants, this should be
cause for concern. Clearly, such an orientation is not enough to support or sustain
community as a social entity through civic engagement and the investment of social capital; even as it might bring a contribution of financial capital.

Virtually all lifestyle migrants have stressed the importance of community in
their decision to relocate. But nearly all tended to focus on aesthetic qualities, specifically characteristics of place, when framing their own understanding of community. Nevertheless, as noted previously, nearly half were actively engaged in
regular activities and service in community organizations. For the rest, community remained more about the aesthetic and an emotional appreciation for geographic place. As the discussion threads indicate, there are a range of voices about
in-migration and growth from both sides. At the same time, the fairly typical discussion excerpted here allows voices to fall out along two familiar lines in local
discourse. On the one hand, you have the view of many longtime residents that
in-migrants represent a colonizing force that is, by nature, unable to share in the
existential insideness of locals. In the words we hear anxiety and even anger over
their sense of loss.

Born and raised in Traverse City, Kathy was in her thirties and worked—perhaps ironically—in tourism promotion (a job that she later left to work for a local
land conservancy). She feels that she has a special connection to the place based on
lived experience and memory that someone moving here could not possibly share.
How could they feel her pain as the place she knew seems to slip inevitable closer
to Anytown, USA?

> Somebody came in the other day, a visitor, and I can't remember where she
> was from—it may have been Chicago. They owned property on Long Lake,
> and they were building. And she said, "How long have you been here," kind

of assuming that everybody that's here came from someplace else. And I said that I lived here all my life. She said, "Wow, do you *appreciate* it?" That made me pause. I really didn't know what to say. I mean, I said that I do appreciate it. I don't know that I appreciate it in the way that you do. It's a different kind of experience. It's an experience that *evolved around me* as opposed to having the contrast between here and some other place.

On the other side, newcomers or would-be in-migrants tend to take a defensive posture by asserting their very right to go where they want. Typically, this assertion of freedom to relocate is made with a clarification that their special status as lifestyle migrants motivates them to protect the quality of life that attracted them in the first place. They are asserting their position as "caring conservers" or "social preservationists" noted earlier. As suggested in research by MacGregor on long-time residents and newcomers in Viroqua, Wisconsin, people are capable of creating community using elements of contemporary society that are typically thought of as antithetical to it—features that include what she characterizes as "an emphasis on personal fulfillment and growth and on expressing oneself through material consumption" much like the orientation of lifestyle migrants as expressed in their quest for a potential self and consumption of place.[13] While research suggests that popular understanding of high rates of in-migration captured in the notion of culture clash—simplistic as it is—does not often capture the actual conditions in these areas, when responses to particular questions of concern over growth or development are considered, the attitude of in-migrants and longtime residents is that there is necessarily what amounts to a kind of clash of ways of understanding how things are and how they should be.

To Kathy, there is a clear contrast between places like Traverse City and metropolitan areas like Detroit. Although I did not find evidence to support her assertion, at least with regards to lifestyle migrants, Kathy believes that too many people coming to the area seem to seek the familiar more than they do the distinct. At the same time, however, there are retailers whose sole purpose is to package and sell something of "local flavor," even if wholly inauthentic. She fears greater development and an incipient uniformity that threatens the distinctive characteristics that define her sense of the local. It is this fear of Anytown, USA, that characterizes virtually all the lifestyle migrants and locals that I have worked with.

[In so many places in America] there's the need to gratify yourself with lots of consumerism because there are not those grounding things to be had in the community. So when you live in the suburbs of Detroit it's not like you can walk across the street and walk along the bay or go for walk in the woods. What do you do? You go to the mall. One of things I've seen going on up here that we have an opportunity to observe because of the way the community is developing, as opposed to the community that's already developed, is that there are all these Applebee's happening . . . the chain stores. You know, Home Depot and Borders [the now defunct bookstore chain]. It's nothing against those stores because they provide a great resource, but it seems that in every facet of the retail business, the mom-and-pop store and the store that reflects the flavor of the community is sort of being sucked dry. The exception is maybe some sort of quaint type businesses that continues to thrive because they offer the tourist some *local flavor*.

With Jack's professional background, his own fear comes with a sophisticated business and legal understanding of the dynamics that drive the development he so loathes. He recently bought a second home in the area with plans to eventually retire here in the coming years, and he feels he has a genuine stake in the character of place. Unlike Kathy, who focuses on the consumptive desires of in-migrants, Jack directs his apprehension at local farmers. Farmers are under a great deal of pressure to sell their land to developers as land values and taxes climb sharply at the same time that the price of their produce falls with increasing overseas competition. He eyes with suspicion both locals and newcomers whose role as consumers might stand in the way of protecting the special properties of this place, the local "flavor" or character.

> I would like to see local communities stand up and say "no," but then they get sued. You've got to have a citizenry [willing to] stand up and say, "We don't mind, we'll pay the taxes. Let the bastards sue, and we'll fight them." But that's what bothers me. It's not even so much growth; they don't give a damn about the environment. The money is coming from Texas or Connecticut? It's not a community situation. It's people who get a demographic map out—and you've got to believe that Traverse City is on a lot of people's maps right now—because they see the population shifts, and some jerk in New York is saying, "We've got to put a Nieman Marcus in Traverse City because it will support it now." You know what I mean? We have a Kmart and a Tom's [a local grocery chain] right here, and they want to put a 200,000-square-foot Meijer's [a midwestern department store chain] store a half a mile away. Why? I've even heard people who are fighting all this growth who are saying, "Gosh, I think it's a good idea. Meijer's has great produce." What's the matter with the lettuce at Tom's! Picket them and say we want better lettuce!

Like many people, Jack recognizes the relationship between beautiful places, desire, consumption, and the potential for destruction. Jack wants to keep it just the way it is, now that he has arrived.

> People are coming here for the reasons that you and I talked about. It's exactly the things that development destroys. It's the open space, clean water, farms, and cherry orchards. But if you're a farmer in today's economy, you can't make it farming. You make your money by selling off property. Those things are sort of antithetical to each other. What I've learned is that you have to survive up here in a friendly fashion. You have to understand that your neighbor's interests—who may be a farmer—are different than your interests as a Downstater who comes up and buys land to enjoy it as opposed to live off it. I don't think that most people come here for a job. You don't

come here because you've heard that the wages are high. You come here for the quality of life, and this has a lot to do with family and community, but it also has to do with the open space, clean water, cherry orchards, the deer, and the turkeys. I didn't come up here to sell off property to make money, so I'm generally opposed to growth. I like it the way it is now, the *character* of this place—that's why I came here.

The desire for a sense of community and concern for place preservation, such as that both Kathy and Jack exhibit, may be a defensive posture taken by lifestyle migrants and others, including longtime residents, against potentially corrosive, market-based forces. It is defense of the ability of individuals and families to construct meaningful accounts, sustainable narratives of self as the basis of individual character and collective identity. It is also a defense for places to retain unique character in the face of sweeping sameness.[14] Even while corporations, reacting to the kinds of demographic and other data to which Jack referred, strive to gain power, profit, and competitive advantage through increased uniformity, and placelessness, individual persons may find greater strength, stability, and personal meaning through engagement with particular places—seeking an experience of belonging and a sense of place based in an appreciation for its distinct character. Despite Jack's anxieties, examples such as the effort to protect Fishtown related in Chapter 9, illustrate how newcomers and longtime residents have joined in the effort to preserve local landmarks and what they understand to be basic elements of this character so that they would not fall victim to the anonymous, strip-mall dominated landscape of Anytown, USA.

CHAPTER 14

Place of Lifestyle Migration

We began our journey with reference to Paul Simon's song "America," which was inspired by his late 1960s visit to the declining industrial city of Saginaw, Michigan. In this melancholy tune, Simon's protagonist shares a sense of longing that we must assume is born of many factors: "I'm empty and aching and I don't know why." Looking outwardly, he counts other travelers on the road and concludes, "They've all come to look for America."[1] Will he and his companion find what they have gone looking for? This is unclear. What is clear is that they had to go on the quest—they had to try. That is the option of elsewhere. Lifestyle migration is a product of broad social, cultural, and technological changes that have taken place over the past half century. The phenomenon appears to grow in total numbers, range of strategies employed, and kinds of places to and from which migrants chose to move, as well as the diversity of migrant demographic characteristics. In addition to the migration detailed in this book, it characterizes a variety of forms of residential tourism (including second home ownership and seasonal relocation) and retirement migration. Lifestyle migration includes increasingly young and solidly middle-class workers and has broadened its reach to new frontiers in developed and developing countries as well as both rural and urban areas.[2]

This book contributes to our understanding of the movement of relatively well-off individuals at all stages of the life course, who relocate either full- or part-time to geographic places made personally meaningful by belief in the potential of both the act of relocation and the places themselves to improve quality of life. Because of the nature of lifestyle migration, the research on which this book is based has drawn on a largely academic literature that documents and interprets belief and behavior within the everyday domains of work, family, and community. My intent has been to situate the lifestyle migration documented here within the work of scholars of migration, work, family, and community. Although providing some appreciation for international applications of the concept, my deliberate focus has been on the migration as observed in the United States.

While in the end there may be no a singular form, most Americans continue to share a largely consistent, normative dream. A normalizing vision of such an American Dream has served as a moral framework. It is a key good that has defined much of a shared cultural understanding of the world and formed an overall motivation for American society while defining the very bonds of community within which some common culture is shared. This framework has allowed people to determine in their everyday lives what is of value, what is good, what should be done, and what to support or reject. It is like a horizon that in relation to people are capable of taking a stand. Principally, the dream has provided an answer to the question of why individuals should work hard, make sacrifices, and believe in the power of determined effort, money, and their capacity and right to realize future rewards for themselves and their families. After serving to build an industrial economy that shaped the course of the twentieth century and despite recent challenges to its foundational elements, this dream persists as a moral framework but may hold far less relevance than in the past.

A *Time* cover from September 2010 proclaims that Americans should be "Rethinking Homeownership." The story's author, Barbara Kiviat, asks whether, even while the United States government has promoted home ownership as a bedrock social and economic value for more than half a century, "a nation of cul-de-sacs lead[s] to the American Dream or to a paralyzed, debt-ridden labor force."[3] Increasing insecurity among the middle class, who helped to shape the meaning of that dream and made it their own, has hastened its erosion. Today, as suggested by my work with lifestyle migrants, people in the United States seem increasingly less certain about how to construct the relationship between their economic life and an essential quest for deeper values, the human spirit.

People approach this dilemma in diverse ways. I have focused on lifestyle migration as one possible reaction—and this migration is not uniform. There are many expressions and experiences. As my research has shown, however, there are consistent themes. Listening to the stories of these migrants tells us something about strategies that people may follow before moving that ultimately were not enough as they reflect back on those lives from the vantage provided by relocation and the hindsight supplied by passing time. We have seen how people may try to compartmentalize their lives in order to manage conflicting desires, obligations, and commitments. An old model of career devotion, the way of Whyte's "Organization Man"—who willingly, devotionally belonged to the company—declines further in the face of economic restructuring and globalizing instability. There is a new imperative for the middle class to establish more individually meaningful and relevant priorities and values. A revised dream may emerge that embraces opportunities of enhanced freedom and flexibility—a free-agent lifestyle—even while it tries to preserve some of the promises and desires of the old, including meaningful ties to community or what we may characterize as the cultivation of *roots*.

Although relative economic hardship on a mass scale suggests that the act of relocation as a basic element to the phenomenon of lifestyle migration has been slowed in the immediate term, the values inherent in narratives of the migrants in this and other studies—taken against the larger backdrop of evidence from other scholarship and as evident in popular culture—suggests a shift that will endure. This can be characterized in part as a move from an ethic of self-denial, which characterized much of the twentieth-century world of work, to one of self-fulfillment. Other related shifts might include going from normative social definitions of success to individualized notions and from a concern for obtaining a higher "standard of living" to achieving better "quality of life." While this may be taken as both new and positive in many ways, it may in fact be a furthering of the individualism and insularity that encouraged the cul-de-sacs that observers like Kiviat question.

Among distinct aspects of a modern self, beyond the sometimes disengagement with community that characterizes America's peculiar notion of freedom, is a sense of inwardness, uniqueness, and concern with authenticity—a feeling that one must aspire to be true to inner selves. Americans are encouraged to explore inwardly for meaning and to find their moral source. This quest for deeper values, we are told, is to be found in manner of living. Fulfillment depends on a quest to identify inner selves and to live a life, design a lifestyle that resonates with that self.

What distinguishes lifestyle migrants from others on a path that might be described as self-help is that they identify a need to start over that relocation either enables or enhances. Through the experience of vacations, people come to recognize that new places, together with change of routine, can be renewing—even therapeutic. A principal part of the understanding of lifestyle migrants is the importance of place in shaping everyday life and constructing a sense of self. At its most basic, their decisions about *where* to live are also about *how* to live. We have seen how place came before work choices, requiring migrants to follow a process of *making it work*. Lifestyle migrants tell travel stories. As narratives of personal discovery, they embody movement through time and place. They describe feelings of losing a sense of control and the search to find it. As we have seen, this may involve passing through seemingly *liminal* states that lead to real or imagined reorientation to the good. In this process, particular places are chosen as refuge. Here in the Grand Traverse region, Up North can be more than location taken in geographic terms. It is a moral position, an orientation to the good that has spatial dimensions. Being Up North is believed to be a state of refuge or asylum from other places and ways of being. In this refuge, lifestyle migrants believe that they can realize potential selves through the *option of elsewhere*.

With parallels to long-standing traditions of pursuing the simple life, this begins with identifying one's own core values and getting back to basics. In their stories, we often hear about a desire to put family first and a need to "take back" a life. Getting at core values involves exploring the inner self as a source of guidance. Numerous social scientists across a number of disciplines have underscored the significance of declining sources of shared meaning. Lifestyle migrants show how people attempt to be true to self, using a notion of quality of life as a kind of moral compass. Moral questions must go beyond right behavior or obligation to principles and standards that guide action and tell us what we should do. In this larger sense, the moral includes asking what it is good to be, what is fulfilling, what makes a life worth living and provides self-respect and dignity. Lifestyle migrants show how this means having faith, trust in self, fidelity to one's promises and convictions, commitment, and sincerity of intent.

The quest is not just about leaving something and someplace behind; it is not easily pinned down as "escape." It is about value affirmations. It is about choosing to start over so as not to be or become "entrenched" or "stuck" in lives that many felt they never really chose for themselves but rather had happen to them. It is about seeking places seen to resonate with and support a lifestyle commitment.

We can see from lifestyle migrants how their relocation and an accompanying re-orientation is not only made within a space of questions about what is good and bad, what is worth doing and what is not, but also how it is bound up with their bearings in the world, with space and more significantly with place. Nurtured attachment to place becomes essential for how they locate themselves in a moral, social, and material landscape and find their way.

Finding or believing in a place of refuge or asylum can be essential to people at certain crucial, watershed points in their lives. As we have seen, vacations may provide temporary time out of normal time as an opportunity to imagine other possibilities. More lasting refuge should offer time and place for reimagining and envisioning new directions. Lifestyle migrants describe experiencing refuge in feelings of rootedness and connectedness to particular places. The belief that we can remake ourselves and our lives through sheer force of will is an essential part of an American ethos. It is likely grounded in America's cultural heritage of migration and starting over in the circumstances of its development as a nation based on immigrant dreams and a frontier experience. This suggests, in fact, a kind of paradox.

In the accounts of lifestyle migrants, we see a tension between two simultaneous desires. On the one hand is a desire for retreat from the world expressed in the need to find personal refuge in order to take back lives and protect family from potentially corrosive forces of change. On the other hand is a desire for engagement with the world through wanting to experience more intimate expressions of human community and the need to feel belonging, in a personally meaningful way, to something bigger, whether that is community or the physical landscape.

People deal with this tension in different ways. In characterizing their reactions, we cannot confine people either to a view wherein middle-class American families become heroic moralists struggling to maintain traditional values and bourgeois ideals against rising dissolution of familiar bonds, or to an opposing perspective where they have become withdrawn resigners from the complexities of an increasingly diverse, multicultural world. Lifestyle migrants in this project are people who attempt to live their lives in the best possible way they can in the only way they feel that they can while being true to self. Nevertheless, given prevailing socioeconomic and demographic conditions, there is the inescapable risk that their behavior can exclude diversity and difference, exacerbate social and economic inequities expressed in spatial separations, and create what amounts to spontaneous gated communities based on clusters of people with similar backgrounds and ideals. Some worry that this is but one of many factors contributing to what has been called the "clustering" of America—a phenomenon discovered, interestingly, through marketing research made possible by fine-grained statistical data and high technology called geodemographics.[4] It seems that most Americans have been busily sorting themselves at least since the 1970s into increasingly homogeneous zones found not at the regional or state levels but rather at the microlevel of city and neighborhood.

Some scholars have long suggested that in societies such as the United States, a "community of limited liability" may emerge when the "centrifugal" forces—to which I have earlier referred—tear at countervailing "centripetal" tendencies that keep people rooted. In this scenario, relocation becomes a more reasonable alternative to remaining in any one place in the face of unmet needs. According to the sociologist Morris Janowitz (who coined the term in 1952) and demographer John Kassarda, "in a highly mobile society, people may participate extensively in local institutions and develop community attachments yet be prepared to leave these communities if local conditions fail to satisfy their immediate needs or aspirations."[5] The concept emphasizes the voluntary, the intentional, and particularly the contingent and differentiated involvement of community residents.

In terms of attachment, community of limited liability suggests that largely instrumental values and self-interest—as opposed to affective bonds based on interpersonal relationships within neighborhoods—characterize the basis of commitment to community. Clearly such limited liability tied to calculated individual outlay has real implications for communities ever more in need of real commitment and sustained investment from residents. Reporting on her research in the American Midwest, Sonya Salamon documents swift suburbanization of rural and still largely agrarian places where newcomers tend toward a *moral minimalism* such that they "may live in a small community but not belong to it," preferring instead to cultivate only loose connections and to engage only with the most "porous" of local institutions in order to maximize personal autonomy and freedom.[6] Despite the contingent attachment suggested by limited liability and moral minimalism, can local community remain important to residents (newcomer and old-timer alike) as a site for the realization of *shared* values in support of social goods such as mutual trust, norms of civility, the collective care of youth, and protection of cherished places?

At this juncture, studies of lifestyle migration like that presented in this book run alongside those that concentrate on matters of "work and family" in their shared interest in questions of social capital in both community and family, civic engagement, community building, and the extent to which these may be affected by profound changes in everyday life as result of economic restructuring and changing work and family dynamics.[7] Similarly, research into the "family-friendly community" recognizes that particular places may become potentially important resources, as well as obstacles, for families trying to adjust to changing demands of work as expressed in the accounts of lifestyle migrants. Research by the sociologist Stephen Sweet and others finds that community residential selection may represent an *adaptive strategy* at the family level taken in response to host of current or anticipated life-course "stressors" and thus shaped not matters such as not only job conditions but also residential environments that are perceived to support current and prospective family needs.[8]

Quoted in the introduction to Alan Wolfe's examination of the moral values of everyday America, former secretary of labor Robert Reich voiced a typically liberal-minded concern that the more affluent of the United States may be "quietly seceding from the large and diverse publics of America into homogenous enclaves, within which their earnings need not be redistributed to people less fortunate than them."[9] This is akin to the phenomenon that Wolfe calls "middle-class withdrawal." In the introduction to an updated edition of *Habits of the Heart*, Robert Bellah and his coauthors comment on the possible withdrawal of privileged social classes into real and virtual lifestyle enclaves.[10] All of this occurs within the broader context of relentless mergers and breakups in companies that further disintegration in local social and economic ties—many of which have been built through long-time communities of work. Corporate volatility can lead to a kind of placelessness at the top that creates a wealthy class cut loose from commitment to any particular place and transformed into a kind of "roaming frontiersman" or the "itinerant professional vandal" roundly vilified in the essayist Wendell Berry's lyrical but acerbic accounts, who may be kin to the somewhat hapless nomads who voluntarily slip in and out of the places examined in Kilborn's *Reloville*.[11]

The phenomenon of lifestyle migration—in all its forms—should be explored in this wider framework as a potential expression of the changing nature of such fundamental social and cultural categories as work, family, and community. Importantly, recent research by the geographer Sam Scott on economic expatriates in Europe is critical of a focus in the migration literature on *privileged* forms of career-based mobility. In his own case, Scott argues that skilled international migration—though still relatively limited when compared with other forms of labor migration—has become a "normal" middle-class activity rather than something confined to a professional, economic elite.[12] In a similar way, research by others in the area of growing international retirement migration among the middle class of developed nations suggests the same process of normalization in what would have been considered, a short time ago, truly exceptional behavior.[13]

The study of lifestyle migration presented here is situated in a broad field of studies concerned with identity and, among other things, the desire for particular geographic places as a "consumable," an attachment to a rural ideal, or the attraction of natural amenities.[14] In addition, it fits together with studies of travel-inspired entrepreneurship and tourism-related migration.[15] The connection between international tourism and migration has been largely neglected, but evidence of the increasing role that both economic and cultural globalization plays in producing modified forms of leisure, work, retirement, and community provides further impetus for researchers of lifestyle migration to document the phenomenon in a variety of contexts around the world.

Within an emerging literature focused on the phenomenon of lifestyle migration, there are several key reasons cited for why these individuals and families chose to relocate. These factors, or motivations for moving, provide a reasonable means of clarifying areas of focus within the field of migration research. Notably, however, these motivating factors are neither mutually exclusive nor fully inclusive. As we have seen in the accounts of migrants here, these factors include: quality or pace of life; qualities of geographic place (especially natural environment or "amenities"); qualities or character of human community (including "culture" and architecture); overall cost of living (especially availability of comparatively inexpensive land); and climate.

As with other forms of migration, factors such as these effectively "pull" migrants to certain places and/or "push" them out of others. While such things as an assumed "slow pace of life" might encourage a lifestyle migrant to relocate to a *destination* community (a pull factor), embedded in this may be the migrant's feeling that the *origin* community is too "fast paced" (a push factor) thus encouraging relocation to a place believed supportive of a lifestyle commitment to live a slower and presumably less stressful life. Research by scholars of work and family on topics such as job or life satisfaction—and their relationship—contributes to an understanding of factors in the motivation of lifestyle migrants. In addition to specific studies of satisfaction with one's job, more general studies of overall life satisfaction have been one of the most frequently studied outcomes of conflict in the domains of work and family. Not surprisingly—as would be expected given the narratives of lifestyle migrants—findings in these studies have indicated an inverse relationship in which the greater the level of conflict, the lower the level of life satisfaction.[16]

Given the longing of many lifestyle migrants to use relocation to purposefully rebalance work and family commitments, for example, through starting their own business or employing sophisticated forms of telecommuting, research on lifestyle migration benefits from—and may contribute to—ongoing research involving work and family integration and "boundary theory" such as studies done by sociologist Christina Nippert-Eng, whose work follows earlier inquiries into mutually dependent domains of home and work and their role in individual identity formation.[17] Research in this area includes investigations into increasingly complex issues of identity made possible by workplace flexibility and technology, including potential areas of conflict and "blurring" in the domains of work and family that may arise.[18]

This book extends the understanding of noneconomic migration and relocation decision making by examining important moral dimensions from a perspective informed by social, cultural, and historical insight. This understanding is brought to bear on considerations of personal motives and social meaning of the phenomenon of lifestyle migration. It suggests the need for an *integrated* ethnographic view that combines the perspectives of the production- and consumption-side explanations of migration, bringing together considerations of economic and structural factors and decision making understood in terms of consumption choices. Appreciating the significance of lifestyle migration depends on being able to separate out factors ranging from possible changes in people's propensity to relocate, greater salience of certain residential preferences, and the economic and structural changes that can have either enabling or constraining effects on the process. It also depends on being able to find a framework for reintegrating these factors into a story that results in a coherent whole.

My intent has been to explore the mutually implicating impact felt by people and absorbed by places of social and cultural changes in an emerging economic order distinct in important ways from an industrialized economy that has defined the United States over the past century. My particular understanding of these changes comes from talking with lifestyle migrants—a group of people who have proven themselves especially articulate about how they chose to respond to characteristic challenges and opportunities born of this shift.

A professor of law, Margaret Radin has developed the concept of "property for personhood" (introduced briefly in Chapter 9), which resonates strongly with both the commonsense understandings of the people with whom I have worked in this project as well as my interpretation of their experiences. Radin asserts that as social scientists and concerned citizens, scholars interested in these issues need to pay close attention to how things fundamental to the person may be commodified or, conversely, made inalienable. She makes a compelling case that proper self-development—what we are calling personhood in this context—requires that people have some reasonable security (in the sense of predictability and constancy) and control over certain things in their external environment, which would include those places people call "home."

Radin's vision consists of a world where "market-inalienability would protect all things important to personhood."[19] While such a utopian ideal is likely impossible to put into practice within the present socioeconomic system, her proposal recognizes and elucidates the fundamental connection between place and personhood—local and individual character—so essential to my discussion of lifestyle migration. Defining property for personhood raises the issue of potentialities for being and emerges from a fear for possible loss of the physical or symbolic resources that make up this potential. While Radin recognizes the limits of her argument for "universal non-commodification," she holds that the logic of economic or legal authorities that characterizes a neoliberal form of capitalism that has increasingly shaped economic policy in the United States over the past half-century "stifle[s] the individual and social potential of human beings through its organization and production, distribution, and consumption, and through its concomitant creation and maintenance of the person as a self-aggrandizing profit- and preference-maximizer."[20] Alternatively, Radin refers to a kind of "human flourishing" to describe different conceptions of necessary and sufficient conditions for construction of personhood. In this way, "an inferior conception of human flourishing disables us from conceptualizing the world rightly."[21]

This is precisely how corporate refugees turned lifestyle migrants such as Alan describe struggling along in an economic and, ultimately, cultural system that made it impossible for them to "live their lives properly." As Radin notes, "Market rhetoric, the rhetoric of alienability of all 'goods,' is also the rhetoric of alienation of ourselves from what we can be as persons."[22] Similarly, Charles Taylor recognizes that despite this rhetoric, perhaps the most urgent and powerful cluster of demands that we would recognize as being essential to basic moral concern is "the respect for the life, integrity, and well-being, even flourishing, of others."[23] Radin understands that "*the terms in which* human life is conceived matter to human life."[24] The idea that words matter to being is an important point to make. Like Coombe, Radin is concerned with the impact of social discourse and law on potentialities for being. If the "discourse of fungibility [that anything can be substituted for or replaced] is partially made one's own, it creates disorientation of the self that experiences the distortion of its own personhood."[25]

What does it mean to experience one's self as commodity or "ignored cost"? Is this the experience of so-called disposables in the contingent, just-in-time workforce? Corporate executives have spent at least twenty years extolling the virtue of using global markets to set the price for employees. Once viewed as a pillar of stability and corporate paternalism, IBM has referred to their per diem workers, in ironic reference to its focus on computer hardware, as "the peripherals." According to one former temp: "You're just a fixture—a borrowed thing—that doesn't belong there." Other companies refer to full-time staff as "core workers" to distinguish them from growing ranks of leased employees. In an age of so-called flexibility, universal market discourse "transforms our world of concrete persons, whose uniqueness and individuality is expressed in specific personal attributes, into a world of disembodied, fungible, attribute-less entities possessing a wealth of alienable, severable 'objects.'"[26] As noted earlier, today's workers are asked to think of themselves as a set of disembedded skills, the *portfolio self*, rather than as a complete and integral individual with a particular, discrete job. Popular self-help books assure today's workers that the secret to personal success is to begin thinking of themselves "as a product that is being offered in the marketplace for labor."[27]

The anthropologist Melissa Fisher has documented the practices of Wall Street women, for example, who define a *self-work* ethic wherein work is defined and has value insofar as it provides an opportunity to acquire marketable skills and a venue for creating a network of social ties that may be used to either hasten professional ascent or stave off sudden descent. In the wake of the 2000 dot.com bust and heightened anxiety about work without well-defined career paths, Fisher documents how these women were constructing new definitions of success, sometimes after becoming New Economy refugees who sought to "rewire" their lives by creating new lives and new careers outside of corporate jobs—in a manner akin to lifestyle migrants.[28]

Similar to what we are expected to accept as persons, those responsible for marketing specific locations are also encouraged to treat physical places as a product that is being offered in the marketplace. As noted by geographers Chris Philo and Gary Kearns, places are treated "not so much as foci of attachment and concern, but as bundles of social and economic opportunity competing against one another in the open (and unregulated) market for a share of the capital investment cake."[29] In market discourse, particular places are regarded as little more than commodities to be consumed "that can be rendered attractive, advertised, and marketed much as capitalists would any product."[30] Social scientists need to appreciate "the constituents of this discourse—considering as we do the various turns that the discourse takes for different 'actors' in the process—and their varying practical consequences."[31]

Returning, finally, to Radin's argument, we find that she suggests that a better view of personhood, distinct from one inherited from the historical subject/object dichotomy and consistent with the dialogic and material understanding of personhood basic to my discussion, "does not conceive of the self as pure subjectivity standing wholly separate from an environment of pure objectivity."[32] Rather, Radin's notion of "contextuality" asserts that both social and physical contexts should be acknowledged as integral to personal individuation. Context is fundamental not simply as surrounding information but as costructure, or "cotext" in what I have described as an essentially *narrative* construction of self. This asserts the existential relationship between personhood and context—person and place—and the overlapping nature of individual and local character.

Conditions of flexibility and hyperconnectedness characteristic of life in what many consider to be a postmodern and, increasingly, postindustrial world offer opportunities and challenges to both individual and local character, the construction of self and place. In this context, distinct places are ever more valuable and valued.

As suggested by lifestyle migrants, preservation of places as anchors to identity—as moorings to sense of self—is critically important as a defense against the corrosion of persistent change on both distinct character of particular places and lasting character of the self. As in the case of the neighbor's fence referred to in Chapter 9, it is erected in violation of a sense of place with consequences for personhood, described as nothing less than "darkly oppressive."

We have seen how lifestyle migrants recognize the importance of place for personhood. In compelling narratives of relocation, they show us how embodied experience gives them meaningful, personally constitutive connections to place and an intangible spirit of history that resides in particular places as local character. It is about something greater than themselves and of striving to find relative stability for a sense of self on which to base an individual account, a moral narrative of self, in the spatial order.

Analogous to deep currents in American traditions of simple living and transcendence, lifestyle migration as we have examined it in this book is about personal reform and even redemption. The idea that the rural and small-town places serve as the cultural repository of all that is authentic, simple, and good is a persistent force in American life. Nostalgia and imaginings play a role here, but the motivation for pursuing these and other strategies is one of reorienting oneself to the good as a manner of living, as a lifestyle. The faith of urban-to-rural lifestyle migrants in the capacity of these places to shape experience and support personal reorientations toward an authentic self, a simpler life in tune with core values, and an individualized notion of the good drives them to relocate.

EPILOGUE

Reinvent the Pie

Patterns of migration in the United States during the first decade of the twenty-first century have exhibited continuation of a general directional trend that began in the late twentieth century with overall movement of population from the Northeast and Midwest to the South and West—a shift from the so-called Snow Belt to the Sun Belt. However, the United States is presently experiencing the lowest migration rates since World War II. Housing sales are down dramatically over the past several years. Many empty nesters are either unable or opting not to relocate upon retirement. Further, many young Americans appear to be moving in much smaller numbers and buying fewer houses than a few years ago—perhaps due to insecurity about jobs and inability to obtain credit. In fact, many would-be empty nesters continue to provide shelter for adult children who may have little choice but to remain at home.

What's Next for Migration in America?

According to data from the US Census Bureau's Current Population Survey, the largest declines have been in long-distance moves of more than one hundred miles—a fact with an especially big impact on the broader economy given that these relocations are an especially important engine for regional growth.[1] For would-be commuter migrants—those who move within one hundred miles from origin communities and jobs—rising gasoline prices have had a dampening effect on relocation. While comparatively inexpensive gas helped to fuel suburbanization for decades—contributing to environmental degradation and traffic congestion in the process—we may be at a tipping point where transportation costs have a meaningful effect on relocation decisions. Current statistics on migration suggest how rapidly changing housing and labor market conditions, together with consumer energy prices, can affect population shifts.

According to the demographer William Frey, we may be witnessing a "migration correction" in the wake of a housing market gone bust and an associated "migration bubble" having subsequently burst in the middle of the first decade of the twentieth century—a double-barreled downturn fired by easy credit and speculative stimulation of market prices in many southern cities such as Phoenix, Las Vegas, and Tampa in general and, in particular, many exurban areas around the country.[2] Many places with the most prerecession overbuilding have seen equally dramatic drops in housing prices and in-migration. As we learned earlier, labor migration from Michigan to these 1990s and 2000s Sun Belt boomtowns has slowed in light of falling home values and rising unemployment—conditions too much like places in the state of would-be migrants. Latest data available through annual subnational population estimates from the Census Bureau suggests that through the beginning of twenty-first century's second decade, trends of the late 2000s have continued and, by Frey's estimates, will raise the prospect of a "'new normal' about where people decide to locate."[3] As we saw in Chapter 6, such "new normal" states have been reached before.

Here we are returned to conjecture about what might be the next (or "fifth") migration to follow the suburbanization that largely defined patterns of twentieth-century residential development in the United States. Robert Fishman—whose thesis is that we are likely to see renewed appreciation for the city and an era of re-urbanization—would no doubt find support in data that suggests that many large metropolitan areas have grown faster than suburbs (and especially exurbs) during the last several years. Close examination suggests, however, that many of the positive numbers in urban areas may be due to natural increase, immigration from other countries countering domestic out-migration, and what some have called "windfall staying" of would-be migrants unable to leave given the effects of an economic crisis that began in 2007.[4] For his part, Jack Lessinger—as a protagonist for the rise of an exurban "Penturbia," as he calls it—would find little comfort in recent demographic data available for these locales. As with most migration phenomenon during the 2000s, when it comes to migration to areas beyond the traditional suburb, that decade is split between a very different first six years and the years that followed 2007's vivid reversal of fortunes. The most recent information available suggests that the least dense, outer suburbs—the exurbs—have seen extremely low growth continue since that fateful year.[5]

In consideration of these numbers and in light of broader changes, an urban and regional planner from the University of Michigan, Christopher Leinberger, has declared the "fringe suburb" dead. Importantly, Leinberger holds out no hope that even after economic recovery the exurb will make a comeback as he holds that we are witness to a "profound structural shift" as significant as that which took place in the 1950s when suburbs boomed at the expense of cities.[6] Even by the 1960s, more Americans lived in the suburbs than the central cities. Just twenty years later, the balance of jobs in the United States had shifted to the suburbs as well. Another ten years and the country had become dependably suburban with a solid majority of the population calling them home.[7] Those facts are dramatic, but what of today? Leinberger is unequivocal in his statement that: "For 60 years, Americans have pushed steadily into the suburbs, transforming the landscape and (until recently) leaving many cities behind. But today the pendulum is swinging back toward urban living, and there are many reasons to believe that this swing will continue. As it does, many low-density suburbs and McMansion subdivisions . . . may become what inner cities became in the 1960s and 70s—slums characterized by poverty, crime, and decay."[8]

Drawing on compelling research on consumer preferences, Leinberger has reason to believe that the shift that we have seen away from rapid exurban growth is long lasting given what he characterizes as a major demographic event wherein both Baby Boomers and Millennials are developing a lifestyle preference for urban downtowns, micropolitan areas, or thoughtfully constructed suburban town centers. Thus, we may have pent-up demand for walkable, centrally located neighborhoods with mixed-used, higher-density development and forms of "alternative transportation" that would allow for essentially car-free living on a day-to-day basis. Areas that have tended to fare better through the economic turmoil, attracting (or at least keeping) residents and seeing less (if any) decline in housing prices have all or most of these characteristics.[9] Although the historian Lewis Mumford declared urban density obsolete nearly a century ago in a world that was already being made hyperconnected by advances in transportation and communications, today that density is becoming desirable again. What were disadvantages of inner-city districts during the long period of suburbanization—including its pedestrian scale, housing stock, retail and manufacturing facilities, reliance on mass transit, and diversity of residents—have emerged as distinct advantages for our current age. The same properties of place that in one period were taken to be "outdated" and undesirable by self-proclaimed suburbanites may now offer the opportunity for urban renewal through shifting consumer demand and emerging migration trends.

A National Association of Realtors study of community preferences produced in 2011 found that a majority of the survey sample selected a description of a representative "smart-growth" community as their ideal place to reside. This ideal included a mix of various types of housing and businesses, sidewalks and public transportation, and was widely preferred over the typical "sprawl" community that defines typical suburban development with only single-family homes sited on large lots located far from everything else—places of work, schools, businesses, recreational sites—so that residents depend on driving.[10] While speaking directly to the fate of metropolitan areas in light of recent data showing some in-migration—including to those places that lost population during the early 2000s—Frey concludes that it is those places that avoided overheated housing markets and fostered diversified economies that have benefited and will continue to benefit through sustained growth in the future.

Leinberger's pronouncement of exurbia's decay is as strident as Jack Lessinger's earlier prediction of its ascendency, which was indeed dead right for the 1990s and early 2000s. Frey is less inclined to the dramatic flourish.[11] For his part, he leaves open the possibility of changes in preference—though he is fairly sure that, at least in the short term, America's young are unlikely to set their sights on the exurban frontier: "The fact that the outer suburban [i.e., exurban] growth has continued to falter two years after the recession ended calls into question whether today's younger generations will hold the same residential preferences as their forebears. It is possible that the new financial risks they face, along with increased environmental and economic concerns, will change perceptions of where to find their version of the American Dream."[12]

Joel Kotkin, demographer and professor of urban development, isn't convinced that we are likely to see a major event through shifting preferences for community type. Thwarting the hope of new urbanists who find confidence in predictions of Fishman and others for a robust reurbanization, Kotkin predicts a simple "reversion to type" following a sustained economic recovery wherein trends underway in the first part of the 2000s recover and continue with the suburbs rebounding as the predominant destination for movers.[13] Even Kotkin, however, suggests that "we need to look at current suburbia not as a finished product, but something beginning to evolve from its Deadwood phase."[14] Specifically, Kotkin appears to embrace the notion that while the suburb may remain the primary category, any particular suburb could succeed or fail in attracting migrants and retaining residents based on how well these places can learn from "our ancient sense of the city" and, in particular, how well leaders recognize "the need for community, identity, the creation of 'sacred space,' and a closer relation between workplace and home life."[15]

On these final points, I find that I am in thorough agreement with Kotkin. In fact, the three vignettes of lifestyle migrants that make up the rest of this epilogue—drawn from my follow-up research over the past two years with key project participants—suggest that the needs that Kotkin identifies may be essential to America's next act. As Mumford described for earlier periods of migration, today's trends may be seen as the result of feedback from the preceding period—most recently the suburban sprawl that came to define the American landscape during the twentieth century. As Mumford noted, the impact of great phases of migratory flow on American society has always come not by way of population redistribution per se but rather from materialization of the predominant lifestyle that migrants in each period have pursued and the cultural ideals that were accordingly expressed.[16]

Central to this book is the question of how people choose to respond to everyday struggles between contending obligations and visions of the good life. Where do people find moral orientation at a time of shifting social and cultural categories and diminished importance in traditional sources of shared meaning? Following the integrative approach that I have employed in this book as a whole, I tend to think that as far as lifestyle migration is concerned we will continue to see the same underlying tensions being worked out in the choices that individuals and families make in their attempt to negotiate the challenges and opportunities of an ever-altered cultural, social, and economic landscape. Whether relocation decisions lead to rural areas, small towns, exurbs, suburbs, or urban centers does not change the factors that motivate lifestyle migrants. Kotkin correctly identified a fundamental set of needs much like those that we have seen in the accounts of lifestyle migrants—regardless of the prevailing residential pattern. I would say that a fifth migration in America will be distinguished not as much as any singular pattern of *where* migrants choose go but rather by the compelling *motives* that they have for relocating, they ways in which they *frame* their decisions, and the lifestyle choices that they make for starting over in these communities.

Three Vignettes

LIVING IN TWO PLACES AT ONCE

Although Susan has moved away from Northern Michigan, she has kept close ties to place and maintains a lifestyle commitment to reinventing work in her life. Several years ago, Susan left the area mere weeks after the birth of her daughter. As we sit on the deck of her second home—situated in a lakeside resort community that she shares with another family by splitting use evenly over the year—Susan explains how she went to live with her mother in Toledo, Ohio, when her relationship with the child's father deteriorated badly. Following a home birth with a local midwife, Susan spoke of how she dreamed of homeschooling her daughter and deepening a close connection to place through what she would teach her daughter about the land: "I saw this place as an incredible one in which to grow up, to *live* in. My ideas about this have not changed." For more than a year after the breakup, Susan returned to the area only to appear in court: "This place became kind of painful. It tore me apart because there was part of me that belonged here and still loved it." In the years since these disputes were settled, Susan has started returning to the area with her daughter.

> What was interesting is that at that point, I thought I was done with this place—thought I needed to make a new life elsewhere. And I did settle down there [in Toledo], bought a house, and started a business. But I couldn't stay away from here. My daughter asks, "When can we move back to Michigan," and I say that I've got a house and a job, but I never say no because I still have dreams. This was a place that I needed to be once—where I started over. Now it is a place that I need to be for my daughter. It is my desire to give her this life—living in a healthy, safe, empowering sort of place. She was born a couple of miles from here in Leelanau County. So, it will never leave me now. Before it was a place that I was drawn to and now it is home—her home. There will always be that connection.

Susan had come to this area after losing faith in the direction of the company to which she once felt that she very much belonged. This was a break that left her searching for meaning outside the world of work. After her quest led her to the study area and a desire to root herself in the landscape of this place, she worked a variety of cobbled-together jobs sometimes, she says, "knocking on doors looking for work to appear." Work at this time in her life was a means to an end, a way of being able to stay in the area. As she planned to have a child and make a family, however, she wanted work that could provide for her not only financially but also through fostering greater connections. It wasn't until after she moved from the area—returning to her natal home in Toledo—that she made that connection. Now Susan works closely with her mother in a business that they started together. She described how this began: "I have a degree in business and I'm sort of entrepreneurial, so I said to my mother 'Let's start a business,' and she got really excited.

She was getting close to sixty-five but wanted to keep working. I wanted to know what she wanted to do. I'd help run whatever business fit that."

Starting from her mother's appreciation for a real need of contemporary families to have support when caring for elderly parents—and with her mother's savings—they bought a franchise centered on elder care: "So, it's a combination of our two circumstances, backgrounds, and education. We combined what we had and grew it. I needed to own my own business if I was going to homeschool my daughter, and it gives my mother the flexibility that she wants in retirement." Susan explained how she homeschools her daughter while she works—keeping her daughter with her the whole time. She was emphatic in describing how this was a "natural" thing for mothers to work with their families.

> Haven't mothers always worked with their families through history? There's not a separation. I'm a mother. I take care of my child. Let me do the work that needs to be done. That's our life. It's just all together—melding together. This brings out parts of me that I didn't know that I needed to work on like relationship skills. I wouldn't have ever chosen this kind of work, but as I get older I realize that it rounds out my whole life. When I started out it was a means to an end—something to get me back on my feet. But now it is something to take me to the *next page*.

Susan's success with the business allowed her to buy into the second home that she and her mother now share and from which they continue to run the franchise during their periodic trips away from Toledo for a month or more at a time. Susan describes her evolved sense of place:

> There is less and less of a separation between here and Toledo. When I got in the car yesterday and came Up North, I didn't even think about it. It was just like driving to work. It has gotten so easy to connect the two now. This is a really good feeling because all that time that was so stressful before. I think that it was also the stress of being away from here—the feeling that it was not my home anymore. It was tearing me apart. Now, however, things have gotten better with my daughter's father and the places are melding together. When we arrived here last night it was like we had just left. I guess that for now we're living in two places at once.

BACK TO THE LAND

It was a cool morning in late July 2010 when I pulled into a narrow paved driveway in Leelanau County that disappears over a ridge into thick woods a short distance from Lake Michigan. As I stepped from my car, Carl seemingly emerged from the undergrowth. He had recently purchased this large plot of land with his second wife, Maeja. He and Liz divorced a few years earlier after fifteen years of marriage. It was amicable. As it turned out, they were on different paths, and though she shared their original desire to start over through lifestyle migration, she wasn't willing to take the steps that Carl now took. At the time of my visit, he was just

Beach scene within view of Susan's shared second home
in Leelanau County. Photo by Brian Hoey

completing a raised wooden platform for what would eventually be a small house
of largely recycled materials. I brought my hammer along to lend a hand to the
day's effort, but after a few years without much conversation, he and I were too
busy catching up to drive many nails.

Sitting on the platform's edge, gazing over a clearing that—with a few gnarled
apple trees in need of pruning—appears to have once been an orchard, Carl spoke
of the passion that drew him to the area a decade earlier: "Land has always been
important—it's the primary source of my feeling that this place is home. My co-
nundrum had become how to find a way that I could live closer to the land—on
the land—without having to *own* it. So, I've been looking for a piece for which I
could become caretaker." I would later learn that he and Maeja bought the plot in
cash—nearly all their savings—from a local bank who had repossessed it from its
previous owner. After the market crashed, the bank apparently jumped at their as-

tonishingly low offer—preferring a bird in hand. While now technically holders of the whole parcel, unusual deed restrictions define only a few, limited building envelopes and warrants that the rest of the land is set aside as a commons and nature preserve. Such restrictions stifled interest from other potential buyers, who chafed at the limitations, but they seemed tailor-made to Carl and Maeja, for whom the usual pattern of subdivision of large plots "uses land up without building community" through shared use and caretaking.

Thinking in terms that would resonate with the quest of many back-to-the-land migrants of a generation or more ago—for whom independence or self-reliance was a paramount goal—I wondered if Carl intended on being self-sustaining through what cultivation the land (and deed restrictions) might allow. He set me straight: "We are not an island. We grow up hearing that we should somehow not have to depend on other people. Those who most think that they're independent are, in fact, most dependent on others—whom they don't even know. We are always connected, and we need to be aware of those connections." How was it that he had come this much further down the road in the quest to more completely fulfill an earlier lifestyle commitment? "About four years ago, I realized that I was giving too much to my job. I realized that I needed to do something different. Actually, I was working three different jobs and was never getting caught up. This was taking away from my ability to enjoy the root reason for my being Up North, which was to get back to the land and a lifestyle where work and life are more in balance. So this has been about rebalancing." Shortly before his divorce, Carl quit his primary job and focused initially on his piano business. What he really wanted, however, was to explore other work and the opportunities that might come with this searching. He began volunteering with the local land conservancy—work that stoked his passion for place. In a short while, this became a full-time, paying job where he was given oversight of the conservancy's volunteer projects. When the bottom fell out of the economy, however, the local nonprofit sought ways to cut back without laying off workers through initiatives such as job sharing. Carl went part-time and took three months of leave. As it turns out, all that time allowed him to find this parcel and navigate the complexities of the unorthodox deed. Thinking about their decision to pare down their lives and living space to the essentials, Carl exclaimed: "What we're doing may seem odd, but it's going to become more normal. You see it in a family downsizing from a suburban McMansion to something like a 1,500-square-foot home. To them, it is a radical move, but it's the same process."

Two years later, when I return for a visit in July 2012, Carl and Maeja had finished a charming house, a well-appointed outhouse, and a tool shed that have been built either through cash-and-carry or—preferable to them both—arrangements of barter with other community members. Today, they live without a mortgage in just a few hundred square feet—though, to be clear, there is little separation in their minds between what is "inside" and "outside" in their living arrangements. It is on this general theme that my visit began. Almost immediately upon arrival, I found myself in a spirited conversation about zoning. It turns out that local ordinances require that living space in a structure deemed a "dwelling unit" must be at least eight hundred square feet. I hadn't thought about such a thing before, and

Carl standing in front
of the structure that he
and his second wife built
in Leelanau County.
Photo by Brian Hoey

it seemed odd to me that a person would not be allowed more discretion when it
came to such matters. Clearly, the building that they called home was more than
adequate for two people to live, but by square footage it is less than half as large
as what was necessary to call it a house. I came to learn that it was such seemingly
mundane matters of local ordinance that had pushed the former landowner into
bankruptcy when he was forced to build into the parcel a quarter-mile-long, engi-
neered road that could accommodate fire trucks.

   With the sound of birds ever present through open windows, we relaxed in
their cozy structure made of recovered wood and other recycled materials, and
insulated with organic sheep wool batting. Carl spoke to me of what I now understand is an essential thread throughout ongoing transformation in the lives of these

lifestyle migrants: "I had separated place from community for a long time. I came here for the place. Now, however, my focus has shifted to seeing how *integrated* they must be." The tumult that had roiled the established economic order throughout the state gave Carl and Maeja the sense that the time was ripe to see and do things differently—both individually and collectively. During my visit two years earlier, Carl had asked me in what I thought Michigan might now be a leader—if not the auto. He preempted my thoughts to assert that agriculture was poised to surpass this once defining industry in terms of monetary impact. Certainly there is evidence that this sector's growth and impact has increased tremendously in a relatively short time. Carl mentioned a fact of which I was already aware—that people in the study area had agreed, through a ballot initiative several years earlier, to tax themselves in order to preserve farm land and support local farming operations.

We also talked about the Grand Vision plan, which has brought together the five counties of my study area into a long-term, grassroots planning effort that coordinates local citizens, government, and business with state-level agencies. The Grand Vision found its beginning in an unlikely place. During my early research, a proposed bypass road and bridge across the Boardman River—designed to lesson traffic around downtown Traverse City—was approved by local government and federally funded. Following an intense and protracted debate about the proposal that I witnessed through a number of heated public forums, the plan was effectively scrapped in 2004. Thereafter, in a surprising turn of events, funds were reappropriated to be used for a long-term planning process that would serve the entire region. In this way, the status quo vision of good economic development—so often based on building infrastructure such as roads and bridges—had been completely transformed through an extraordinary showing of public support and volunteerism organized to create a collective vision of the area's future.

Like many others with whom I spoke during my visit in the summer of 2012, Carl asserted that—whether a formal outgrowth of the Grand Vision or not—a robust local food movement was taking off in Northern Michigan. People spoke to how this might be "relocalizing" the economy, encouraging a broad examination of lifestyle choices, and putting people in touch with one another in ways that surprised many. Further, a local currency was started at roughly the same time that the Grand Vision was born, and now "Bay Bucks" is growing in popularity as a way of keeping exchanges local. Whereas US currency could leave the area, Bay Bucks could not—except as souvenirs.

Carl was convinced that a growing number of people—fed up with the status quo—were willing not only to hope or imagine change but to do something to make it happen. He referred to the growing number of piano work clients who were open to bartering. Forced to explain his reluctance to take cash payment for his services, he is frequently led to explain the lifestyle choices that he has made. Carl explains that after initial confusion, many people get a wistful sparkle in their eyes. "Our problems today stem from a basic disease of disconnection," he says. He has given quite a few subsequently interested people tours of the land and living arrangements that he and Maeja now call home. While most are not ready for such an apparent leap, others have initiated a broad change in lifestyle inspired by what they have seen. On this Carl says: "This may not be the model, but it is a way to honor at least what I know to be true," as he points to his chest. "It is a way toward what is true. It may not be the end point, but it gets us out of the egocentric vision of exchange among people and allows for greater possibilities of connection."

REINVENT THE PIE—OR DIE

My time with Mike always begins with a cup of coffee. It is not only a gesture of welcome but also a wholehearted extension of his work ethic. In the process of acquiring my drink, he will pause to greet customers, clear a table, and check on his employees behind the counter. It all happens without apparent self-consciousness. Rather, it is what needs to be done for him to feel that things are good. In the summer of 2010, after he and I were finally settled in a relatively quiet corner catching up, I asked Mike to tell me how he's weathering the economic storm. Although I expected a report on his bottom line—after all, he is a business man—he began enthusiastically sharing his newfound knowledge of Michigan agriculture. In turn, I am taught about how Michigan State University is working with growers to develop hardier strains of cherries, apples, and blueberries. Mike has learned the fine points of Michigan agriculture because he has committed his entire business to buying Michigan products—much of these coming from the immediate geographic area: "We buy as much as possible in the state. We try to do our part. We buy something like a million pounds of fruit and other agricultural products in the state every year. The economic impact of paying the distributor, who is paying the processor, who is paying the grower, who is paying the employees, is that it all stays right here in Michigan." Today, he claims that more than 95 percent of his products—from the fruit, flour, and sugar in the pies to the table tops in his stores on which people have their own slice—comes from both small and large Michigan companies.

Mike explains that because the state has borne the brunt of the financial tempest, a "take-care-of-ourselves mentality" now breeds healthy localism. While he had always considered his business one that supported community by providing opportunity for local people through well-paying jobs in his store, the theme of local was now front and center and principal to his marketing: "You know, we are 'proudly made in Michigan.' We are the local guy, but Applebee's or Panera we're not. We try to preach to our franchisees that 'Hey, you're a local business. We share the same name, but we want people in your community to be proud of you for what you do *there*. That drives everything, even the bottom line." This doesn't appear to be simple branding, as Mike invoked big-picture ideas and switched to speaking about how here in Traverse City, people had for years assumed that big employers would just stay "because they've always been here" and that the community didn't need to make investments in itself. Fortunately, however, it seems that Traverse City and the surrounding area is a lot further along in thinking about such investment than many other places: "I think we have vision," Mike asserts. When Mike stated emphatically—"If you start a business, you embrace it. You don't leave it. Even if you're just sponsoring an event in the community, you still

Poster displayed near the door of the Grand Traverse
Pie Company stores. Photo by Brian Hoey

live it"—I realized (perhaps again) that for him there is little separation between his business and the values that led to his dramatic career change and lifestyle migration.

While most other businesses in the state were recoiling from shock, Mike found inspiration for growth: "Up until the last several of years, I really didn't want to grow. There are a lot of hassles with franchising, but if the brand grows and has success and can stimulate the local economy, then why not? Yes, we open every day and have to make pies—have to make a living—but that's only part of calling this a successful business." Being successful means making personal and economic investments in local community that lead to positive change and through serving as a kind of model, an inspirational story of what is possible. This led him to consider how he and Denise had progressed in their commitment to the business, community, and values that motivated their lifestyle migration. He reflects back on his early life: "You know, when you're born and raised in Lansing [Michigan], a union town, you put in so many years of service and then you put savings into a cabin or a boat come retirement. That's *not* the world that we live in anymore." Mike wanted to emphasize how he wasn't building a business on which he could retire or, more importantly, so that his kids could follow in his footsteps. To clarify, he spoke of how he had just recently been having lunch with his son Bobby—then a junior at Michigan State University in urban and regional planning—and Bobby said, "You've taught me that you can be whatever it is that you want." For Mike, "that's so much more than leaving them this business. It is leaving them the model, the *vision*."

Two years later, in the summer of 2012, I was back in the pie shop catching up again with Mike's news and doing my best to simply keep up with him as he moved around the store—getting a feel for things and tending to everyone's needs—before heading next door to his office for a meeting with his "numbers person" in order to look at the performance of more than a dozen stores, both franchised and corporate, scattered around Michigan and neighboring states. In the past year and a half, they had closed a total of six locations. At 9 a.m., the Traverse City shop was lively with breakfast and pie orders being filled. At the counter, a notice explained why cherry pie prices had jumped. Mike's comment of two years before about the need to develop hardier fruit varieties seemed prescient now as up to a 90 percent of the local tart cherry crop was lost earlier that spring due to unseasonably warm weather followed by a frost.

In the numbers meeting back in the office, the three of us took seats around a table in a small conference room. In front of us were stacks of printed tables and charts with figures that the two of them had spent an hour trying to interpret. What did the numbers mean? The recession meant that Mike looked much more closely at the data: "What's happening in the market there? I don't know when Panera opened, but we can probably find that here." Eventually, it was clear: The strategy of introducing gourmet salads and deli sandwiches—in order to directly confront Panera, a bakery-style chain with over sixteen hundred locations in North America—was a success. The figures on pie, however, didn't look as good. In fact, Mike's business partner, who joined us later, explained that *whole* pie sales had been going down industry-wide over the past few years. Despite this, everyone was clear on the need to get back to this "core of the brand" even while addressing broader menu choices. After all, their stated mission as a company is for "Warming Hearts and Community through Pie." Back in the franchise office—not far from a placard that reads "Love What You Do" as a kind of informal company motto—there's another sign that proclaims, simply, "Pie Can Do It."

Following this declaration, the next two hours were spent contemplating how it might be possible—and even necessary—to innovate the traditional, staid pie. With a social scientist in the room for this meeting, the conversation broadened to a discussion of changing demographics and cultural trends. Younger customers were coming into the stores for salads; could they be tempted by pie as well? What, in particular, of Millennials? Had they developed an expectation for self-centered customization born, perhaps, of an infinitely variable suite of apps on their iPhones? What about a hand-held pie—shaped like a slice—which can be personalized on-site? "We need to do some serious R&D on this," Mike asserted. I did not mention my own sense that a drop in whole pie sales seemed a sort of chilling confirmation of the thesis of those social scientists who decry a loss of community in America. If people are not buying and sharing pies, wouldn't individualizing the desert only serve to exacerbate the erosion of social capital? Perhaps, but in an odd echo of my opening chapter—which explores the essential adage of a robust capitalism, "Reinvent or Die"—the economic imperative for Mike's business seemed clear: *Reinvent the Pie.*

Having not stopped for lunch and with all this talk of food, by 2:30 in the afternoon our stomachs were audibly growling. Mike decided to take me to his new downtown store, where he intended to check-in with the manager there. While navigating abundant traffic in a nearly vain attempt to find a parking spot at the height of the widely acclaimed Traverse City Film Festival, Mike got a call on his cell phone—it went to voicemail. Later, as we walked to his pie shop a few doors from the festival's main venue at a refurbished mid-twentieth-century theater, he returned the call from the owner of the pie shop in California that had started his lifestyle dreaming nearly twenty years earlier. Commenting on the call, he explained that he continues to work with her on innovative recipes—including a viable gluten-free crust—as part of what he only half-jokingly refers to as the "Fraternity of Pie." Once we were seated in his other Traverse City store—and noticing my obvious admiration for the beautiful wood table at which we were enjoying our sandwiches—he explained that it was his commitment to Michigan business that allowed for him to acquire the tables. In so doing, he made an unexpected but deeply personal connection: It turns out that the man with whom he had contracted was a materials recycler—much like the supplier for Carl and Maeja's cabin—who used wood from the original ceiling rafters of the old Lansing Armory. This was the place where Mike's mother once went to USO dances in the 1940s. As I previously noted, Mike deliberately finds ways to connect the personal and the professional. Mike's mom became their first bookkeeper when the pie shop opened—allowing family and work to be purposefully integrated while giving her meaningful work late in life.

Looking pensive, he reflected on what all this meant to him—the business and the choices that he made to get here. Mike laid out a brief personal history of the

Mike standing in front of his downtown store on Front Street, Traverse City. Photo by Brian Hoey

business: "When I started out, it was all about 'Is this going to work?' It was only later that we could look at the people around us, the suppliers and others, and begin to think more seriously about how we could integrate the business with the community." He explained that when he and Denise had started, it was about rejecting the lack of commitment to employees and loss of attachment to community by his large corporate employer as a different economic order emerged. There had been passion to do something else at that time, but the passion hadn't yet been defined. He described how they had outlined an economic engine, that is, to "make the best pie," because it seemed likely that this could make money in the area. This day, however, that passion had been defined and honed by the fires of recession. Mike was now passionately committing his business to the support of other local businesses, and Denise had started and was working with a variety of local nonprofits that support such unambiguously right causes as ending child abuse.

Earlier in the day, when I had been behind the counter at the original pie shop,

I literally ran into Denise on that busy morning, as she was prepping for baking seventy-five pies that had been previously made by foster kids giving their time as part of a project to raise money for the local land conservancy. Seeing me, she reflected: "I'm hardly back here anymore. I miss it, but I've moved out into the community work." Looking back on the decision to expand the business to other locations and franchising, Denise explained that it was especially hard when some franchisees "didn't get it," as she described. "This is all about heart, about community—through pie. The ones that get that do well. The company has been moving that way—an even greater commitment to community." Speaking about how he had now chosen to find suppliers engaged in sustainable agriculture or working for social justice (the case with the small company supplying his coffee), Mike reflected on how he was changed by the lifestyle commitment that he and Denise had made sixteen years earlier: "I used to be an old generation capitalist. Now, I see that trickle-down doesn't work. We need to be willing to set the table so that others have a chance. I'm not drinking the Kool-Aid anymore."

APPENDIX 1

Methodological Considerations

Using aggregate, census-type data, most studies of migration in the United States have focused on providing relatively distant macrolevel explanations of causes and consequences of observed migration patterns.[1] That is to say, these studies have generally attempted to speak from a bird's-eye view to broad trends and, specifically, to quantitative assessments of population movement between different areas of the country. A limited number of scholars have taken a microlevel approach in an attempt to get closer to the ground so as to explore processes of migration decision making and examine an array of economic and noneconomic issues that may weigh on those decisions.[2]

At this level, discussions typically focus on motivation and attempt to place individual or family choice behavior within a field of *constraining* and *enabling* factors from the proximate and personal to the social and structural. These include the availability and quality of information about destinations, extent and nature of individual social networks, personal characteristics such as ability to accept risk, and the social, economic, and demographic characteristics of the household. Here research on lifestyle migration shares interest with and contributes to studies on work and family decision making affecting residential migration, job-related relocation, and a household "career hierarchy" wherein calculations are made as to whose career will take priority.[3]

Foundational, microlevel data for this book was gathered through in-depth, open-ended interviews with in-migrants to study area communities who relocated beginning as early as 1980. Interviews emphasizing personal background, reasons for leaving a job and relocating, the process of relocation decision making, and the means of negotiating individual identity after the move were conducted with a total of 128 individuals (see Appendix 2 for the Initial Interview Guide). Formal interviewing—where an appointment was made in which I would meet with the interviewee using an interview guide—was an important part of this research in that it allowed me access to some individuals who would otherwise not have been available given schedules and inclinations regarding participation in the project. It also provided a practical way to compare details across individual stories.

A number of these interviews led to more thorough study of particular cases. This involved extended, informal follow-up conversations and observation in everyday work and family life of this core group of participants. While a larger sample allowed me to consider a range of personal backgrounds and relocation experi-

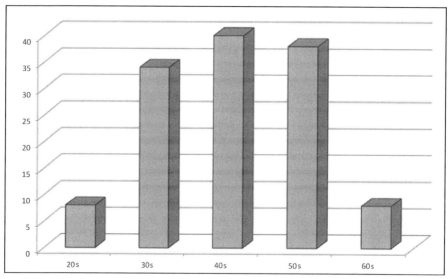

Figure A.1 Age of participants

ences, I maintained frequent contact with four individuals and eight families who relocated within the five years prior to the start of my fieldwork in 2000. The more formal initial interviews were scheduled with individuals responding either to fliers posted at local businesses such as grocery stores, theaters, bookstores, and restaurants or local newspaper, television, and radio reports on the project. These persons then helped to identify potential participants, many of whom after my contact with them joined the study to form the overall sample assembled largely through word of mouth and the loose social networks that emerged among newcomers.

Reflecting demographics of in-migrants to the area, study participants were white and generally what would be objectively classified as middle class. Participants were largely professionals, including managers, accountants, lawyers, social workers, and those in fields related to health care. Almost half found or made work after relocation in a field they considered a significant departure from their record of employment or field of study. Nearly 60 percent saw at least an initial drop in income from prerelocation levels ranging from as little as 5 and to as much as 40 percent. Forty percent started their own business, ranging from home-based consultancies to retail shops with several employees. Of the remaining participants, most found either salaried or hourly wage work in the local government, school system, community college, or hospital or in a wide variety of local businesses. Nearly 20 percent worked two part-time jobs in order to meet income goals.

Of a total of 128 formal participants, roughly even amounts (30 percent) were in their thirties, forties, and fifties respectively, with slightly more than half female (see Figure A.1). Nearly 30 percent were married with grown children no longer living at home full-time. There was a roughly even split among the remainder between those married with young children, married with school-age children, married with no children, and single (see Figure A.2). Approximately 60 percent of

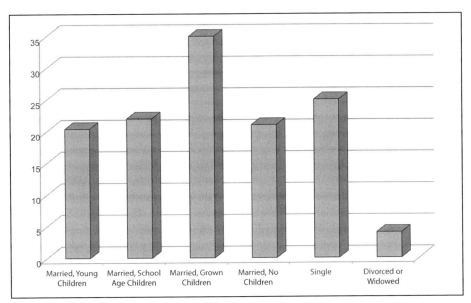

Figure A.2 Marital status of participants

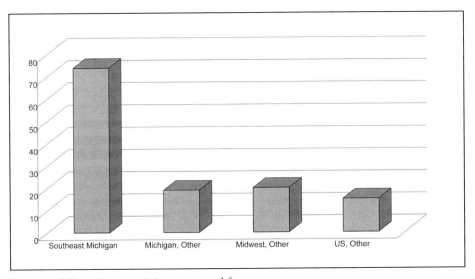

Figure A.3 Locations participants moved from

participants relocated from southeastern Michigan, while the rest were split evenly between other parts of Michigan, the Midwest more generally, and the United States at large (see Figure A.3). Eighty percent of migrant areas of origin were outside urban cores but still classifiable as metropolitan. Seventy percent had vacationed in the study area either as children or as adults. Approximately 60 percent of participants moved to the study area within the previous five years.[4]

Many of the profound social changes taking place in the realm of work and family in the United States remain only partially understood—if at all. This is the reason that the Alfred P. Sloan Foundation funded the research on which this book is based. Despite this shortage of knowledge, there has been no lack of political rhetoric about American families being under siege and about the inadequacy in our communities for meeting the challenges facing American society. Non-anthropologists increasingly employ ethnographic techniques native to this discipline in part as a response to the relative lack of genuine understanding about why these changes are taking place, the meanings these changes have for people, and how people are choosing to react to them in their everyday lives. Working in the United States, these researchers contribute to a more complete picture of social problems and trends by adding to knowledge already derived from polling, statistical studies, media analysis, and journalistic inquiry.

While anthropology is the disciplinary home of ethnographic approaches—as noted in my preface to the book—because of historical peculiarities in the development of the discipline, anthropologists have been outnumbered in the discussion of social change in the United States when compared to contributions made by economists, demographers, political scientists, and sociologists. Anthropologists have tended to work in settings deemed more exotic than the suburban middle class. Over the past thirty-some years, anthropologists have challenged the assumptions and biases on which this deficiency is based.

Donald Messerschmidt's 1981 edited volume on anthropological work in North America was one of the first detailed looks into the methods and issues of study by ethnographers working in their own society. In his introductory chapter, Messerschmidt addresses the continuation of established theoretical roots and methodological traditions of the profession in so-called work "at home."[5] On the whole, contributors to this volume found that approaches long used in cross-cultural settings can be applied at home with additional considerations for more team and multidisciplinary approaches. In my own case, I have essentially followed the same approach that I used in earlier fieldwork among largely involuntary migrants in Indonesia, but I recognize that my place as participant-observer is substantially different here than it was there. In the current project, although there are differences in life experience between informants and myself, I can be considered "native."

Might the fieldworker serve as a key informant in his or her *own* culture? I think so. That was my experience in fieldwork conducted for this book as I became a significant member in the community of study—living and working in a way that was simply impossible when I was in Indonesia. Fieldworkers conducting research in their own culture may provide vital functions otherwise available only from natives while doing work within other cultures. These include having perspective as the anthropologists learn fragments of the system before comprehending their place in the larger system as well as hypothesis reduction, which is normally assisted by the native key informant who helps to reduce explanations to a researchable few.[6]

Native anthropologists ideally combine an observer's impartiality as a professional with the cultural expertise of a native who remains emotionally and intellectually involved in the events and beliefs of study.[7] The training and sensitivity of a professional ethnographer should allow one to cut through the naturalness of native categories—effectively making what might be taken-for-granted familiarity, unfamiliar—though we must be wary of biases of familiarity that could lead a native ethnographer to regard popular culture, for example, as trivial and unworthy.

In a similar vein, the oral-historian Valerie Yow speaks to meaning making both in how the subject of research interprets experience and how researchers interject themselves in this process, both as observers and as narrators themselves.[8] More broadly, all researchers—and perhaps especially ethnographers—by their very presence in the field help to give shape to the phenomenon that they observe. I have always contended that such "reactive effects," that is, how people respond to our presence, are themselves important forms of data. Yow suggests seeing such work as fundamentally collaborative—a notion put fully into practice in the work of my colleague, the anthropologist Luke Eric Lassiter, at Marshall University.[9] Similarly to Yow, I followed a method that allowed informants to tell me their stories in a life-history approach so that I could see the process by which—as narrators—they constructed identity through autobiographical storytelling. Beyond the initial interview, my informants choose what to discuss, decided how to treat the topic, and drew their own conclusions, thus giving their own continuity to the story.

In the treatment of informant narratives as accounts and my own notes of our encounters, I use a theme analysis approach much like that suggested by anthropologist Sherry Ortner, whose enduring notion of "key symbols" and "scenarios" I have always found helpful.[10] In addition to examining the text of these narratives for themes, I have also attempted to be aware of meta- or master-narratives that form composite understandings shared by members of a larger group.[11] I have, for example, looked at understandings of career in corporate America through my work with those lifestyle migrants I have called "corporate refugees" on the basis of their own descriptions of their experience.

The anthropologist John Van Maanen reminds us that ethnographies like this book are themselves narratives and—as with the narratives of individuals included within—they are experientially driven and purposefully shaped by the ethnographer. The interpretive process entailed in going from fieldwork data to the written account is about translating experience—of those participating in the research as well as those conducting that research—into texts. Van Maanen has gone so far as to assert that ethnography "is the peculiar practice of representing the social reality of others through the analysis of one's own experience in the world of these others."[12]

Although concerned specifically with documentary fieldwork, Robert Coles has shown how any attempt to represent reality is necessarily an interpretation despite the fact that there is a tendency among readers or viewers of such work to accept it at face value—to view it as a somehow autonomous reality. A child psychiatrist and author of countless books concerned with human moral and spiritual reasoning, Coles's point is that objectivity is a myth. The representation of life entails some subjective distortion given that the lived world is complex and ambiguous when compared with the comparative neatness required of an account of the research on which it is based. In the end Coles asserts, "Through selection, emphasis and the magic of narrative art, the reader or viewer gets convincingly close to a scene, a subject matter and sees the documentary as one of many possible takes, not the story, but a story."[13] In this spirit, I attempt to provide a compelling story of lifestyle migration that reflects the subjective, lived experience of those with whom I have worked.

APPENDIX 2

Initial Interview Guide

BIOGRAPHICAL INFORMATION

Okay, we're going to warm up with some very basic biographical kinds of information so we have some background for later questions. Many of these beginning questions will only require a brief response, but feel free to explain anything further should you feel the need.

- What was the date and place of your birth?
- Where did you grow up?
- How long did you live there?

If s/he is from the study area:

- Why did you leave originally?
- Why have you come back to the area?
- How has the area changed?
- How do you feel about those changes?
- What do you remember most about this place?
- Please describe to me what it was like here so that I can imagine what it was like.

See if s/he mentions moving around. If so, have him/her explain both why these moves were made and how s/he felt about them.

- How about your parents?
    - Where are they living/did they live?
- Do you recall your parents having any dominant concerns when you were growing up, things that they might have thought were very important or even that seemed to preoccupy their time?
- What were these things?
- Could you describe them for me?
- What was the level of formal education or training that your parents had?
- How would you describe their income or socioeconomic status when you were growing up?
- What is your level of formal education or training?
- How would you define your current level of income or socioeconomic status?

WORK, HOME, AND FAMILY LIFE

Okay, we're going to shift gears. Now we're going to focus more close on work and family kinds of questions with regard to your life since becoming an adult . . .

- How would you describe your present job?

- How long have you had this job?
- Have you had this job since you moved to the area?

Get clarification if s/he has changed jobs since moving to study area.
- What do you most like/dislike about what you do?
- Do you expect to remain in this job for the foreseeable future?
- About how many hours per week would you say you spend doing work directly related to this job?
- If we were to discuss the work that you were doing before moving to the area, how would you describe this job and your feelings toward it?
- Would you say that there were differences between the job you had before moving here and the job you have now?
- People will sometimes choose an occupation in order to accommodate the demands of family. Would you say that this has been the case for you in choosing a job?
- Please describe your family to me (not natal family).
- Where do family members spend most of their time?
- Do you usually look forward to being at home while you are at work?
- What kinds of chores do you do at home?
- Do you consider these activities "work?"
- How are they the same or different than "work?"
- If you had more time to spend either at home or at work, or perhaps somewhere else, where would you choose to spend more time?
- Do you feel that you have enough time to pursue activities that you value and enjoy?
- How about before your move to this area?
    - Would you say that how you spent your time was more or less the same or somehow different to now? Please explain.
- Aside from activities that are specifically work and/or family related, what other things do you engage in outside of work and family responsibilities? [If a prompt is required: For example, do you participate in any local organizations?]
    - If so, how important is it to you that you participate in these organizations?
- Have your routines changed since your move?
    - If so, please explain how you feel that they have changed.
- How long have you lived in your current place of residence?

Get clarification on where else s/he has lived if current place of residence is not the first and only residence in the study area.
- If you have moved, why did you move from that/those location(s) to where you are now?
- On the whole, would you say that you are happy with your current place?
    - What things do you like/dislike about it?
    - What would you change?
    - What kinds of things do you think would make those changes possible/practical?
- How about before your move to the Traverse City area?
    - Were you happy with your place of residence?
    - What would you have changed then?
    - What sorts of considerations went into choosing that place of residence?
    - What kind of relationship did you have with neighbors?
- How was the decision made to move to the Traverse City area?
    - Could you please describe for me how you made that decision?
    - What sort of things were important to you in that decision-making process?
    - Were there differences in how you and your family/your spouse/your household felt about the move? How so?

- What would you say the best things are about living in this area?
- What would you say are the worst things?
- Would you say that these things are different or the same as your expectations before moving here?
- Suppose that you/your family (household) was able to double your level of income, what—if anything—would you change about your style of living?
    - For example, would you remain in this present place of residence?
    - Would you remain in this area?
    - Why or why not?
- How important is it that you be near relatives?
    - Did this issue come into your decision making? Please explain.
    - Are there any in the area?
    - If so, who?
- Have you ever had to take on additional work—aside from your principal job—in order to meet financial demands placed on you by your family?
    - What were the circumstances at that time?
    - How did you feel about the experience of taking on this additional work?
    - Was this ever necessary before you moved?
- What sort of schedule do you have at work?
- How flexible is it?
- Would you say that you are able to take time to do more at home or at work when you need to?
- Could you bring work home from your job if you wanted to?
- What would or do you like/dislike about being able to do this?
- What kinds of work do you bring home? How often?
- Before you moved what was your work schedule like?
- Did you ever work at home? Why or why not?
- How often do you find yourself thinking about work while you are at home doing things around the house?
    - Do you find this to be a distraction?
    - If s/he works at home: How would you describe your working at home?
- Would you consider it an ideal situation?

Notes

PREFACE
1. Hoey (2003).
2. Rogerson (1999:983).
3. Excerpt from promotional brochure for the 2nd Annual Michigan Legislative and Business Leaders Public Policy Forum, Traverse City, MI, September 2000.
4. Michigan is a state surrounded by water—leading some to refer to it as America's "third coast" after the Atlantic and Pacific coasts. Two peninsulas are formed by Lakes Huron, Michigan, and Superior. In local vernacular, there is an Upper Peninsula and a Lower Peninsula to distinguish these two parts of the state divided by a channel connecting Lake Huron and Lake Michigan. The Lower Peninsula is what most Americans recognize as the state of Michigan. The Grand Traverse region is located in the northwestern part of the Lower Peninsula.
5. Brown-Saracino (2009:252).
6. Veblen (1965 [1899]).
7. Bradshaw (1994).
8. Wolfe (1998).
9. A more detailed discussion of methodological considerations can be found in Appendix 1. A copy of the initial interview guide may be found in Appendix 2.

CHAPTER 1
1. Simon, Paul. "America," from *Bookends*, Simon and Garfunkel. Columbia CK 66003, 1968, LP.
2. Burns (2010).
3. For a discussion of themes underlying my understanding of this option, see Jasper (2000), Leach (1999), and Morrison and Wheeler (1978).
4. United Van Lines (2008).
5. Florida (2009).
6. Belden, Russonello, and Stewart (2011).
7. Buchholz and Buchholz (2012).
8. Meilhan quoted in Tuttle (2012).
9. French (April 3, 2009).
10. French and Wilkinson (2009), French (April 2, 2009).
11. Quoted in French (April 2, 2009).
12. French and Wilkinson (2009).
13. Boulding (1966).
14. Beckley (2005).
15. Schumpeter (1976 [1942]).

CHAPTER 2

1. Davidson (1990).
2. Bender (1982).
3. Ortner (1997:62).
4. Ortner's (1997) approach, which she considers "radically delocalized," traces the members of a single high school class and finds among them an enduring sense of community, although her subjects exhibit 100 percent mobility from the place they lived when in high school together roughly forty years prior. What she follows is community on the move as a "structure of feeling," à la Raymond Williams, or a "community of the mind" located in the real lives, practices, and systems of relations; in other words, the persistence of an idea of community despite the lack of immediacy and participation that we normally associate with ideal community that is geographically located.
5. Hummon (1990:179–80) is referring to Gusfield's *Community: A Critical Response*.
6. Ibid., p. 38.
7. Geertz (1973:12).
8. See Fricke (1997).
9. MacGregor (2010).
10. Ibid., p. 8, emphasis added.
11. Brown-Saracino (2009:8).
12. MacGregor (2010:9).
13. Ibid., p. 33.
14. Ibid., p. 35.
15. For discussions of place marketing, see Edmondson (1998), Kearns and Philo (1993); Rogerson (1999), and Ward (1998). Hummon's (1990:27) study on community ideology and identity also provides useful insight into how popular views of community are the product of both direct, individual experience and enculturation as well as how they originate from how residents (and others) "read," literally and figuratively, from community icons, slogans, and authoritative community imagery and community landscape by "interpreting the social and symbolic messages encoded in the styles and other features of the built environment."
16. Gillett and Gamble (1998:423).
17. Quoted in Holdrich (2005).
18. Gillett and Gamble (1998:423).
19. Bellah et al. (1996).
20. Jackson (2008); see also Osbaldiston (2013).
21. I subsequently learned how this phrase was immortalized in country music fame through the songwriting of Pikeville, Kentucky, native Dwight Yoakam. Yoakam's tune "Readin,' Rightin,' Route 23," from a 1987 album titled *Hillbilly Deluxe*, speaks to a childhood experience of leaving Appalachia from his hometown just off Route 23 in the coalfields of eastern Kentucky at a very young age. Among its lyrics are the following lines:

    They learned readin,' rightin,' Route 23
    To the jobs that lay waiting in those cities' factories

22. See Richardson (2007).
23. Powell (2007).
24. Wakefield and Wakefield (1980).
25. Leelanau County Association of Commerce (1924).
26. Reporting in his *Algic Researches*, Henry Rowe Schoolcraft (1839) translated the word as "delight of life" in the context of a story he called "Leelinau, or the Lost Daughter, an Odjibwa Tale." The tale itself concerns a Native American girl who, from a young age,

preferred the company of spirits in an enchanted grove of pines where she sought quiet contemplation and refuge from the everyday. Eventually, she becomes so charmed by the place and its otherworldly inhabitants that she disappears, apparently joining them on some ethereal plane. Over time, the name has become Leelanau and the translation has become disconnected from the tale itself.

27. Aron (1999); Sears (1989).
28. At the same time, there are fundamentally material aspects of personhood. These material aspects involve embodiment as a basic or "ontological" feature of personhood, which is to say that it has to do with our very existence. This simply speaks to the fact that we have a physical body that must be situated in a world of material things. We are always oriented in physical space through our being embodied. Embodiment entails the way persons negotiate everyday lives through their physicality, and how they mediate, interpret, and interact with both social and physical environments. In this way, this materiality is as fundamental to being and human subjectivity as is our sociality—our relationship with others in society. See Csordas (1990) and Scheper-Hughes (1994).
29. For a discussion of the idea of key symbols, see Ortner (1973). I discuss my use of symbols in a thematic analysis of individual and meta narratives in Appendix 1.
30. See Bourdieu (1977).
31. Taylor (1989). See also Bellah et al. (1996) and Wuthnow (1996).
32. For a discussion of this particular notion of "quest," see MacIntyre (1984:203–4).

CHAPTER 3
Epigraph: Steinbeck (1962:3).
1. Johnson and Beale (1998:23). See Shi (1985).
2. See Shi (1986).
3. Shi (1985:6).
4. Turner (1966 [1894]:200).
5. For discussions of the symbolic power of places understood as "frontier," see Cuba (1987); Limerick (2000); Smith (1950); and White et al. (1994).
6. Bell (1994).
7. Cuba (1987:164).
8. Jacobson (2002:3). Useful to an understanding of the essential importance for personhood of "place," as material space made culturally meaningful, are early works by human geographers such as Edward Relph (1976) and Yi-Fu Tuan (1974) on similar ideas of lived experience of place, "existential insideness" or "topophilia," and the meaning of placelessness for self. See also Edward Soja (1989) on subjectivity and the ontological priority of a connection between spatiality and being, as well as Kent Ryden (1993) for a highly readable, humanistic, and folkloric approach to place where stories of place are simultaneously expressions of self.
9. Bell (1994:7).
10. See Hoey (2007) for a discussion of such positive environmentalism in the context of late nineteenth century reform of asylums for the insane—including one constructed according to these principles located in my study area of Northern Michigan.
11. Fishman (1987).
12. Glacken (1967); Macy and Bonnemaison (2003).
13. MacIntyre (1984:212).
14. Ibid., p. 205. See Sennett (1998).
15. Certeau, (1984:115).
16. Johnstone (1990:5,134).
17. Gray (1989:59).
18. Taylor (1989:22, emphasis added).

19. Heat-Moon (1982); Herzog (1999); Steinbeck (1962).
20. Brown-Saracino (2009:10). See also Lawrence-Zúñiga (2010) for a discussion of this motivation and the tensions that it can create.
21. Aron (1999). See also Sears (1989).
22. At the same time, vacationing was becoming an important way of demonstrating achieved status in having not only the financial capacity to indulge in this kind of leisure but also the personal capacity to appreciate the sublime beauty of natural scenery at the place of destination. Being on holiday in these places became a way of distinguishing the tourist as a person of "breeding and sophistication . . . a member of the 'refined and cultivated' classes" (Aron [1999]:130).
23. Galani-Moutafi (2000) and Noy (2004). See also Neuman (1992).

CHAPTER 4
1. See Baudrillard and Poster (2001:25).
2. For more on this phenomenon, see Balfe (1999); Hall and Müller (2004) and McIntyre et al. (2006).
3. See Clark and Officer (1962) who speak directly to "the Line."
4. According to the Traverse City Convention and Visitors Bureau's own accounting of the origin of visitors to the area, 70 percent were found to originate from elsewhere in Michigan, another 20 percent were from other midwestern states including Ohio, Indiana, Illinois, and Wisconsin, and the remaining 10 percent originated in another part of either the country or the world.
5. Rink (1999:10).
6. Quoted in Wakefield (1977:36–37).
7. Wakefield (1988).
8. It was during the 1920s that the area began having its annual Cherry Festival, which now brings close to half a million to the area in July, when the crop is generally ready to be harvested.
9. Gamble and Gillett (1998).
10. McGillivary (2012).
11. The lyrics of the song "Boomtown" are shown at the beginning of Chapter 13.
12. Heath (2001).

CHAPTER 5
1. Kilborn (2009).
2. Goodwin (1993:147).
3. Ibid. See also Kotler et al. (1993).
4. See Burgess (1982).
5. Bell (1994:240).
6. Hummon (1990) has noted the role of local institutions in shaping local as well as outsider perceptions of a place.
7. Gillis (1996); Putnam (2000).
8. Whyte (1956).
9. Sweet (2006); see also Sweet and Meiksins (2008).
10. Darrah et al. (2007).
11. Gillis (1996:232).
12. Shweder (1998).
13. Sennett (1998:31).
14. As far as I can tell, the original use of the term "downshift" was by Amy Saltzman (1991) in *Downshifting: Reinventing Success on a Slower Track*. Although it may have been previously used, Saltzman made it her own.

15. Pink (2001).
16. Families and Work Institute (2003).
17. Paine (2006). See also Zemke et al. (2000). This observation, however, appears in contrast to assertions by Buchholz and Buchholz (2012).
18. Bell (1994).
19. See Vidich and Bensman (1958). See also Hummon (1990).
20. See Taylor (1989).
21. Wuthnow (1996:4).
22. There is conflicting research regarding both the amount of leisure time average Americans now enjoy (as well as the income they take home). Although in *The Overworked American: The Unexpected Decline of Leisure*, Juliet Schor (1991) finds that there have been dramatic increases in work hours compared to leisure time over the past generation, studies such as those of John Robinson and Geoffrey Godbey (1999) have found that collectively the US population has as much as six more hours a day per person, on average, than in the 1970s. They note that retirees, however, realized most of the gain and that ultimately much of the time gains people have received are not *experienced* as leisure. Economists Ellen McGrattan and Richard Rogerson (1998) find that census data since 1950 also shows that with leisure time the question is not so much more or less but rather for who. For people aged twenty-five to fifty-four, there was more than a 20 percent increase in hours worked while for those sixty-five to seventy-four, the hours were reduced 50 percent.
23. Reich (2000).
24. Bell (1994:23).
25. Taylor (1989:23, emphasis in original).
26. Ibid., p. 5.
27. Bellah et al. (1996:99).
28. Wuthnow (1996:46).

CHAPTER 6
Epigraph: Stocking (1990:93, 147).
1. Heubusch (1998:43). Heubusch excludes any places that are part of a designated Metropolitan Statistical Area in the US Census, which puts these micropolitans outside the "metro squeeze and beyond suburban sprawl." Furthermore, the micropolitans must contain at least fifteen thousand residents with at least forty thousand in the surrounding county. Traverse City has just over fifteen thousand residents and is in a county of nearly seventy thousand.
2. For studies of skilled, tech-oriented laborers, see, for example, Beaverstock (2001) and Ong (2003). For studies on the international migration of well-heeled retirees, see, for example, Casado-Diaz (2006); Sunil et al. (2007); Williams et al., (1997).
3. Benson and O'Reilly (2009, *Lifestyle*; 2009, "Migration").
4. See, for example, Burnley and Murphy (2004) and Osbaldiston (2012).
5. Costello (2007).
6. Ullman (1954).
7. McGranahan (1999); McGranahan and Sullivan (2005); McGranahan (2008). The role of natural amenities in migration behavior has been investigated by other scholars in the United States including Carlson et al. (1988); Clark (1991); Comartie (2001); Greenwood and Hunt (1989); and Rudzitis (1999). Amenity migration in the broader international context is documented by such scholars as Moss (2006) in an edited volume on the subject for mountainous areas in a range of countries.
8. See Berry (1976); Williams and Sofranko (1979).
9. Jobes (1992).
10. Nearing and Nearing (1970).

11. Jacob (1997).
12. United States Environmental Protection Agency (1972:iii, 1).
13. For an early discussion of what he called "elements of structural conduciveness," see Smelser (1962).
14. Calvin Beale, a researcher at the Economic Development Division of the US Department of Agriculture, is generally attributed with discovering the turnaround or, at the very least, noticing that population estimates between 1970 and 1973 indicated that population growth in nonmetropolitan areas on the whole was greater than in metropolitan areas. Beale's (1975) paper on the "revival of population growth in non-metropolitan America" stimulated a series of studies both in the United States and eventually abroad. Brian Berry (1976; 1980:14) provided a term and general definition for the phenomenon. Berry describes the gain of nonmetropolitan areas as a process of "counterurbanization" as it occurred in direct opposition to a historical tendency toward the increasing population concentration we know as urbanization. For Berry, counterurbanization is "a process of population deconcentration; it implies a movement from a state of more concentration to a state of less concentration."
15. British geographer Anthony Champion (1989), whose work is concerned with the analysis of population distribution trends in industrialized nations, has noted that the idea of a clean break has been challenged by four basic and progressively more restrictive definitions of what might be considered necessary in order to constitute a clean break from past trends. These definitions include considerations that such a break should only be recognized if relevant growth (1) is not merely "spillover" from metropolitan areas; (2) is not leading to the emergence of new metropolitan areas; (3) is not taking place as new urbanized areas or settlements; and (4) is not merely a relocation of urban lifestyles to nonurban settings but rather is a change from an urban to a rural or "neo-rural" lifestyle.
16. Both Hummon (1990) and Cuba (1987) discuss a generally "anti-urban" sentiment that prevails among Americans in terms of their community preferences and ideals. Specifically, Hummon notes that for those who are dissatisfied with where they are and want to relocate someplace else, they more often than not would choose a smaller, less urban location.
17. See Fishman (2005) and Lessinger (1986; 1991). See also Wolf (1999).
18. Mumford (1925).
19. Ibid., p. 130.
20. Ibid.
21. Ibid., p. 131.
22. See Baumgartner (1988).
23. Mead (1949:454).
24. Yi-Fu Tuan (1974) believed that suburbanization is a reaction to the city and a stage in the process of urbanization, a frontier in its eventual expansion.
25. Fine (1989:4).
26. Wolf (1999).
27. See Wolf (1999) for application of Lessinger's model.
28. Lessinger (1987:33).
29. Ibid., p. 34. In a similar manner, Mumford suggested that the early twentieth century conservation movement in the United States grew out of a desire to "repair the evils of the first migration," specifically the wasteful use of *natural* resources. We can also see some similarity with Brown-Saracino's "social preservationist" type in the context of urban gentrification.
30. At least in some respects, Lessinger's work reflects assertions made in Alvin Toffler's book *Third Wave*, published in 1980, that predicted the creation of a postindustrial lifestyle in the American countryside where people would be able to be connected electronically to work and would value careful use of resources and protection of the environment.

31. Fishman (2005:359).
32. Brown-Saracino (2009).
33. Ibid., p. 9.
34. Fishman (2005:363).
35. Ibid., p. 265. See also Lawrence-Zúñiga (2010) on preservationist attitudes among historic home owners.
36. Jobes (2000). For generally consistent findings for the characteristics of in-migrants presented in research on noneconomic, urban-rural migration, see Fuguitt et al. (1989); Ghose (1998); and Judson et al. (1999). At least one recent study has branded these migrants members of the "new middle" or "service" class—a cohort with residential preferences strongly influenced by a rural ideal. Jobes also found that lifestyle migrants were especially likely to no longer be integrated in to permanent, dependable, supportive groups, including family, neighborhood, church, and community. Echoing assertions by Robert Putnam and others, Jobes concludes that this is a consequence of an overall decline in traditional forms of community. See also Putnam (2000).
37. Thrush (1999:49).
38. Kilborn (2009).
39. Joinson (1998:63). At one time, corporate assistance in job relocation extended only so far as moving day. During the 1970s, I moved three times by the time I was eight, as the child of a career IBM employee, so I have some direct experience with this—my mother used to tell my father it must be time to move because the freezer needed defrosting. More recently—at least in better economic conditions than the past several years—there has been a trend toward providing more of what are called transition support services in order to help meet varied family concerns, including "identifying resources in the new location and helping families re-create their lifestyle" (ibid., p. 68). As stated by the CEO of a "mobility services" company, the bottom line, as it were, in today's business of job relocations is that "there's closer scrutiny of the economic impact of a move and what it does to quality of life" (quoted in ibid., p. 70).
40. Moen (2001).

CHAPTER 7

1. Gini (2000:8).
2. In 1989 the Bureau of Labor Statistics developed the following conceptual definition: "Contingent work is any job in which an individual does not have an explicit or implicit contract for long-term employment." Polivka and Nardone (1989:11).
3. Freedman (1985:35).
4. Martin (1999).
5. Saltzman (1991).
6. In his work in the Silicon Valley presented at the American Anthropological Meetings in 2000 entitled "Techno-Missionaries Doing Good at the Center," Charles Darrah (2000:5) describes some of the unique ways that this place has developed as a community with its own distinctive culture of work. Among his findings he notes that while the idea that people "seek a grander meaning to their jobs is certainly not new, . . . historically most such claims have argued that the work is valuable to society. What is perhaps distinctive in the accounts of work in Silicon Valley is that work transforms that society to the extent that others embrace its products, services, and outlooks. The process is essentially one of conversion to a new way of seeing and acting."
7. Rybczynski (1991).
8. See Yankelovich (1982) and Moen (2001).
9. The term "Me, Inc." is attributed to Tom Peters, a business consultant quoted in Murray (2000).

CHAPTER 8
Epigraph: MacCannell (1999:5–6).
1. Hummon (1990:21).
2. Hochschild (1997).
3. Rieff (1987).
4. Robinson and Godbey (1999:314).
5. For a range of discussions on consumer behavior and desire, see the edited volume by Roger Rosenblatt (1999). Remarkably, one point that Rosenblatt makes in his chapter is that directly or indirectly, 90 percent of the US workforce is in the business of producing consumer goods and services.
6. For an overview of anthropological studies of consumption and commodities and a discussion of its importance to the discipline, see Miller (1995).
7. Bonner (1997:169).
8. Lasch (1977).
9. For a detailed discussion of idealized popular and academic views of the family, see Skolnick (1991). See also Coontz (1992).
10. Philo and Kearns (1993:3).
11. Landor Associates (2001; emphasis added).
12. Knudson (1999).
13. Ibid.
14. Savageau (2000).
15. Williams (1973:248).
16. Philo and Kearns (1993:3).
17. Tarrant (2001:5).

CHAPTER 9
1. Low (1994:66).
2. Ryden (1993:252).
3. Csordas (1990); Scheper-Hughes (1994).
4. Leach (1999); Sennett (1998).
5. Bellah et al. (1996); Putnam (2000); Wuthnow (1996).
6. Quoted in Yaeger (1996:10); cf. Soja (1989).
7. Yaeger (1996:10); cf. Ryden (1993).
8. Yaeger (1996:10).
9. Putnam (2000); Bellah et al. (1996); Wuthnow (1996).
10. Taylor (1989:47).
11. Taylor (1989:51); cf. Ricoeur (1992:115) on how narrative presupposes the moral.
12. Ochs and Capps (1996); Hoey (2005; 2006).
13. Bruner (1990); Bakhtin (1981).
14. Taylor (1997); Ricoeur (1992).
15. Hochschild (1997); cf. Markus and Nurius (1986) on "possible selves."
16. Ricouer (1984).
17. Ricoeur (1992:147); MacIntyre (1984); Taylor (1989).
18. Ricoeur (1992:121); Sennett (1998).
19. Green (1999).
20. Altman and Low (1992); Buttimer and Seamon (1980); Hummon (1992); Relph (1976); Seamon (1982); Tuan (1974).
21. Proshansky (1983).
22. Goffman quoted in Milligan (2003:383).
23. Ryden (1993); Tuan (1977).
24. Altman and Low (1992:4).

25. Hay (1998); McAndrew (1998).
26. Fried (1963; 2000); Milligan (1998; 2003).
27. Proshansky (1983).
28. Brown and Perkins (1992); cf. Hoey (2005) on liminality and identity in relocation; Winnicott (1971) on "transitional spaces"; Feldman (1990).
29. Hay (1998).
30. Fried (2000); cf. Milligan (1998; 2003); Sennett (1998).
31. Hummon et al. (1986; 1992).
32. Whyte (1956).
33. Hoey (2005; 2006); cf. Darrah (1994 on the idea of a "bundle of skills."
34. Gillis (1996:232); cf. Martin (1999).
35. Gupta and Ferguson (1992:19–20, emphasis added).
36. See Bellah et al. (1996); Halfacree (1998); Hoey (2007). On New Urbanism, see Frantz and Collins (1999).
37. Boorstin (1974).
38. Echlin (2000).
39. Coombe (1991:1855).
40. Coombe (1991:1866); Taylor (1989).
41. Coombe (1991:1865–66).
42. Low (1994:66).
43. Grosz (1994:142).
44. Gray (1989:53).
45. Ibid., emphasis added.
46. O'Brien (2000:1A).
47. O'Brien (2001:IA).
48. Relph (1976).
49. Hufford (1986:74).
50. Gray (1989:59–60, emphasis added); cf., Gillis (1996); Ryden (1993).
51. Relph (1976:55); cf. Tuan (1974).
52. Stocking (1990:ix, xvxvi).

CHAPTER 10
Epigraph: Bryan (1982:16).
1. Jasper (2000:246).
2. Dudley (1994).
3. Jasper (2000:149).
4. McKay cited in Jasper (2000:84).
5. Gesler (1992:96).
6. See Cosgrove and Daniels (1988); Hirsch (1995); Kearns and Moon (2002).
7. See Rambo (1993).
8. Secunda (2000).
9. For a detailed examination of the meanings of retirement in America, see Savishinsky (2000). In the book, Savishinsky looks at rural men and women as they approach and experience retirement and their efforts to make sense of this often confusing stage of life. He finds that they are deeply committed to defining their own retirement and looks at how these people, as retired, renegotiate their relationships to family, friends, and community. While overall academic in approach, the book has an interesting and decidedly self-help or "how-to" feel.
10. Anderson (1990:8).
11. Quoted in Goode (2001:D7).

CHAPTER 11

Epigraph: Sennett (1998:31, 117).

1. See Bellah et al. (1996:163).
2. Bellah discusses this therapeutic quest for community. This conception of community, while growing out of "an old strand of American culture that sees social life as an arrangement for the fulfillment of the needs of individuals," in the community of interest implicated here, "self-interested individuals join together to maximize individual good." Here "those objects that make up 'the good life,' are still important, but they now take second place to the subjective states of well-being that make up a sense of self-worth" Bellah et al. (1996:134).
3. See Lawrence-Zúñiga (2010).
4. See Hochschild (1997).
5. Gillis (1996).
6. Aron (1999).
7. Giddens (1991).
8. Hall and Williams (2002).
9. See O'Reilly (2000).
10. Waldren (1996).
11. Turner (1967).
12. Turner (1974:38).

CHAPTER 12

Epigraph: *Merriam Webster's Collegiate Dictionary*, 10th ed.

1. See Hochschild (1997) and Nippert-Eng (1996).
2. Bender (1982).
3. LaPorte et al. (1996).
4. Gillis (2000).
5. Balfe (1999:259–60).
6. Ibid.
7. See Snepenger et al. (1995) and Stone and Stubbs (2007).
8. See Nippert-Eng (1996).
9. Luban (2001).
10. Sheehy (1977:364).

CHAPTER 13

Epigraph: Greg Brown, "Boomtown," *The Live One*, recorded live at JR's Warehouse, Traverse City, Michigan, June 1994.

1. In dissertation research in the field of geography conducted in the area of Missoula, Montana, Rina Ghose (1998:iii) applied the theories of rural gentrification to explain the social commodification and consumption of the rural countryside by a wave of equity-rich, educated, middle-class in-migrants possessing a "longing for an Arcadian utopia, a yearning for an imagined, idyllic, bucolic past."
2. See, for example, Davidson (1990); Salamon (2003).
3. See Price and Clay (1980).
4. Everett Ladd (1999:18) defines social capital as encompassing "any form of citizen's civic engagement employed or capable of being employed to address community needs and problems and, in general, enhance community life."
5. Putnam (1995:67).
6. Jobes (2000:4).
7. There are clearly voices of dissent with Putnam's view. Ladd addresses Putnam's findings. Essentially, he concludes that while Putnam's numbers appear correct, his interpretation of the data is flawed—or at least exaggerated. Ladd (1999:18) suggests that "at first glance the

idea of declining civic engagement seems plausible as many older groups have in fact lost ground." However, Ladd points out that associations have always come and gone that there are enough notable counter trends to assure that the concept of citizenship is still viable in America.

8. Like many such forums in subsequent years, TC Talks was discontinued because the webmaster could not control the occasionally uncivil exchanges between some of the regular users. There is no publicly available archive of the forum. The thread here is part of a longer discussion on moving to the area started by John. The discussion weaved in and out of several different topics including the one represented here, which is focused primarily on the meaning of in-migration to the area. I archived my own copies of the relevant threads before the site was shut down.
9. Ozegovic (2000:15).
10. Ibid., p. 13.
11. Ibid., p. 14.
12. Smith (1999).
13. MacGregor (2010:37).
14. See Fried (2000); Green (1999); and Milligan (2003).

CHAPTER 14
1. Paul Simon, "America."
2. See, for example, the edited volume of Benson and O'Reilly (2009).
3. Kiviat (2010).
4. See Bishop (2008); Weiss (1988; 1994).
5. Kasarda and Janowitz (1974:329); Stinner et al. (1992).
6. Salamon (2003:17); see Baumgartner (1988).
7. Bookman (2004); Coleman (1988); Furstenberg (2005); Putnam (2000).
8. Sweet et al. (2005); and Voydanoff (2005).
9. Wolfe (1998:12).
10. Bellah et al. (1996).
11. See Berry (1987) and Kilborn (2009).
12. Scott (2007).
13. See Benson (2013); Gustafson (2002); King et al. (1998); Sunil et al. (2007); and Williams et al. (1997).
14. For studies of "place consumption," see, for example, Hall (1997); Ateljevic and Doorne (2004); and Pettigrew (2007). For studies of the salience of a Rural ideal, see, for example, Buller and Hoggart (1994). For studies on the attraction of natural amenities, see, for example, Green et al. (2005).
15. For studies of travel-inspired entrepreneurship, see, for example, Snepenger et al. (1995) and Stone and Stubbs (2007). For studies of tourism-related migration, see, for example, Hall and Williams (2002).
16. See Beutell and Wittig-Berman (1999); Greenhaus et al. (2003); and Kossek and Ozeki (1998).
17. Nippert-Eng (1996).
18. See, for example, Chesley (2005); and Desrochers and Sargent (2004).
19. Radin (1987:1903).
20. Ibid., p. 1871.
21. Ibid., p. 1885; see Taylor (1989:4).
22. Radin (1987:1871).
23. Radin (1982:4).
24. Radin (1987:1885, emphasis added).
25. Ibid., p. 1907; see Lane (1991).
26. Ibid., p. 1885.

27. Murray (2000:155–56).
28. Fisher (2006).
29. Philo and Kearns (1993:18).
30. Ibid.
31. Ibid.
32. Radin (1987:1904).

EPILOGUE
1. Frey (2010).
2. Frey (2007; 2009).
3. Frey (2012).
4. Frey (2010).
5. Frey (2012).
6. Leinberger (2011).
7. Kasarda (1995); Muller (1981).
8. Leinberger (2008).
9. Leinberger (2008; 2011).
10. Beldon, Russonello, and Stewart (2011:22).
11. Lessenger (1986).
12. Frey (2012). Arthur Nelson (2009), an urban studies professor at University of Utah, has projected housing demand based on consumer preference surveys. His findings suggest that 44.5 million new attached and small-lot housing units—very much distinct from the McMansions of exurbia—will need to be built by 2020 to accommodate demographically-driven demand. Further, his prediction that follows from this, i.e., that 27 million more large-lot homes currently exist than will be needed in 2020, bolsters Leinberger's argument for the relative decline of exurbia. Nelson concludes that more than two-thirds of all new housing units required between now and 2020 will need to be *rental* units as both Baby Boomers and Millennials seek the flexibility of rental over home ownership.
13. Quoted in Alva (2012).
14. Kotkin (2006).
15. Ibid.
16. Mumford (1925).

APPENDIX 1
1. See Jobes et al. (1992); Frey and. Johnson (1998); Pandit and Withers (1999).
2. See Beyers and Nelson (2000); De Jong and Gardner (1981).
3. On residential migration, see Mincer (1978). For job-related relocation, see Bielby and Bielby (1992) and Eby et al. (1999). For "career hierarchy" factors, see Hardill et al. (1997); Pixley (2003).
4. Other studies on urban-to-rural migration suggest similar demographics for noneconomic migration to areas rich in natural amenities. For example, see Fuguitt et al. (1989); Ghose (1998); Judson et al. (1999).
5. Messerschmidt (1981).
6. Hennigh (1981).
7. Kottak (1982).
8. Yow (1994).
9. See Lassiter (2005).
10. Ortner (1989).
11. Metanarrative is discussed by Hobsbawm and Ranger (1983).
12. Van Maanen (1988:ix).
13. Coles (1997:250).

Works Cited

Altman, Irwin, and Setha M. Low. *Place Attachment*. Human Behavior and Environment: The Language of Science. New York: Plenum Press, 1992.

Alva, Marilyn. "Suburbs vs. City? Americans Want Homes with Backyards." *Investor's Business Daily* (2012). *news.investors.com/business-inside-real-estate/052412-612608-slowest-american-migration-since-world-war-two.htm*.

Anderson, Walt. *Reality Isn't What It Used to Be: Theatrical Politics, Ready-to-Wear Religion, Global Myths, Primitive Chic, and Other Wonders of the Postmodern World*. San Francisco: Harper and Row, 1990.

Aron, Cindy Sondik. *Working at Play: A History of Vacations in the United States*. New York: Oxford University Press, 1999.

Ateljevic, I., and S. Doorne. "Cultural Circuits of Tourism: Commodities, Place and Reconsumption." *Companion to Tourism* (2004): 291–302.

Bakhtin, M. M. *The Dialogic Imagination: Four Essays*. University of Texas Press Slavic Series 1. Austin: University of Texas Press, 1981.

Balfe, Judith H. *Passing It On: The Inheritance and Use of Summer Houses*. Montclair, NJ: Pocomo Press, 1999.

Baudrillard, Jean, and Mark Poster. *Selected Writings*. 2nd ed. Cambridge, UK: Polity, 2001.

Baumgartner, M. P. *The Moral Order of a Suburb*. New York: Oxford University Press, 1988.

Beale, Calvin L. *The Revival of Population Growth in Non-Metropolitan Areas*. ERS Report #605. Washington, DC: US Department of Agriculture, Economic Research Service, 1975.

Beaverstock, J. V. "Transnational Elite Communities in Global Cities: Connectivities, Flows and Networks." *Stadt und Region: Dynamic von Lebenswelten* (2001): 87–97.

Beckley, Robert M. "Flint Michigan and the Cowboy Economy: Deconstructing Flint." *Portico* 2005, no. 3 (2005): 14–16.

Belden, Russonello, and Stewart. "The 2011 Community Preference Survey: What Americans Are Looking for When Deciding Where to Live (Conducted for the National Association of Realtors)." Washington, DC, 2011.

Bell, Michael. *Childerley: Nature and Morality in a Country Village*. Morality and Society. Chicago: University of Chicago Press, 1994.

Bellah, Robert Neelly, Richard Madsen, William M. Sullivan, Ann Swidler, and Steven M. Tipton. *Habits of the Heart: Individualism and Commitment in American Life: Updated Edition with a New Introduction*. Berkeley: University of California Press, 1996.

Bender, Thomas. *Community and Social Change in America*. Baltimore: Johns Hopkins University Press, 1982.

Benson, Michaela, and Karen O'Reilly. *Lifestyle Migration: Expectations, Aspirations and Experiences*. Farnham, UK: Ashgate, 2009.

———. "Migration and the Search for a Better Way of Life: A Critical Exploration of Lifestyle Migration." *Sociological Review* 57, no. 4 (2009): 608–25.

———. "Postcoloniality and Privilege in New Lifestyle Flows: The Case of North Americans in Panama." *Mobilities* 8, no. 3 (2013): 313–30.

Berry, Brian J. L. *Urbanization and Counterurbanization*. Beverly Hills, CA: Sage, 1976.

———. "Urbanization and Counterurbanization in the United States." *Annals of the American Academy of Political Science* 451 (1980): 13–20.

Berry, Wendell. *Home Economics: Fourteen Essays*. San Francisco: North Point Press, 1987.

Beutell, N. J., and U. Wittig-Berman. "Predictors of Work-Family Conflict and Satisfaction with Family, Job, Career, and Life." *Psychological Reports* 85 (1999): 893–903.

Beyers, William B., and Peter B. Nelson. "Contemporary Development Forces in the Nonmetropolitan West: New Insights from Rapidly Growing Communities Lincoln County, New Mexico." *Journal of Rural Studies* 16, no. 4 (2000): 459–74.

Bielby, William T., and Denise D. Bielby. "I Will Follow Him: Family Ties, Gender-Role Beliefs, and Reluctance to Relocate for a Better Job." *American Journal of Sociology* 97, no. 5 (1992): 1241–67.

Bishop, B. *The Big Sort: Why the Clustering of Like-Minded America Is Tearing Us Apart*. New York: Houghton Mifflin, 2008.

Bonner, Kieran Martin. *A Great Place to Raise Kids: Interpretation, Science and the Urban-Rural Debate*. Montreal: McGill-Queen's University Press, 1997.

Bookman, Ann. *Starting in Our Own Backyards: How Working Families Can Build Community and Survive the New Economy*. New York: Routledge, 2004.

Boorstin, Daniel J. *The Americans: The Democratic Experience*. New York: Vintage Books, 1974.

Boulding, Kenneth E. "The Economics of the Coming Spaceship Earth." In *Environmental Quality in a Growing Economy*, edited by H. Jarret, 3–14. Baltimore: Johns Hopkins University Press, 1966.

Bourdieu, Pierre. *Outline of a Theory of Practice*. Cambridge Studies in Social Anthropology 16. New York: Cambridge University Press, 1977.

Bradshaw, Sandra S. *Seasons of the Leelanau*. West Bloomfield, MI: Northmont, 1994.

Brown, Barbara, and Douglas Perkins. "Disruptions in Place Attachment." In *Place Attachment*, edited by Irwin Altman and Setha M. Low, 279–304. New York: Plenum Press, 1992.

Brown-Saracino, Japonica. *A Neighborhood That Never Changes: Gentrification, Social Preservation, and the Search for Authenticity*. Fieldwork Encounters and Discoveries. Chicago: University of Chicago Press, 2009.

Bruner, Jerome S. *Acts of Meaning*. Jerusalem-Harvard Lectures. Cambridge, MA: Harvard University Press, 1990.

Bryan, Frank. "Rural Renaissance: Is America on the Move Again?" *Public Opinion*, June/July 1982, 16–20.

Buchholz, Todd G., and Victoria Buchholz. "The Go-Nowhere Generation." *New York Times*, March 10, 2012.

Buller, H., and K. Hoggart. *International Counterurbanization: British Migrants in Rural France*. Aldershot: Avebury, 1994.

Burgess, Jacquelin A. "Selling Places: Environmental Images for the Executive." *Regional Studies* 16, no. 1 (1982): 1–17.

Burnley, I. H., and P. Murphy. *Sea Change: Movement from Metropolitan to Arcadian Australia*. Sydney: New South Wales University Press, 2004.

Burns, Gus. "Paul Simon's 'America' Lyrics Randomly Appearing on Abandoned Structures in Saginaw." *Saginaw News*, December 14, 2010.

Buttimer, Anne, and David Seamon. *The Human Experience of Space and Place*. New York: St. Martin's, 1980.

Carlson, John E., Virginia W. Junk, Linda Kirk Fox, Gundars Rudzitis, and Sandra E. Cann. "Factors Affecting Retirement Migration to Idaho: An Adaptation of the Amenity Retirement Migration Model." *Gerontologist* 38, no. 1 (1988): 18–24.

Casado-Diaz, Maria Angeles. "Retiring to Spain: An Analysis of Differences among North European Nationals." *Journal of Ethnic and Migration Studies* 32, no. 8 (2006): 1321–39.

Certeau, Michel de. *The Practice of Everyday Life*. Berkeley: University of California Press, 1984.

Champion, Anthony G. *Counterurbanization: The Changing Pace and Nature of Population Deconcentration*. New York: Routledge Chapman and Hall, 1989.

Chesley, N. "Blurring Boundaries? Linking Technology Use, Spillover, Individual Distress, and Family Satisfaction." *Journal of Marriage and Family* 67, no. 5 (2005): 1237–48.

Clark, Andrew H., and E. Roy Officer. "Land Use Pattern." In *Great Lakes Basin: A Symposium Presented at the Chicago Meeting of the American Association for the Advancement of Science, 29–30 December, 1959*, edited by Howard J. Pincus, 141–56. Baltimore, MD: Horn-Shafer, 1962.

Clark, David E. "Amenities versus Labor Market Opportunities: Choosing the Optimal Distance to Move." *Journal of Regional Science* 31, no. 3 (1991): 311–28.

Coleman, James S. "Social Capital in the Creation of Human Capital." *American Journal of Sociology* 94 (1988): S95–S120.

Coles, Robert. *Doing Documentary Work*. New York: Oxford University Press, 1997.

Comartie, John. "Net Migration in the Great Plains Increasingly Linked to Natural Amenities and Suburbanization." *Rural Development Perspectives* 13, no. 1 (2001): 27–34.

Coombe, Rosemary J. "Encountering the Postmodern: New Directions in Cultural Anthropology." *Canadian Review of Sociology and Anthropology* 28 (1991): 188–205.

Coontz, Stephanie. *The Way We Never Were: American Families and the Nostalgia Trap*. New York: Basic Books, 1992.

Cosgrove, Dennis E., and Stephen Daniels. *The Iconography of Landscape: Essays on the Symbolic Representation, Design, and Use of Past Environments*. New York: Cambridge University Press, 1988.

Costello, Lauren. "Going Bush: The Implications of Urban-Rural Migration." *Geographical Research* 45, no. 1 (2007): 85–94.

Csordas, Thomas. "Embodiment as a Paradigm for Anthropology." *Ethos* 18 (1990): 5–47.

Cuba, Lee J. *Identity and Community on the Alaskan Frontier*. Philadelphia: Temple University Press, 1987.

Darrah, Charles. "Skill Requirements at Work: Rhetoric versus Reality." *Work and Occupations* 21, no. 1 (1994): 64–84.

———. "Techno-Missionaries Doing Good at the Center." *Anthropology of Work Review* 22, no. 1 (2001): 4–7.

Darrah, Charles., J. M. Freeman, and J. A. English-Lueck. *Busier Than Ever! Why American Families Can't Slow Down*. Palo Alto, CA: Stanford University Press, 2007.

Davidson, Osha Gray. *Broken Heartland: The Rise of America's Rural Ghetto*. New York: Free Press, 1990.

De Jong, Gordon F., and Robert W. Gardner. *Migration Decision Making: Multidisciplinary Approaches to Microlevel Studies in Developed and Developing Countries*. Pergamon Policy Studies on International Development. New York: Pergamon Press, 1981.

Desrochers, S., and L. D. Sargent. "Boundary/Border Theory and Work-Family Integration." *Organization Management Journal* 1, no. 1 (2004): 40–43.

Dudley, Kathryn Marie. *The End of the Line: Lost Jobs, New Lives in Postindustrial America*. Morality and Society. Chicago: University of Chicago Press, 1994.

Eby, Lillian T., Tammy D. Allen, and Shane S. Douthitt. "The Role of Nonperformance Factors on Job-Related Relocation Opportunities: A Field Study and Laboratory Experiment." *Organizational Behavior and Human Decision Processes* 79, no. 1 (1999): 29–55.

Echlin, Bill. "Leland Residents Want to Keep Fishtown Up and Going." *Record-Eagle*, November 5, 2000, 1, 7A.

Edmondson, Brad. "The Place Rating Game." *American Demographics* 20, no. 5 (1998): 14+.

Families and Work Institute. *Generation and Gender in the Workplace*. Watertown, MA: American Business Collaboration, 2003.

Feldman, Roberta M. "Settlement-Identity: Psychological Bonds with Home Places in a Mobile Society." *Environment and Behavior* 22, no. 2 (1990): 183–229.

Fine, Sidney. *Violence in the Model City: The Cavanagh Administration, Race Relations, and the Detroit Riot of 1967*. Ann Arbor: University of Michigan Press, 1989.

Fisher, Melissa S. "Navigating Wall Street Women's Gendered Networks in the New Economy." In *Frontiers of Capital: Ethnographic Reflections on the New Economy*, edited by Melissa S. Fisher and Greg Downey, 209–36. Durham: Duke University Press, 2006.

Fishman, Robert. *Bourgeois Utopias: The Rise and Fall of Suburbia*. New York: Basic Books, 1987.

———. "The Fifth Migration." *Journal of the American Planning Association* 71, no. 4 (2005): 357–66.

Florida, Richard L. "How the Crash Will Reshape America." *Atlantic*, March 2009. *www.theatlantic.com*.

Frantz, Douglas, and Catherine Collins. *Celebration, U.S.A.: Living in Disney's Brave New Town*. New York: Henry Holt, 1999.

Freedman, Audrey. *The New Look in Wage Policy and Employee Relations*. Conference Board Report No. 865. New York: Conference Board, 1985.

French, Ron. "Half of University Grads Flee Michigan." *Detroit News*, April 3, 2009. *www.detnews.com/article/20090403/metro/904030378*.

———. "More Might Go—If They Could." *Detroit News*, April 2, 2009. *www.detnews.com/article/20090402/metro//904020404*.

French, Ron, and Mike Wilkinson. "Leaving Michigan Behind: Eight-Year Population Exodus Staggers State." *Detroit News*, April 2, 2009. *detnews.com/article/20090402/904020403*.

Frey, W. H. "Housing Bust Shatters State Migration Patterns." Washington, DC: Brookings Institution, 2007. *www.brookings.edu/research*.

———. "Bursting 'Migration' Bubble Favors Coastal Metros, Urban Cores." Washington, DC: Brookings Institution, 2009. *www.brookings.edu/research/opinions/2009/03/20-census-frey*.

———. "Population and Migration." In *State of Metropolitan America*, 36–49. Washington, DC: Brookings Institution, 2010.

———. "The Demographic Lull Continues, Especially in Exurbia." Washington, DC: Brookings Institution, 2012. *www.brookings.edu/blogs*.

Frey, William H., and Kenneth M. Johnson. "Concentrated Immigration, Restructuring and the 'Selective' Deconcentration of the United States Population." In *Migration into Rural Areas: Theories and Issue*, edited by P. J. Boyle and Keith Halfacree, 79–106. New York: Wiley, 1998.

Fricke, Tom. "Marriage Change as Moral Change: Culture, Virtue, and Demographic Transition." In *The Continuing Demographic Transition*, edited by Gavin Jones, Robert Douglas, John Caldwell and Rennie D'Souza, 183–212. Oxford: Oxford University Press, 1997.

Fried, M. "Continuities and Discontinuities of Place." *Journal of Environmental Psychology* 20, no. 3 (2000): 193–205.

Fuguitt, Glenn Victor, David L. Brown, and Calvin Lunsford Beale. *Rural and Small Town America*. The Population of the United States in the 1980s. New York: Russell Sage Foundation, 1989.

Furstenberg, F. F. "Banking on Families: How Families Generate and Distribute Social Capital." *Journal of Marriage and Family* 67, no. 4 (2005): 809–21.

Galani-Moutafi, V. "The Self and the Other: Traveler, Ethnographer, Tourist." *Annals of Tourism Research* 27, no. 1 (2000): 203–24.

Geertz, Clifford. *The Interpretation of Cultures: Selected Essays*. New York: Basic Books, 1973.

Gesler, Wilbert M. "Therapeutic Landscapes: Medical Issues in Light of the New Cultural Geography." *Social Science and Medicine* 34, no. 7 (1992): 735–46.

Ghose, Rina. "A Realtor Runs through It: Rural Gentrification and the Changing Cultural Landscape of Missoula, Montana." PhD diss., University of Wisconsin, 1998.

Giddens, Anthony. *Modernity and Self-Identity: Self and Society in the Late Modern Age*. Palo Alto: Stanford University Press, 1991.

Gillett, Mary Bevans, and Sally Gamble. *The Insiders' Guide to Michigan's Traverse Bay Region*. Guilford, CT: Globe Pequot Press, 1998.

Gillis, John R. *A World of Their Own Making: Myth, Ritual, and the Quest for Family Values*. New York: Basic books, 1996.

———. "Our Virtual Families: Toward a Cultural Understanding of Modern Family Life." Working paper, Emory Center for Myth and Ritual in American Life. Atlanta: Emory University, 2000. *www.marial.emory.edu/research/index.html#publications*.

Gini, Al. My Job, *My Self: Work and the Creation of the Modern Individual*. New York: Routledge, 2000.

Glacken, C. *Traces on the Rhodian Shore: Nature and Culture in Western Thought from Ancient Times to the End of the 18th Century*. Berkeley: University of California Press, 1967.

Goode, Erica. "In Weird Math of Choices, 6 Choices Can Beat 600." *New York Times*, January 9, 2001, D7.

Goodwin, Mark. "The City as Commodity: The Contested Spaces of Urban Development." In *Selling Places: The City as Cultural Capital, Past and Present*, edited by Gerard Kearns and Chris Philo, 145–62. New York: Pergamon Press, 1993.

Gray, Rockwell, and Alexander J. Butrym. "Autobiographical Memory and Sense of Place." In *Essays on the Essay: Redefining the Genre*, edited by Alexander J. Butrym, 53–70. Athens: University of Georgia Press, 1989.

Green, G. P., S. C. Deller, and D. W. Marcouiller. *Amenities and Rural Development: Theory, Methods and Public Policy*. Northampton, MA: Edward Elgar, 2005.

Green, R. "Meaning and Form in Community Perception of Town Character." *Journal of Environmental Psychology* 19, no. 4 (1999): 311–29.

Greenhaus, J. H., K. M. Collins, and J. D. Shaw. "The Relation between Work-Family Balance and Quality of Life." *Journal of Vocational Behavior* 63, no. 3 (2003): 510–31.

Greenwood, Michael J., and Gary L. Hunt. "Jobs versus Amenities in the Analysis of Metropolitan Migration." *Journal of Urban Economics* 25 (1989): 1–16.

Grosz, E. A. *Volatile Bodies: Toward a Corporeal Feminism*. Theories of Representation and Difference. Bloomington: Indiana University Press, 1994.

Gupta, Akhil, and James Ferguson. "Beyond 'Culture': Space, Identity, and the Politics of Difference." *Cultural Anthropology* 7, no. 1 (1992): 6–23.

Gustafson, P. "Tourism and Seasonal Retirement Migration." *Annals of Tourism Research* 29, no. 4 (2002): 899–918.

Hall, C. Michael. "Geography, Marketing and the Selling of Places." *Journal of Travel and Tourism Marketing* 6, no. 3 (1997): 61–84.

Hall, C. Michael, and D. K. Müller. *Tourism, Mobility, and Second Homes: Between Elite Landscape and Common Ground*. Clevedon: Channel View Books, 2004.

Hall, C. Michael, and Allan M. Williams. *Tourism and Migration: New Relationships between Production and Consumption*. Dordrecht: Kluwer Academic Publishers, 2002.

Halfacree, Keith. "Migration into Rural Areas: Theories and Issues." In *Neo-Tribes, Migration, and the Post-Productivist Countryside*, edited by Keith Halfacree and Paul Boyle, 200–214. New York: Wiley, 1998.

Hardill, I., A. E. Green, and A. C. Dudleston. "The 'Blurring of Boundaries' between 'Work' and 'Home': Perspectives from Case Studies in the East Midlands." *Area* 29, no. 4 (1997): 335–43.

Hay, Robert. "A Rooted Sense of Place in Cross-Cultural Perspective." *Canadian Geographer* 42, no. 3 (1998): 245–66.

Heath, Tracy. "Small Towns, Big Opportunities." *Site Selection*, March 2001. International Development Research Corporation. *www.siteselection.com/features/2001/mar/smalltowns*.

Heat-Moon, William Least. *Blue Highways: A Journey into America*. Boston: Little Brown, 1982.

Hennigh, Lawrence. "Anthropologists at Home in North America: Methods and Issues in the Study of One's Own Society." In *The Anthropologist as Key Informant: Inside a Rural Oregon Town*, edited by Donald A. Messerschmidt, 121–32. New York: Cambridge University Press, 1981.

Herzog, Brad. *States of Mind: A Search for Faith, Hope, Inspiration, Harmony, Unity, Friendship, Love, Pride, Wisdom, Honor, Comfort, Joy, Bliss, Freedom, Justice, Glory, Triumph, and Truth or Consequences in America*. Winston-Salem, NC: John F. Blair, 1999.

Heubusch, Kevin. "Small Is Beautiful." *American Demographics* 20 (1998): 43–49.

Hirsch, Eric, and Michael O'Hanlon. *The Anthropology of Landscape: Perspectives on Place and Space*. New York: Oxford University Press, 1995.

Hobsbawm, E. J., and T. O. Ranger. *The Invention of Tradition*. New York: Cambridge University Press, 1983.

Hochschild, Arlie Russell. *The Time Bind: When Work Becomes Home and Home Becomes Work*. New York: Metropolitan Books, 1997.

Hoey, Brian A. "Nationalism in Indonesia: Building Imagined and Intentional Communities through Transmigration." *Ethnology* 42, no. 2 (2003): 109–26.

———. "From Pi to Pie: Moral Narratives of Noneconomic Migration and Starting Over in the Postindustrial Midwest." *Journal of Contemporary Ethnography* 34, no. 5 (2005): 586–624.

———. "Grey Suit or Brown Carhartt: Narrative Transition, Relocation and Reorientation in the Lives of Corporate Refugees." *Journal of Anthropological Research* 62, no. 3 (2006): 347–71.

———. "Therapeutic Uses of Place in the Intentional Space of Community." In *Therapeutic Landscapes*, edited by Allison Williams, 297–314. Hampshire, UK: Ashgate, 2007.

———. "Place for Personhood: Individual and Local Character in Lifestyle Migration." *City and Society* 22, no. 2 (2010): 237–61.

Holdrich, Martin. "The Future of Jobs and Employment." *Christian Science Monitor*, January 5, 2005. *www.csmonitor.com*.

Hufford, Mary. *One Space, Many Places: Folklife and Land Use in New Jersey's Pinelands National Reserve: Report and Recommendations to the New Jersey Pinelands Commission for Cultural Conservation in the Pinelands National Reserve*. Publications of the American Folklife Center 15. Washington, DC: American Folklife Center, 1986.

Hummon, David M. *Commonplaces: Community Ideology and Identity in American Culture*. Suny Series in the Sociology of Culture. Albany: State University of New York Press, 1990.

———. "Community Attachment: Local Sentiment and Sense of Place." In *Place Attachment*, edited by Irwin Altman and Setha M. Low, 253–78. New York: Plenum Press, 1992.

Hummon, David M., J. William Carswell, and David G. Saile. "Place Identity: Localities of the Self." In *Purposes in Built Form and Culture Research*, edited by David Saile and William Carswell, 34–37. Lawrence: University Press of Kansas, 1986.

Jackson, Maggie. *Distracted: The Erosion of Attention and the Coming Dark Age*. Amherst, NY: Prometheus Books, 2008.

Jacob, Jeffrey. *New Pioneers: The Back-to-the-Land Movement and the Search for a Sustainable Future*. University Park: Pennsylvania State University Press, 1997.

Jacobson, David. *Place and Belonging in America*. Baltimore: Johns Hopkins University Press, 2002.

Jasper, James M. *Restless Nation: Starting Over in America*. Chicago: University of Chicago Press, 2000.

Jobes, Patrick C. "Economic and Quality of Life Decisions in Migration to a High Natural Amenity Area." In *Community, Society, and Migration: Noneconomic Migration in America*, edited by Patrick C. Jobes, William F. Stinner, and John M. Wardwell, 335–62. Lanham, MD: University Press of America, 1992.

———. *Moving Nearer to Heaven: The Illusions and Disillusions of Migrants to Scenic Rural Places.* Westport, CT: Praeger, 2000.

Jobes, Patrick C., William F. Stinner, and John M. Wardwell. *Community, Society, and Migration: Noneconomic Migration in America.* Lanham, MD: University Press of America, 1992.

Johnson, Barbara. "Culture Clash: The Changes Newcomers Bring Can Be Hard on Natives." *Country Journal* 25, no. 4 (1998): 80.

Johnson, Kenneth M., and Calvin L. Beale. "The Rural Rebound." *Wilson Quarterly* 22, no. 2 (1998): 16–27.

Johnstone, Barbara. *Stories, Community, and Place: Narratives from Middle America.* Bloomington: Indiana University Press, 1990.

Joinson, Carla. "Relocation Counseling Meets Employee's Changing Needs." *HRMagazine* 43 (February 1998): 63, 65–70.

Judson, Dean H., Sue Reynolds-Scanlon, and Carole L. Popoff. "Migrants to Oregon in the 1990's: Working Age, Near-Retirees, and Retirees Make Different Destination Choices." *Rural Development Perspectives* 14, no. 2 (1999): 24–31.

Kasarda, John D. "Industrial Restructuring and the Changing Location of Jobs." In *State of the Union: America in the 1990s,* edited by Reynolds Farley, 215–67. New York: Russell Sage Foundation, 1995.

Kasarda, John D., and M. Janowitz. "Community Attachment in Mass Society." *American Sociological Review* 39, no. 3 (1974): 328–39.

Kearns, Gerard, and Chris Philo. *Selling Places: The City as Cultural Capital, Past and Present.* Policy, Planning, and Critical Theory. New York: Pergamon Press, 1993.

Kearns, Robin A., and G. Moon. "From Medical to Health Geography: Novelty, Place and Theory after a Decade of Change." *Progress in Human Geography* 26, no. 5 (2002): 605–25.

Kilborn, Peter T. *Next Stop, Reloville: Life inside America's New Rootless Professional Class.* New York: Times Books, 2009.

King, R., A. M. Warnes, and A. M. Williams. "International Retirement Migration in Europe." *International Journal of Population Geography* 4, no. 2 (1998): 91.

Kiviat, Barbara. "The Case against Homeownership." *Time,* September 10, 2010, 40–46.

Kossek, E. E., and C. Ozeki. "Work-Family Conflict, Policies, and the Job-Life Satisfaction Relationship: A Review and Directions for Organizational Behavior–Human Resources Research." *Journal of Applied Psychology* 83, no. 2 (1998): 139–48.

Kotkin, Joel. "Suburbia: Homeland of the American Future." *Next American City* 11 (2006): 19–22. *www.newamerica.net.*

Kotler, Philip, Donald H. Haider, and Irving J. Rein. *Marketing Places: Attracting Investment, Industry, and Tourism to Cities, States, and Nations.* New York: Free Press, 1993.

Kottak, Conrad Phillip. *Researching American Culture: A Guide for Student Anthropologists.* Ann Arbor: University of Michigan Press, 1982.

Knudson, Deborah J. "Editorial." *Traverse City: Your Guide to Traverse City and the Surrounding Area* 7 (1999): 3.

Ladd, Everett C. "Bowling with Tocqueville: Civic Engagement and Social Capital." *Responsive Community* 9, no. 2 (1999): 11–21.

Landor Associates. "Brands Are 'the New Religion': Quality and Reliability No Longer Key Factors in Brand Choice." 2001. *www.landor.com.*

Lane, Robert Edwards. *The Market Experience.* Cambridge: Cambridge University Press, 1991.

LaPorte, Paul, Carol LaPorte, and Paul Oppliger. *Life in the North Lane: Living and Working in Traverse City.* Traverse City, MI: Prism Publications, 1996.

Lasch, Christopher. *Haven in a Heartless World: The Family Besieged.* New York: Basic Books, 1977.

Lassiter, Luke Eric. "Collaborative Ethnography and Public Anthropology." *Current Anthropology* 46, no. 1 (2005): 83–106.

Lawrence-Zúñiga, Denise. "Cosmologies of Bungalow Preservation: Identity, Lifestyle, and Civic Virtue." *City and Society* 22, no. 2 (2010): 211–36.

Leach, William. *Country of Exiles: The Destruction of Place in American Life*. New York: Pantheon Books, 1999.

Leinberger, Christopher B. "The Next Slum? The Subprime Crisis Is Just the Tip of the Iceberg. Fundamental Changes in American Life May Turn Today's McMansions into Tomorrow's Tenements." *Atlantic*, March 1, 2008. *www.theatlantic.com*.

———. "The Death of the Fringe Suburb." *New York Times*, November 25, 2011. *www.nytimes.com*.

Leelanau County Association of Commerce. *The Captives, Being the Story of a Family's Vacation in Leelanau County, (Michigan); the Land of Delight*. Grand Rapids: White Printing, 1924.

Lessinger, Jack. *Regions of Opportunity: A Bold New Strategy for Real-Estate Investment with Forecasts to the Year 2010*. New York: Times Books, 1986.

———. "The Emerging Region of Opportunity." *American Demographics* 9, no. 6 (1987): 32–37.

———. *Penturbia: Where Real Estate Will Boom after the Crash of Suburbia*. Seattle: SocioEconomics, 1991.

Limerick, Patricia Nelson. *Something in the Soil: Legacies and Reckonings in the New West*. New York: W. W. Norton, 2000.

Low, Setha. "Cultural Conservation of Place." In *Conserving Culture: A New Discourse on Heritage*, edited by Mary Hufford, 66–77. Urbana: University of Illinois Press, 1994.

Luban, Ruth. *Are You a Corporate Refugee? A Survival Guide for Downsized, Disillusioned, and Displaced Workers*. New York: Penguin Books, 2001.

MacCannell, Dean. *The Tourist: A New Theory of the Leisure Class*. Berkeley: University of California Press, 1999.

MacGregor, Lyn Christine. *Habits of the Heartland: Small-Town Life in Modern America*. Ithaca, NY: Cornell University Press, 2010.

MacIntyre, Alasdair C. *After Virtue: A Study in Moral Theory*. Notre Dame, IN: University of Notre Dame Press, 1984.

Macy, Christine, and Sarah Bonnemaison. *Architecture and Nature Creating the American Landscape*. New York: Routledge, 2003.

Markus, H., and P. Nurius. "Possible Selves." *American Psychologist* 41, no. 9 (1986): 954–69.

Martin, Emily. "Flexible Survivors." *Anthropology News* 40, no. 6 (1999): 5–7.

McAndrew, Francis T. "The Measurement of 'Rootedness' and the Prediction of Attachment to Home-Towns in College Students." *Journal of Environmental Psychology* 18, no. 4 (1998): 409–17.

McGillivary, Brian. "Property Values Decline Once Again: Four-Year Slide Continues in Grand Traverse County." *Traverse City Record-Eagle*, March 4, 2012.

McGranahan, David. *Natural Amenities Drive Rural Population Change*. Washington, DC: Food and Rural Economics Division, Economic Research Service, US Department of Agriculture, 1999.

———. "Landscape Influence on Recent Rural Migration in the US." *Landscape and Urban Planning* 85, no. 3–4 (2008): 228–40.

McGranahan, David, and Patrick Sullivan. "Farm Programs, Natural Amenities and Rural Development." *Amber Waves* 3, no. 1 (2005): 28–35.

McGrattan, Ellen R., and Richard Rogerson. "Changes in Hours Worked since 1950." *Federal Reserve Bank of Minneapolis Quarterly Review* 22, Winter (1998): 2–19.

McIntyre, Norman, Daniel R. Williams, and Kevin McHugh. *Multiple Dwelling and Tourism: Negotiating Place, Home and Identity*. Cambridge, MA: CABI, 2006.

Mead, Margaret. "The Contemporary American Family as an Anthropologist Sees It." *American Journal of Sociology* 53, no. 6 (1948): 453–59.

Messerschmidt, Donald A. "On Anthropology 'at Home.'" In *Anthropologists at Home in North America: Methods and Issues in the Study of One's Own Society*, edited by Donald A. Messerschmidt, 3–14. New York: Cambridge University Press, 1981.

Miller, D. "Consumption and Commodities." *Annual Review of Anthropology* 24 (1995): 141–61.

Milligan, M. J. "Interactional Past and Potential: The Social Construction of Place Attachment." *Symbolic Interaction* 21, no. 1 (1998): 1–33.

———. "Displacement and Identity Discontinuity: The Role of Nostalgia in Establishing New Identity Categories." *Symbolic Interaction* 26, no. 3 (2003): 381–403.

Mincer, Jacob. "Family Migration Decisions." *Journal of Political Economy* 86, no. 5 (1978): 749–73.

Moen, Phyllis. *The Career Quandary*. PRB Reports on America 2, no. 1. Washington, DC: Population Reference Bureau, 2001.

Morrison, Peter A., and Judith P. Wheeler. "The Image of 'Elsewhere' in the American Tradition of Migration." In *Human Migration: Patterns and Policies*, edited by William H. McNeill and Ruth S. Adams, 75–84. Bloomington: Indiana University Press, 1978.

Moss, Laurence A. G. *The Amenity Migrants: Seeking and Sustaining Mountains and Their Cultures*. Cambridge, MA: CABI, 2006.

Muller, Peter O. *Contemporary Suburban America*. Englewood Cliffs, NJ: Prentice-Hall, 1981.

Mumford, Lewis. "The Fourth Migration." *Survey Graphic* 7 (1925): 130–33.

Murray, Alan. *The Wealth of Choices: How the New Economy Puts Power in Your Hands and Money in Your Pocket*. New York: Crown Publishers, 2000.

Nearing, Helen, and Scott Nearing. *Living the Good Life: How to Live Sanely and Simply in a Troubled World*. New York: Schocken Books, 1970.

Nelson, A. C. "The New Urbanity: The Rise of a New America." *Annals of the American Academy of Political and Social Science* 626, no. 1 (2009): 192–208.

Neuman, Mark. "The Trail through Experience: Finding Self in the Recollection of Travel." In *Investigating Subjectivity: Research on Lived Experience*, edited by Carolyn Ellis and Michael C. Flaherty, 176–201. Newburg Park, CA: Sage Publications, 1992.

Nippert-Eng, Christena E. *Home and Work: Negotiating Boundaries through Everyday Life*. Chicago: University of Chicago Press, 1996.

Noy, Chaim. "This Trip Really Changed Me: Backpacker's Narratives of Self-Change." *Annals of Tourism Research* 31, no. 1 (2004): 78–102.

O'Brien, Bill. "TC Man Sues Neighbor to Restore His View of the Bay." *Record-Eagle*, January 23, 2000, 1, 3A.

Ochs, Elinor, and Lisa Capps. "Narrating the Self." *Annual Review of Anthropology* 25 (1996): 19–43.

Ong, Aihwa. "Cultural Citizenship as Subject-Making: Immigrants Negotiate Racial and Cultural Boundaries in the United States." *Current Anthropology* 37 (1996): 737–51.

O'Reilly, Karen. *The British on the Costa del Sol: Transnational Identities and Local Communities*. London: Routledge, 2000.

Ortner, Sherry B. "On Key Symbols." *American Anthropologist* 75 (1973): 1338–46.

———. *High Religion: A Cultural and Political History of Sherpa Buddhism*. Princeton Studies in Culture/Power/History. Princeton, NJ: Princeton University Press, 1989.

———. "Fieldwork in the Postcommunity." *Anthropology and Humanism* 22, no. 1 (1997): 61–80.

Osbaldiston, Nicholas. *Seeking Authenticity in Place, Culture, and the Self: The Great Urban Escape*. New York: Palgrave Macmillan, 2012.

———. *Culture of the Slow: Social Deceleration in an Accelerated World*. Bassingstoke: Palgrave Macmillan, 2013.

Ozegovic, Jack. *Northern Spirits Distilled: Stories and Memories of the Upper Midwest*. North Liberty, IA: Ice Cube Press, 2000.

Paine, J. W. *Cross-Generational Issues in Organizations*. Sloan Work and Family Research Network, Boston College, Boston, 2006. *wfnetwork.bc.edu*.

Pandit, Kavita, and Suzanne Davies Withers. *Migration and Restructuring in the United States: A Geographic Perspective*. Lanham, MD: Rowman and Littlefield, 1999.

Pettigrew, Simone. "Place as a Site and Item of Consumption: An Exploratory Study." *International Journal of Consumer Studies* 31, no. 6 (2007): 603–8.

Philo, Chris, and Gerry Kearns. "Culture, History, Capital: A Critical Introduction to the Selling of Places." In *Selling Places: The City as Cultural Capital, Past and Present*, edited by Gerry Kearns and Chris Philo, 1–32. New York: Pergamon Press, 1993.

Pink, Daniel. *Free Agent Nation: How America's New Independent Workers Are Transforming the Way We Live*. New York: Warner Books, 2001.

Pixley, Joy. "Prioritizing Careers." In *It's about Time: Couples and Careers*, edited by Joy Pixley and Phyllis Moen, 183–200. Ithaca, NY: Cornell University Press, 2003.

Polivka, Anne E., and Thomas Nardone. "On the Definition of 'Content Work.'" *Monthly Labor Review* 109, no. 12 (1989): 9–16.

Powell, Douglas Reichert. *Critical Regionalism: Connecting Politics and Culture in the American Landscape*. Chapel Hill: University of North Carolina Press, 2007.

Price, Michael L., and Daniel C. Clay. "Structural Disturbances in Rural Communities: Some Repercussions of the Migration Turnaround in Michigan." *Rural Sociology* 45, no. 4 (1980): 591–607.

Proshansky, H. M., A. K. Fabian, and R. Kaminoff. "Place-Identity: Physical World Socialization of the Self." *Journal of Environmental Psychology* 3, no. 1 (1983): 57–83.

Putnam, Robert D. "Bowling Alone: America's Declining Social Capital." *Journal of Democracy* 6, no. 1 (1995): 65–78.

———. *Bowling Alone: The Collapse and Revival of American Community*. New York: Simon and Schuster, 2000.

Radin, Margaret. "Property and Personhood." *Stanford Law Review* 34 (1982): 957–1015.

———. "Market-Inalienability." *Harvard Law Review* 100 (1987): 1849–937.

Rambo, Lewis R. *Understanding Religious Conversion*. New Haven, CT: Yale University, 1993.

Reich, Robert B. *The Future of Success*. New York: A. Knopf, 2000.

Relph, Edward Charles. *Place and Placelessness*. London: Pion, 1976.

Richardson, Pete. "Two-Tier Kin: Imagining and Contesting Familism in a UAW Local." *Journal of Anthropological Research* 61, no. 1 (2007): 73–93.

Ricoeur, Paul. *Time and Narrative*. Vol. 1. Chicago: University of Chicago Press, 1984.

———. *Oneself as Another*. Chicago: University of Chicago Press, 1992.

Rieff, Philip. *The Triumph of the Therapeutic: Uses of Faith after Freud*. Chicago: University of Chicago Press, 1987.

Rink, Jim. "The Grape Northwest: Old Mission and Leelanau Peninsulas Lead the State in Vineyard Numbers and Visiting." *Michigan Living* 82, no. 1 (1999): 10–13.

Robinson, John P., and Geoffrey Godbey. *Time for Life: The Surprising Ways Americans Use Their Time*. University Park: Pennsylvania State University Press, 1999.

Rogerson, Robert J. "Quality of Life and City Competitiveness." *Urban Studies* 36, no. 5–6 (1999): 969–85.

Rosenblatt, Roger. Consuming Desires: Consumption, Culture, and the Pursuit of Happiness. Washington, DC: Island Press, 1999.

Rudzitis, Gundars. "Amenities Increasingly Draw People to the Rural West." *Rural Development Perspectives* 14, no. 2 (1999): 9–13.

Rybczynski, Witold. *Waiting for the Weekend*. New York: Viking, 1991.

Ryden, Kent C. *Mapping the Invisible Landscape: Folklore, Writing, and the Sense of Place*. American Land and Life Series. Iowa City: University of Iowa Press, 1993.

Salamon, Sonya. *Newcomers to Old Towns: Suburbanization of the Heartland*. Chicago: University of Chicago Press, 2003.

Saltzman, Amy. *Downshifting: Reinventing Success on a Slower Track*. New York: HarperCollins, 1991.

Savageau, David. *Places Rated Almanac, Millennium Edition*. Foster City, CA: IDG Books Worldwide, 2000.

Savishinsky, Joel S. *Breaking the Watch: The Meanings of Retirement in America*. Ithaca, NY: Cornell University Press, 2000.

Scheper-Hughes, Nancy. "Embodied Knowledge: Thinking with the Body in Critical Medical Anthropology." In *Assessing Cultural Anthropology*, edited by Robert Borofsky, 229–42. New York: McGraw-Hill, 1994.

Schoolcraft, Henry Rowe. *Algic Researches, Comprising Inquiries Respecting the Mental Characteristics of the North American Indians*. New York: Harper and Brothers, 1839.

Schor, Juliet B. *The Overworked American: The Unexpected Decline of Leisure*. New York: Basic Books, 1991.

Schumpeter, Joseph Alois. *Capitalism, Socialism, and Democracy*. 1942. 5th ed. London: Allen and Unwin, 1976.

Scott, S. "The Community Morphology of Skilled Migration: The Changing Role of Voluntary and Community Organisations (VCOs) in the Grounding of British Migrant Identities in Paris (France)." *Geoforum* 38, no. 4 (2007): 655–76.

Seamon, D. "The Phenomenological Contribution to Environmental Psychology." *Journal of Environmental Psychology* 2, no. 2 (1982): 119–40.

Sears, John F. *Sacred Places: American Tourist Attractions in the Nineteenth Century*. Amherst: University of Massachusetts Press, 1989.

Secunda, Victoria. *Losing Your Parents, Finding Your Self: The Defining Turning Point of Adult Life*. New York: Hyperion, 2000.

Sennett, Richard. *The Corrosion of Character: The Personal Consequences of Work in the New Capitalism*. New York: W. W. Norton, 1998.

Sheehy, Gail. *Passages: Predictable Crises of Adult Life*. New York: Bantam Books, 1977.

Shi, David E. *The Simple Life: Plain Living and High Thinking in American Culture*. New York: Oxford University Press, 1985.

———. *In Search of the Simple Life: American Voices, Past and Present*. Salt Lake City: Peregrine Smith Books, 1986.

Shweder, Richard A. *Welcome to Middle Age! (And Other Cultural Fictions)*. The John D. and Catherine T. MacArthur Foundation Series on Mental Health and Development. Studies on Successful Midlife Development. Chicago: University of Chicago Press, 1998.

Skolnick, Arlene S. *Embattled Paradise: The American Family in an Age of Uncertainty*. New York: Basic Books, 1991.

Smelser, N. *Theory of Collective Behavior*. New York: Free Press, 1962.

Smith, Henry Nash. *Virgin Land: The American West as Symbol and Myth*. Cambridge, MA: Harvard University Press, 1950.

Smith, Mark. "The Gentrification of Leelanau County." *Northern Michigan Journal*. 1999. *www.leelanau.com/nmj/winter/smith99.html*.

Snepenger, David J., D. Johnson Jerry, and Rasker Raymond. "Travel-Stimulated Entrepreneurial Migration." *Journal of Travel Research* 34 (1995): 40–44.

Soja, Edward W. *Postmodern Geographies: The Reassertion of Space in Critical Social Theory*. New York: Verso, 1989.

Steinbeck, John. *Travels with Charley: In Search of America*. New York: Viking Press, 1962.

Stinner, W. F., N. Tinnakul, S. Kan, and M. B. Toney. "Community Attachment and Migration Decision Making in Nonmetropolitan Settings." In *Community, Society, and Migration: Noneconomic Migration in America*, edited by William F. Stinner, Patrick C. Jobes, and John M. Wardwell, 47–84. Lanham, MD: University Press of America, 1992.

Stocking, Kathleen. *Letters from the Leelanau: Essays of People and Place*. Ann Arbor: University of Michigan Press, 1990.

Stone, Ian, and Cherrie Stubbs. "Enterprising Expatriates: Lifestyle Migration and Entrepreneurship in Rural Southern Europe." *Entrepreneurship and Regional Development* 19, no. 5 (2007): 433–50.

Sunil, T. S., V. Rojas, and D. E. Bradley. "United States' International Retirement Migration: The Reasons for Retiring to the Environs of Lake Chapala, Mexico." *Ageing and Society* 27, no. 4 (2007): 489–510.

Sweet, Stephen. "Job Insecurity." *Sloan Network Encyclopedia*. 2006. *workfamily.sas.upenn.edu/wfrn-repo/object/5m03mp4t9kb3719h*.

Sweet, Stephen, and Peter Meiksins. *Changing Contours of Work: Jobs and Opportunities in the New Economy*. Thousand Oaks, CA: Pine Forge Press, 2008.

Sweet, Stephen, Raymond Swisher, and Phyllis Moen. "Selecting and Assessing the Family-Friendly Community: Adaptive Strategies of Middle-Class, Dual-Earner Couples." *Family Relations* 54, no. 5 (2005): 596–606.

Tarrant, Ellyn. "Editor's Note." *Northern Home* 6, no. 2 (2001): 5.

Taylor, Charles. *Sources of the Self: The Making of the Modern Identity*. Cambridge, MA: Harvard University Press, 1989.

———. "Leading a Life." In *Incommensurability, Incomparability and Practical Reason*, edited by Ruth Chang, 170–83. Cambridge, MA: Harvard University Press, 1997.

Thrush, Glenn. "Something in the Way We Move." *American Demographics* 21, no. 11 (1999): 48–52+.

Tuan, Yi-Fu. *Topophilia: A Study of Environmental Perception, Attitudes, and Values*. Englewood Cliffs, NJ: Prentice-Hall, 1974.

———. *Space and Place the Perspective of Experience*. Minneapolis: University of Minnesota Press, 1977.

Turner, Frederick Jackson. *The Significance of the Frontier in American History*. 1894. Reproduced by University Microfilms. Washington, DC: Government Printing Office, 1966.

Turner, Victor. *The Forest of Symbols: Aspects of Ndembu Ritual*. Ithaca, NY: Cornell University Press, 1967.

———. *Dramas, Fields and Metaphors: Symbolic Action in Human Society*. Ithaca, NY: Cornell University Press, 1974.

Tuttle, Brad. "Gen Y's Take on Car Ownership? 'Not Cool.'" *Time*, May 2, 2012, *moneyland.time.com*.

Ullman, Edward L. "Amenities as a Factor in Regional Growth." *Geographical Review* 44, no. 1 (1954): 119–32.

United States Environmental Protection Agency, Environmental Studies Division. *The Quality of Life Concept: A Potential New Tool for Decision-Makers*. Washington, DC: Environmental Studies Division Environmental Protection Agency, 1972.

United Van Lines. *Great Lakes Region Sees More People Leaving; West, Southeast Welcome Residents*. Fenton, MO, 2008.

Van Maanen, John. *Tales of the Field: On Writing Ethnography*. Chicago Guides to Writing, Editing, and Publishing. Chicago: University of Chicago Press, 1988.

Veblen, Thorstein. *The Theory of the Leisure Class, 1899*. New York: A. M. Kelley, 1965.

Vidich, Arthur J., and Joseph Bensman. *Small Town in Mass Society; Class, Power and Religion in a Rural Community*. Princeton, NJ: Princeton University Press, 1958.

Voydanoff, Patricia. "The Effects of Community Demands, Resources, and Strategies on the Nature and Consequences of the Work-Family Interface: An Agenda for Future Research." *Family Relations* 54, no. 5 (2005): 583–95.

Wakefield, Lawrence. *All Our Yesterdays: A Narrative History of Traverse City and the Region*. Traverse City, MI: Village Press, 1977.

———. *Queen City of the North: An Illustrated History of Traverse City from Its Beginnings to 1980*. Traverse City, MI: Village Press, 1988.

Wakefield, Lawrence, and Lucille Wakefield. *Sail and Rail: A Narrative History of Transportation in the Traverse City Region*. Traverse City, MI: Village Press, 1980.

Waldren, J. *Insiders and Outsiders: Paradise and Reality in Mallorca*. Oxford: Berghahn Books, 1996.

Ward, Stephen V. *Selling Places: The Marketing and Promotion of Towns and Cities, 1850–2000*. Studies in History, Planning, and the Environment 23. New York: Routledge, 1998.

Weiss, Michael J. *The Clustering of America*. New York: Harper and Row, 1988.

———. *Latitudes and Attitudes: An Atlas of American Tastes, Trends, Politics, and Passions: From Abilene, Texas, to Zanesville, Ohio*. Boston: Little, Brown, 1994.

White, Richard, Patricia Nelson Limerick, and James R. Grossman. *The Frontier in American Culture*. Berkeley: University of California Press, 1994.

Whyte, William Hollingsworth. *The Organization Man*. New York: Simon and Schuster, 1956.

Williams, Allan M., Russell King, and Tony Warnes. "A Place in the Sun: International Retirement Migration from Northern to Southern Europe." *European Urban and Regional Studies* 4, no. 2 (1997): 115–34.

Williams, James D., and Andrew J. Sofranko. "Motivations for the Inmigration Component of Population Turnaround in Nonmetropolitan Areas." *Demography* 14, no. 2 (1979): 239–55.

Williams, Raymond. *The Country and the City*. London: Chatto and Windus, 1973.

Winnicott, D. W. *Playing and Reality*. New York: Basic Books, 1971.

Wolf, Peter M. *Hot Towns: The Future of the Fastest Growing Communities in America*. New Brunswick, NJ: Rutgers University Press, 1999.

Wolfe, Alan. *One Nation, After All: What Middle-Class Americans Really Think about, God, Country, Family, Racism, Welfare, Immigration, Homosexuality, Work, the Right, the Left, and Each Other*. New York: Viking, 1998.

Wuthnow, Robert. *Poor Richard's Principle: Recovering the American Dream through the Moral Dimension of Work, Business, and Money*. Princeton, NJ: Princeton University Press, 1996.

Yaeger, Patricia. *The Geography of Identity*. Ann Arbor: University of Michigan Press, 1996.

Yankelovich, Daniel. *New Rules: Searching for Self-Fulfillment in a World Turned Upside Down*. New York: Bantam Books, 1982.

Yow, Valerie Raleigh. *Recording Oral History: A Practical Guide for Social Scientists*. Thousand Oaks, CA: Sage, 1994.

Zemke, Ron, Claire Raines, and Bob Filipczak. *Generations at Work: Managing the Clash of Veterans, Boomers, Xers, and Nexters in Your Workplace*. New York: Amacom, 2000.

Index

agency, 14, 60, 72, 78, 97, 168
agriculture, 34, 38, 62, 168, 186, 202–3, 208
Alfred P. Sloan Foundation, vii, xv, 212
Alger, Horatio, 112
alienation, 62, 100, 129, 189–90. *See also*
    lifestyle migrants: dispossession expressed
    by
amenities, 18, 41, 59, 61–62, 168, 187
America (Simon), 2–3, 9, 17, 182
American culture
    anti-urban sentiment, 224n16
    belief in self-mastery and, 9, 17, 26,
        86–87, 111–12, 185
    belonging and, 27
    centrifugal tendencies, 10, 31, 111, 130,
        183, 185
    centripetal tendencies, 10–12, 31, 130,
        183, 185
    conception of community, 228n2 (chap.
        11)
    contrast between work and family
        domains, 87
    democracy, 57, 105, 111
    expressed in consumption, 86, 105
    faith in market, 111–12
    faith in redemption, 9, 141, 191
    faith in starting over, 9–10, 17, 26
    freedom, 17, 29, 55–59, 65, 105, 130, 184
    frontier concept, 8, 23, 26–27, 30, 52,
        62–63, 65–66, 70, 185
    home-centeredness, 149
    idealization of small town, 52, 191
    ideals of simplicity, 15–16, 25–26, 50, 53,
        62, 101, 141, 152, 184
    immigrant history and, 111–12, 185
    individual discretion, 58, 157, 201
    longing, 3, 11, 16, 31, 53, 182, 188
    personal fulfillment, 139
    pie as key symbol of, 49–50, 206

    practice of self-definition through work,
        50, 93
    rural ideal, 23, 25, 90, 95, 187, 229n14
        (chap. 14)
    self-made individual, 57, 112
    simplicity as theme, 25–26, 50, 62
    success stories, 112. *See also* success
    therapeutic ideal, 15, 57, 86, 139, 228n2
        (chap. 11)
    travel narrative as expressing, 17–18,
        29–30, 90, 162–63
American Dream, 5, 14, 83
    career path and, 94–95
    erosion, 183
    home ownership and, 53, 66, 87, 183
    as key symbol, 52–53
    as moral framework, 52–53, 182–83
    as viewed by Millennials, 195
anthropology, vii, 11, 99, 117, 212
    collaborative, 213
    concept of postcommunity, 11–12
    ethnographic approaches, viii, xii, 11–12,
        70, 188, 212–13
    fieldwork, vii–viii, 11–12, 14, 53, 118,
        210, 212–13
    history of, vii, 212
    interpretive, 213–14
    native anthropologists, 212
    perspective on place, 117
    reactive effects in fieldwork, 213
    study of culture, 12–13, 23
    understanding of landscape, 117–18
    views of social action, 23, 85
Arendt, Hannah, 96–97, 132
Aron, Cindy, 30, 143
asylum, 30, 150, 162, 184–85
authentic self
    core values and, 96, 108, 147, 155–56,
        160, 184, 191